The Foresight Wholefood Cookbook

The Foresight Wholefood Cookbook

NORMAN AND RUTH JERVIS

AURUM PRESS

Foresight Association for the Promotion of Pre-conceptual Care is a registered charity (no. 279160).

For more information, write to Foresight, The Old Vicarage, Witley, Godalming, Surrey GU8 5PN.

Note: Neither Foresight, Mrs Belinda Barnes, the authors, nor any members of their families derive any financial benefit from the sale of any product mentioned in this book. Brand names are given solely to help readers. Part of the proceeds from the sale of this book are being donated to the Foresight Research Fund.

Published by Aurum Press Limited, 33 Museum Street, London WC1A 1LD

First published in 1984 by Roberts Publications Limited, 225 Putney Bridge Road, London SW15 2PY

ISBN 0 948149 42 6

Typeset by Phoenix Photosetting, Chatham, Kent
Printed by Mackays of Chatham Ltd, Kent

Contents

Foreword

The notion of pre-conception care is as old as the hills, although we tend today to speak of it as something new, almost revolutionary. In the Book of Judges, chapter 13, one reads, 'An angel of God appeared to the wife of Manoah and said, "You are barren and have no child. But from now on take great care. Take no wine or strong drink, and eat nothing unclean. For you will conceive and bear a son".' The child subsequently born was Samson, renowned for his strength and stamina.

Perhaps part of the price we are paying for over-emphasizing the importance of modern science and technology is the risk of losing our common sense – certainly in matters affecting health. How absurd it is when detailed scientific research, often at great cost, claims to prove that 'we reap what we sow'; if we eat live foods we live, if we eat dead foods we die.

Anyone familiar with animal husbandry or breeding will know of the importance of pre-conception health in the breeding stock – in the male as well as in the female of the species. Many rural societies in our present world have long known and practised such health cultivation before conception. We in Great Britain are particularly plagued by a rising tide of degenerative diseases, poor reproductive efficiency amongst them.

Sufficient is known already for us confidently to state that much of present day failure in reproduction – inability to conceive, inability to hold on to a pregnancy, difficulties during childbirth, and less than perfect offspring – is directly related to malnutrition and other forms of pollution. We do indeed reap what we sow. It is heartening, therefore, to see a reawakening of interest in this all-important aspect of human health. The courage, dedication and tenacity of those who are cultivating Foresight ideas in our society deserves full recognition and credit. Pre-conception care will one day play its part as ante-natal care does today, and physical nutrition is the cornerstone of such care.

Having personally worked with couples preparing themselves for conception, for more than twelve years now, I have long felt the need for a book such as this. I have no hesitation in recommending this carefully produced wholefood cookbook to all those who, in varying ways, are associated with preparation for pregnancy. If they use it as their guide to nutrition, not only before, but during and after pregnancy, they will be well on their way to having a 'bespoke' baby – healthy in every way – the greatest joy of any parents.

Dr James Witchalls, MB, BS(Lond), LRCP, MRCS, D.Obst.RCOG

Introducing Foresight

True good health is becoming increasingly rare in our Western society. Since 1945 degenerative diseases have markedly increased, and more people suffer from allergy and depression. The highest rates of spina bifida in the world occur in South Wales, Scotland and Northern Ireland. Infant mortality figures for Britain compare poorly with other European countries, and show that our unborn babies are at risk now. 1984 figures showed 3,643 were stillborn, 6,037 died during the first year and 13,546 had congenital malformations which are not reversible. Add to this the cleft palates, club feet, hyperactivity, learning difficulties and allergic syndromes (e.g. eczema, asthma, hay-fever and headaches) and there is an even greater total of heartbreak and suffering. Many of these latter problems follow premature birth, low birth weight or early feeding problems leading to failure in breast-feeding.

One in six babies born today in Britain is likely to be disadvantaged by physical or mental handicap, allergy or a learning disability (e.g. dyslexia, autism, hyper-activity) which will show later. One pregnancy in four ends in miscarriage. Foresight Association believes that much could be done with nutrition and education of both prospective parents to prevent the onset of these disabling conditions.

Where a family has already suffered a tragedy, parents often ask themselves why and what they could have done to prevent this.

Those of us who feel reasonably healthy and cannot believe that our life style can possibly harm our unborn children may do well to look around us at our family and friends and their children. Are they all perfectly healthy? Look back into the family tree and trace out the patterns of health and allergy. Is there room for improvement?

We who have learnt from Foresight carry an urgent message of hope to so many anxious parents.

What is Foresight?

Foresight Association for the Promotion of Pre-conceptual Care is a registered charity formed to give every baby the opportunity of starting life in perfect health. Foresight aims to ensure that each baby enters this world free from congenital abnormality or mental damage. Foresight believes that with proper care for both parents *before* conception, the problems of birth defects and child ill-health can be tackled before they start.

Foresight works with prospective parents through enlightened health profes-sionals in the expanding network of Foresight Pre-Conceptual Clinics. Sym-pathetic doctors who appreciate the Foresight approach lead these clinics which, of necessity, are privately run.

The work of Foresight is educational as well as practical, and includes research.

Following three Foresight Symposia in London and many regional Teach-ins, some forty Foresight Clinics are now operating around Britain. Foresight publications explain how its aims can be achieved by caring parents who choose to assume responsibility for their own and their family's good health. A subscription to Foresight and *Guidelines for Future Parents* make the ideal gift for newlyweds. Donations help Foresight research. Teaching cards are being prepared to spread the message among schoolchildren.

Foresight members are helped in their quest for better health for all the family, kept informed of training programmes, research work and progress, and do invaluable public relations work.

How does Foresight help parents?

The Foresight approach covers four main areas, which are:
- Improved nutrition – the reason for this book!
- Protection from pollution (from heavy metals and poisonous chemicals).
- Combatting allergy.
- Discouraging the use of common social poisons (e.g. alcohol, smoking, the Pill, tranquillizers, sleeping pills, etc.).

Many authorities have recently drawn attention to the part played by environmental lead in causing stillbirth, congenital damage to the brain and central nervous system, and mental retardation. Various methods of assessment in the USA have shown correlation between lead levels in children and hyperactivity and learning difficulties. Foresight believes that the detection and cleansing from the system of toxic metals (lead, mercury, cadmium and aluminium) prior to conception is vital to the health of the baby.

Where allergies exist, malabsorption syndromes are often found – i.e. the nutrients in the foods eaten may not all be assimilated and used by the body: malnutrition is often the result. This may be due to the lack of the necessary digestive enzymes or to candidiasis infections. So Foresight advocates the detection and treatment of allergies and infections, and the adoption of a balanced wholefood diet which avoids the individual's known allergens. Sometimes it may be advisable to rebalance the nutritional status with vitamin and mineral supplements to help normalize the metabolism. Hair, sweat and/or blood analyses are helpful in revealing the unique nutritional status of essential minerals in the individual and the presence of toxic metals.

At their nearest Foresight Pre-Conceptual Clinic, intending parents can receive a comprehensive medical overhaul. This will include screening for the detection of these potential health hazards. They will receive appropriate counselling and treatment, with follow-up sessions to monitor progress. Thus, together with their clinician, they will provide the vital data for Foresight's five-year Research Project.

There is no joy equal to that experienced by the healthy mother confident that, with loving foresight, she has done everything in her power to contribute to her baby's total well-being. She may enjoy a serene healthy pregnancy, free from nausea, constipation or any other problems; an easy natural birth; and long breast-feeding of her contented, alert, thriving baby who grows into a fit, intelligent, responsible, healthy and happy adult. I speak from personal experience – our Foresight children and grandchildren are our happiest achievement. Hopeful grandparents may like to give their children the cost of Foresight Clinic counselling; this could pay dividends in the family health inheritance as well as in happiness!

Happiness is a Foresight family

Colin and Judy are intelligent but impecunious Foresight parents who became members when they were engaged. They both worked at a day centre for the mentally and physically handicapped, so they were extra aware of the problems of birth handicap. Seeking help from Foresight before many Foresight Clinics were in operation, they shopped around for a sympathetic NHS doctor and maternity hospital, and sent their hair for analysis.

Judy's hair analysis chart revealed a toxic level of copper (from using the contraceptive pill) and a little cadmium (from smoking) and some deficient trace minerals, including manganese. Colin was also a smoker, and his hair chart showed some toxic cadmium and deficient mangense. Both claimed to be wholefood enthusiasts, and their good zinc levels bore this out.

Faithfully they carried out the recommended individual supplementation programmes for six months, and studied all the Foresight literature. Judy had stopped smoking two years before, and Colin cut down his cigarettes. Shortly before conceiving, Judy had her last alcoholic drink, and then enjoyed a pregnancy in extremely good health, free from morning sickness (and without any drugs).

Baby Joy was born on the expected day, with only a whiff of gas and air to ease her arrival, with tired but delighted parents together welcoming and sharing her first two hours of newborn life. Joy was a perfect 6 lb 13 oz at birth, and is now contentedly thriving as her serenely competent and loving mother breast-feeds her on demand.

Despite cramped housing conditions, with no possibility of a washing machine to help her, Judy has suffered no post-natal depression, and is thoroughly enjoying motherhood. Colin is justifiably proud of them both, and is quick to express his gratitude to Foresight.

Pre-conceptual care for fertility

Enlightened farmers do not gamble with the health of their stock. They realize that better feeding and care of both sire and dam before mating produces higher fertility, fewer losses, healthier offspring – and greater profit. Do we value our babies less than their lambs, calves and foals? Surely a better start in life is the most worthwhile gift money could buy? The cost of pre-conceptual care will be a valuable investment in their family's health. Wise parents attending Foresight Clinics may also be contributing to the improved health of our nation by providing data (confidentially) for Foresight Research.

A healthy plant starts from a healthy seed. The ovum and sperm will be less healthy from parents whose eating patterns and life-style deplete their nutritional resources and good health. Smoking, alcohol and drugs all multiply the effects of poor nutrition, and thus increase susceptibility to infections which could also endanger foetal development.

Where many adverse factors coincide, nature usually overrules to produce infertility. But between infertility and truly healthy reproduction is a shadowy phase where conception may occur, but maximum health is unlikely. This is another reason for consolidating a good diet and healthier life-style for several months before conception.

Usually, by the time a woman knows she is pregnant, the first five to six weeks growth of the foetus has already taken place. This is the most vital period for the laying down of the major organs. The raw materials needed for this crucial stage will have been drawn from the mother's body stores. Improved feeding during pregnancy, though commendable, is too late to make up the deficiencies occurring at the time of conception.

This is the case for pre-conceptual care. Prevention of handicap is better than cure.

Nutrition for Health

The relationship of food to health

Sir Robert McCarrison, pioneer nutritionist, said 'I know nothing so potent in maintaining good health in laboratory animals as perfectly constituted food; I know of nothing so potent in producing ill-health as improperly constituted food'. This too is the experience of stock-breeders. Is man an exception to a rule so universally applicable to the higher animals?

McCarrison's work was unique in that it showed how human health is related to the wholeness of food. In recent years research has shown that healthy people of any ethnic group who change from their natural traditional wholefood diet to a Western-style diet develop the degenerative, non-infectious diseases now common in Europe and North America. These diseases include dental decay, obesity, arthritis, allergic syndromes, gastro-intestinal disorders (appendicitis, peptic ulcer, diverticulosis, constipation, cancer of the colon), coronary heart disease, haemorrhoids, varicose veins, mental illness, birth defects and lactation failure.

In 1982 the National Advisory Committee on Nutrition Education (NACNE) Report recognized the irrefutable links between diet and disease. It recommended improving the average diet by:

- Reducing fat consumption, from dairy fats (in milk, cream, butter and cheeses), from meats, delicatessen foods, fried foods, and from the consumption of cakes, biscuits, pastries and rich foods.
- Reducing total sugar consumption, especially from cakes, biscuits, sweets, ice-creams and soft drinks as well as in tea and coffee.
- Reducing salt consumption – so avoid adding salt at table.
- Significantly increasing the fibre content of meals, by including more wholegrain cereals, vegetables and fruits.

This book embraces all of these principles.

Good nutrition helps every area of our lives

Good nutrition helps build not only a healthy body, but also a resilient healthy mind and good emotional balance, which can cope better with the stresses of everyday life. For the brain and endocrine glands are nourished by the same food, water and air as the rest of the cells in the body. In addition our diet affects our physical appearance, our energy levels, our intellectual and creative abilities, our mental health and general feeling of well-being. It even affects our ability to enjoy love and sexuality.

Health is also affected by our thoughts – our emotions, our hopes and fears, our loves and hates; whether we think positively or negatively; whether we have faith or fear. Stress is a component of life. Stress may easily increase our nutritional requirements beyond their availability in today's 'normal' diets. The natural

protective immune response will be depressed, and we will become more suscept-
ible to infections, allergies, mental problems and to more serious illness if our
nutritional stores are too low to allow God's natural self-defence mechanisms to
be implemented.

Why a 'normal good diet' can be deficient

There are a variety of reasons today why our daily food is lacking many vital
nutrients. Modern farming methods may prevent the plants from taking up
manganese because of liming. The minerals may be depleted from the soil
because artificial fertilizers do not supply the complete range of minerals taken
out by previous cropping (e.g. zinc and selenium). Nutrients may be removed
during processing (e.g. the refining of whole wheat to white flour results in
considerable losses of many trace minerals and vitamins (see page 14). Commercially frozen green vegetables lose zinc, manganese and calcium (but home
freezing does not). Crop spraying with insecticides prevents manganese absorption from food. Food additives may affect the balance of vital nutrient uptake.
The heat of cooking affects the B complex and vitamin C. Many water-soluble
minerals and vitamins are thrown away with the cooking water.

Furthermore, common social poisons (caffeine, nicotine, alcohol, etc.) and the
Pill increase the requirement of some minerals and vitamins. Exposure to pollu-
tants increases the need for protecting nutrients.

The nutrients in foods relate to soil

Health-building begins with the living soil, for the full nutritional value of
wholefoods depends on the availability of the trace minerals as well as basic
nutrients in the soil from which they originate. So believed my father, Robert
Atkinson Reddell, founder of Enton Hall Health Hydro, where the bio-dynamic
composted vegetable garden was the essential source of the fresh vital salads and
vegetables served daily there. These were complemented by eggs and milk
organically produced on the home farm.

Traditionally over the centuries, food crops were always grown this way,
returning to the soil all the waste left over from its production, adding the
farmyard manure – 'The Law of Return'. Fresh locally grown vegetables and
fruit were enjoyed in their seasons; home-baked bread was made from stone-
ground local wholewheat flour; poultry and livestock were reared naturally;
chemical fertilizers, pesticide sprays and dusts were unknown. The hard labour
of man working with the laws of nature produced healthy herds and crops on
fertile soils; natural predators controlled the pests. Man had no need to study
nutrition for healthy eating.

'Progress' has brought us far beyond this Utopian self-sufficiency. Farming
and marketing methods have changed, and the Law of Return is rarely obeyed. In
listing rich food sources of nutrients (see page 12), we acknowledge past
research to help guide food selection. But the precise nutrient value of any specific
food sample will depend upon many factors: the geographical location, the soil,
the fertilizers and pesticides used and the production methods employed.

The value of organically grown food

Organic produce really is preferable, when we can obtain it. The Gerson Diet for cancer relies on it. We who enjoy good health may cope well without it, but some reach the point in ill-health or allergy where they need bio-dynamic food i.e. organically grown on compost-fed soil, without chemical fertilizers and un-sprayed by any insecticides, pesticides, herbicides, fungicides or sprout-ing inhibitors.

If you have a garden and grow your own vegetables, this is the best way. Tracking down organic produce can be difficult (see page 192-3).

Where organic produce is unobtainable, ask your greengrocer for unsprayed produce. Some aware farmers use biological control (natural predators) and companion planting instead of chemicals, and more will follow when we increase the demand for it.

The use of chemical sprays on fruit, vegetables and salads is a cause for great concern, as is cereal crop aerial spraying. Some apples and lettuces, particularly, may have been sprayed many times during growth – and most chemical residues are toxic and cumulative. Brassicas and soft fruits are commonly sprayed too – the consumer's distaste for greenfly and caterpillars is to blame, rather than the grower.

Washing in acidulated water (1 tbsp cider vinegar to 1–2 pints water) helps remove surface contamination from salads, vegetables and fruit, but plants absorb a proportion of the spray.

There is an organic lotion concentrate available, especially made for washing off chemical sprays, which is useful for soft fruits as well. Apples can be scrubbed with hot water. Otherwise peel your fruit and avoid lettuce unless grown without sprays.

Happily, a good wholefood diet does help protect us from these poisons (see page 183).

The need for fibre

While peeling apples may be a necessary expediency, eating wholefoods will provide the right balance of nutrients and fibre. The bran is still there in 100% wholemeal flour and bread, crushed and whole grains; fibre is naturally present in potato, tomato and apple skins, pulses, vegetables and salads. It makes better sense to eat the whole food the way nature provides it rather than separate the parts and then eat added bran.

Healthy food need not be expensive

Wholegrains, sea vegetables, dried peas and beans (pulses) are really cheap nourishing foods. Soups and stocks can use up bones and outer vegetable leaves, saving waste. Most people spend more than they need to on meat (see Proteins page 8) – by economizing here the budget should stretch to buy more vegetables and wholemeal bread. Cutting down on bought cakes, pies, biscuits and sweets helps finance the free-range eggs, nuts, fresh and dried fruits and salads. Buy fruit, vegetables and salads in season, when they are less expensive, and save on tinned goods. Water is cheaper than bought squashes and colas. Baking our own wholefood pies, biscuits, cakes and sweet snacks can save money too.

Home baking takes time, but our wholefood way of eating can save preparation time too. Salads are quickly prepared and need no cooking. Potatoes are better left unpeeled. Soups can be quickly made from left-overs. Fresh and stewed fruit or yoghurt are quicker to prepare than puddings or pies. What could be quicker than a bowl of wholefood muesli and some raw fruit? Nuts are nature's convenience food – instant quick nourishment. Slow cookers and vacuum jars can simplify long cooking and time spent on duty in the kitchen. Check you health food store for packeted foods made from wholefoods.

Avoiding the usual instant packeted or tinned convenience foods will eventually save time nursing sick children. 'Fast food = quick sick' is a slogan with a ring of truth!

Enlist the children's help with preparation; they may find the 'cup' recipes easier than 'weights'. Active participation in its creation adds to the enjoyment of eating a new dish. All our grandchildren love salads, beansprouts, muesli and wholefoods, having always seen us enjoy these foods. Example helps. Our little ones eat salad in their fingers as it is more pleasurable for them to manage independently. For reluctant youngsters, make 'collage' pictures with salad ingredients on the plate – a face, a flower, a fish, etc. Good feeding habits are the foundation of future good health.

The next chapter gives more practical help.

How we can build healthy families from wholefoods

The health of all the family depends on the food we eat. How we look, how we feel, how long we retain our youthful vitality despite the passing years, largely relates to our diet. Every part of our bodies – eyes, brain, bones, teeth, glands, heart, muscles, blood, skin, hair – is built from the food and water we consume and the air we breath. What we choose to eat is important. So is the life-style and eating habits we adopt and then pass on to our children. Family health and happiness is in the homemakers' hands as they plan and shop, prepare and cook, serve and eat with their family.

Healthy meals, intelligently chosen and prepared with loving care, will taste different from the devitalized foods made from white flour and the processed foodstuffs which are liberally seasoned with salt or sweetened with sugar (and perhaps have chemical 'enhancers') to disguise their lack of flavour. Make the change-over from traditional to wholefood cooking gradually to win the approval of the sceptical members of the family.

Man has evolved from a wholefood diet which supplies both known and presently unrecognized nutrients. The use of supplements should never be a substitute for a balanced wholefood diet. A lifetime of better nutrition can prevent the development of many diseases. The choice is ours.

Cooking is caring! Enjoy participating in your family's good health.

Proteins

Western man consumes 50% more protein than his body needs. Eating too much protein is not only costly and wasteful, but puts an unnecessary strain on the liver and kidneys; and it can lead to a tendency to rheumatism, arthritis and other health problems.

Protein requirements vary according to the number of body cells which are being built or repaired, so those needing more than the recommended minimum protein intake are:
- Expectant mothers.
- Nursing mothers.
- Babies; they need more protein in relation to their body weight, as they are growing fast.
- Children, especially at times when they are growing fast.
- Convalescents, for the repair of broken bones and burnt tissue, or after undergoing surgery, for wound healing.

Combining foods to give better value protein

By combining selective groups of protein foods lacking in different amino acids, better value protein can be obtained. The complementary protein groups are:
- Animal protein (milk, yoghurt, cheese, eggs, meat, fish, poultry or dried milk powder) with wholegrain cereal or vegetable protein.
- Wholegrain cereal protein (wheat, bread, pasta, wheatgerm, flour, rice, corn, barley, oats, etc.) with animal or pulse protein.
- Pulse protein (peas, beans, lentils, soya beans or soya products, peanuts) with wholegrain cereal, nut or seed protein.
- Nut and seed protein (brazil nuts, almonds, sunflower seeds, sesame seeds, pumpkin seeds, etc.) with pulse or animal proteins.

Bread and beans, eaten together, give a better resultant protein than meat! So does bread and cheese. Similarly most traditional pairs of foods – fish and chips, roast beef and Yorkshire pudding, rice pudding, macaroni cheese, spaghetti bolognaise, cornish pasties – all give better value protein by their combinations of complementary protein groups.

No meat is actually necessary in a health-promoting diet. In fact recent research has shown how athletes perform better on diets containing lower amounts of protein (especially animal protein) as there then is less excess to be excreted as urea. But vegetarians may risk zinc deficiency.

The best sources of dietary protein
- 'Free-range' eggs.
- Fresh fish from unpolluted water.
- Cooked dried beans with wholegrains, or sprouted beans and grains.
- Wholemeal bread with farmhouse (unprocessed) cheese.
- Wholegrain cereals with nuts and milk or yoghurt, i.e. muesli.
- Game (free from any danger of drug residue).
- Organ meats – heart, brains, sweetbreads, tongues – which contain less cholesterol than muscle meats.
- Soya beans, which have the advantage of containing lecithin, the natural emulsifier and controller of cholesterol, and very little saturated fat.
- Butcher's meat: 'free range' fresh poultry and lamb are the best.

Fats and oils

Fats and carbohydrates are the energy fuel foods. While proteins, starches and sugars all supply energy at the rate of 4 kcal/gm, fats and oils supply energy at the rate of 9 kcal/gm – i.e. more than twice as fattening! (The other commodity in the energy table is alcohol, supplying 7 kcal/gm.)

Oils are fats which are liquid at room temperature, sometimes due to a higher content of polyunsaturates.

The only animals which are fat in the wild are those exposed to icy temperatures and those ready for hibernation. This fat provides a food store and insulation against the cold. If we eat a lot of fat, we need to work very vigorously to burn it up. Many people consume as much as 40% of their calorific intake in fat, which is excessive.

Some fat in the diet (around 3-5%) is essential for health, for the absorption of vitamins A, D and E and to provide vitamin F (the essential fatty acids, which are found in polyunsaturated fats). The Hyper-Active Children's Support Group has researched the lack of essential fatty acids as a possible cause of hyperactivity, and found a correlation in many cases. Read *Super Nutrition for Healthy Hearts* by Richard Passwater to learn why we need balanced low amounts of both animal and vegetable fats for good health.

The butter or margarine controversy remains. Butter can be the natural product which has been consumed for hundreds of years (but avoid these butters containing colourings). Margarine is produced by a chemical process to make the oil solid at room temperature. The best margarines are the soft polyunsaturated vegetable margarines, low in cholesterol, and free from artificial chemicals (read the label and check). Butter has a unique flavour, but is high in cholesterol. Compromise with Butter Plus (p. 171).

Cold-pressed vegetable oils, high in vitamin F, are best used sparingly in salad dressings, special nutritional drinks or cream substitutes where they are not spoilt by heating. Store them in a cold place. Rancid fats and oils are toxic and should be thrown away. For cooking, use the cheaper vegetable oils which have a longer shelf life. The best source of valuable polyunsaturated oils is found in wholegrain cereals, seeds, fish, avocado, fresh raw nuts, sunflower and safflower oil. (See also under vitamin F.)

Hidden fat is present in many foods – e.g. nearly all cheeses, eggs, fish, meats (even lean meat!), pastry, cakes, biscuits, ice-cream – and even more in potato crisps and roasted peanuts!

Carbohydrates

Starches and sugars, together called carbohydrates, need B vitamins for their metabolism into energy. Nature adequately provides these B vitamins in whole carbohydrate foods, but refining processes seriously deplete them.

It has been shown that there is a direct connection between the consumption of refined carbohydrates and many diseases prevalent today. This 'saccharine disease' includes gastric and duodenal ulcers, diabetes and hypoglycaemia, dental decay, diverticulosis, haemorrhoids, varicose veins, coronary heart disease, appendicitis, obesity and cancer of the colon.

Our bodies evolved to extract glucose slowly from complex carbohydrates, i.e. natural cereals, vegetables, pulses, fruits and nuts. Man had lived for thousands of years before refined sugar was ever produced. For the body's fuel, the purest, most highly refined carbohydrates – i.e. white sugar (sucrose) and dietary glucose – are far from ideal. It is comparable with putting petrol into a wood-burning stove!

Consider: a whole yard of succulent sugar-cane would take about half an hour to chew, leaving you well satisfied from a good snack containing many vitamins and minerals, good natural energizing carbohydrate with a little protein and fat, and lots of fibre. This yard of sugar-cane, in processing, is stripped of all its nutrients, leaving only pure sucrose – one white sugar lump. Truly a junk food which contains nothing other than energy!

Sugars

1. First and best are the naturally occurring fruit sugars found in sun-dried and fresh sun-ripened fruits – grapes, pears, peaches, apples, bananas (very ripe), etc; raisins, sultanas, dates, figs, prunes and apricots.
2. Honey is best unpasteurized, see page 13. It is sweeter than sugar and contains many vitamins, minerals and enzymes. Use in moderation.
3. 'Raw cane sugars' are sucrose, but as a result of less processing, still contain some nutrients. They are produced in Barbados, Mauritius and the Demerara area of Guyana; look for the country of origin on the pack. In order of preference, these are:
   • Molasses sugar, sticky, granular, almost black, with a strong molasses flavour and the least refined of all the sugars we can buy.
   • Muscovado sugar, soft, sticky, granular and dark brown, containing a little less molasses.
   • Light Muscovado sugar, paler and more refined.
   • Demerara sugar, naturally crystallized sugar with a golden colour.

All other sugars (also sucrose), are highly refined and usually white. Where they are brown, they have been coloured.

Fructose, or 'fruit sugar' as we purchase it, is as highly refined as ordinary white sugar, denuded of all its nutrients. Its advantages are that it is one and a half times as sweet as sucrose, and is more slowly metabolized.

How sugar (sucrose) affects us

In ordinary people, the excessive consumption of refined sugar leads to demands for extra insulin to process the extra blood-sugar arriving in the bloodstream. Repeated high sugar intake overstimulates the pancreas and the adrenals, as they strive to maintain the blood-sugar concentration within healthy limits. When the adrenals become stressed, the pancreas may become over-stimulated and produce too much insulin. This produces a dramatic drop in the blood-sugar level, and rebound hunger brings a craving for more sugar as the energy level flags. So a dependence on sugar can be established with the widely swinging 'highs and lows' on the way to hypoglycaemia. Or the pancreas may become exhausted, fail to produce sufficient insulin to keep the balance, and lead the way to diabetes.

In the long run, eating sugar and sweets makes people tired rather than energetic, as it depletes the body's supply of the B vitamins needed to convert it into energy.

When we give our children sweets 'as a treat' or 'to keep them quiet', we pave the way for them to become irritable, uncooperative, troubled with spots and rashes, colds, catarrh – and even become hyperactive or slow learners!

Starch

'Give us our daily bread'. The staff of life around the world is the locally grown cereal or starch crop. We have bread made from wheat; the Scots have oatmeal porridge; the Red Indians, maize; the Africans, yams; the Irish, potatoes; the Asians, rice. Barley, millet, buckwheat and rye also make their appearance.

As nature provides it, the cereals other than maize are balanced whole foods, containing the complex carbohydrates which the body needs for the slow, steady production of blood-sugar for energy (like wood for the wood-burning stove). Protein, roughage, vitamins, minerals and even essential fatty acids all naturally occur to produce a good, balanced, sustaining, whole, starch food.

Where there is a history of allergy, bio-dynamically grown whole grains, sprouted or cooked whole – or flaked and used as in the muesli and kruska recipes – may be better tolerated than bread or flour made from the same grains. Locally grown 'soft' organic wheat contains less gluten than the hard Canadian wheat, and so is less likely to produce a gluten sensitivity.

While a cave-man diet (see page 186) excludes all cereal grains, bread is a traditional food which has been happily consumed by man for thousands of years. It is a good food when made from the whole of the grain as God provided and nature intended, grown on organically fertilized soil (and free from fungicide sprays). This is why this book advocates the use of 100% wholemeal flour – made from the whole grain including the outer bran covering, the growing point of germ, and the starchy centre.

Comparison with white bread

In the production of white flour, a tremendous nutrient loss occurs. Dr. Henry Schroeder, M.D. working on trace mineral metabolism, points out that white flour (as opposed to whole wheat flour) contains only '23% of the thiamine (B1); 20% of the riboflavin (B2); 19% of the nicotinamide; 29% of the pyridoxine (B6); 50% of the pantothenic acid; 33% of the folic acid; and 14% of the vitamin E.' He further points out that of the trace elements there remains only '13% of the chromium; 9% of the manganese; 19% of the iron; 13% of the cobalt; 10-30% of the copper; 17% of the zinc; 50% of the molybdenum and 17% of the magnesium'.

In wartime Britain, white bread, by law, had four nutrients added back into it – calcium from powdered chalk, iron and two B vitamins, thiamine and niacin. This has recently been reduced to only three. How poorly white flour and white bread compare with 100% wholemeal!

Concentrated nutrient sources

These good foods and nutrient concentrates may be used to enhance a good wholefood diet when necessary. We advise the use of the foods more regularly than the more concentrated nutrients, as over-consumption of one nutrient can create an increased need for others in order to maintain a good balance.

ALFALFA SPROUTS: These are easy to grow (see chapter on salads and beansprouts), and particularly rich in vitamin K and nearly every vitamin and mineral. Valuable as a living food full of enzymes and amino acids, as are the other sprouted seeds, beansprouts, etc.

BONE-MEAL (prepared for human use): This powder is a very good source of calcium, phosphorus, manganese, copper, nickel and fluoride – all essential for building strong teeth and bones, and is a useful supplement for those allergic to milk. It can be contaminated by traces of lead, so choose carefully.

BREWER'S YEAST POWDER: This is an excellent source of the B complex vitamins, containing 17 vitamins, 16 amino acids and 14 minerals and one of the best sources of RNA (a nucleic acid that helps the body's immune system). Because brewer's yeast has a high phosphorus to calcium ratio, it is advisable to mix it with powdered milk. Another high protein food, but one to use in small amounts as more and more people are becoming allergic to yeast through overdosage with it.

COLD-PRESSED SAFFLOWER, SUNFLOWER AND 'ALL BLEND' OILS: These polyunsaturated oils are rich sources of essential fatty acids (see 'fats and oils' and 'vitamin F'). Use sparingly. Needs vitamin E.

CRUDE BLACK MOLASSES: The first extraction of sugar from sugar-cane. It contains the B complex vitamins: biotin, folic acid, inositol, pantothenic acids, B_1, and B_2, as well as vitamin E, and is rich in potassium, iron, copper, magnesium, phosphorus and calcium.

DESICCATED LIVER: This vacuum dried beef liver is prepared at low temperature, so most of the nutrients are conserved. It is rich in vitamins of the B complex, A, C and D, calcium, copper, iron and phosphorus.

GOAT'S MILK: Goat's milk, yoghurt and cheese, hygenically produced, is a palatable alternative to cow's milk, being more easily digested and found to be more suitable for some people suffering from eczema and other allergies.

HONEY: While all honey is organic, nectar from flowers unsprayed by insecticides and pesticides, gathered by healthy bees (winter-fed on honey, not sugar) is much the best, so I buy unpasteurized honey from a hot sunny country. Honey contains natural sugars which are slowly released into the bloodstream, and is predigested by the bees. Containing traces of many minerals and vitamins, honey is a digestive aid, a wholesome source of energy and sweetness, and being bactericidal, is useful as a first-aid application to burns and cuts. Use in moderation.

KELP AND DULSE: Powdered seaweeds and one of the best sources of iodine. They are also rich in calcium, magnesium, vitamins D, E and K and the B complex. Being salty in taste, it is a nutritious salt substitute – but use sparingly; like brewer's yeast, it has an unusual flavour!

LIVE NATURAL YOGHURT: Preferably Bulgarian. This is the best way to take milk, as the protein is pre-digested. At its best made from raw milk – preferably goat's milk. It is useful for re-introducing the beneficial bowel bacteria after the use of antibiotics – or use miso.

MISO: A naturally fermented soya purée, containing lactic acid and enzymes. Stir into stocks and soups just before serving.

SEAWEEDS OR SEA VEGETABLES: Fresh dried, these are even better than kelp and dulse. They are a balanced source of minerals and vitamins, including B_{12}, and may be powdered after crisping in a slow oven. While protective and curative in cases of heavy metal exposure, they are gentle on the kidneys, so are good natural chelators. Worth acquiring a taste for! (see page 62).

SPIRULINA: The powder made from this alga is a valuable food supplement. Spirulina contains perfect protein (comparable with egg, but without the disadvantage of the cholesterol), is a rich source of vitamin B_{12}, and is high in iron. It is also a valuable source of gamma-linolenic acid (an essential fatty acid).

WHEATGERM: Best when raw and unstabilized. Wheatgerm contains the B vitamins, folic acid, niacin, pantothenic acid, B_1, B_2 and B_6 as well as vitamin E, phosphorus, iron, magnesium, selenium and zinc. It is high in protein and is a wonderful food for those who can tolerate wheat.

Rich food sources of minerals and vitamins

In nutrition, trace elements are even more important than vitamins, because it is generally believed that they cannot be synthesized by living matter as can vitamins. The minerals in foods depend on the soil from which they originated. As with vitamins, many minerals are lost in processing and food preparation, and may be thrown away with the peelings or the cooking water!

CALCIUM: Milk, yoghurt, cheese (both cow's milk and goat's milk), soya milk; turnip tops, broccoli, mustard and cress, cabbage, sea kale, sea vegetables, watercress; shellfish, especially cockles, shrimps, whitebait, sprats and sardines; blackstrap molasses; soya beans, haricot beans; sesame seeds, dates and figs; powdered milk, bone-meal*, dolomite*; raw muesli cereal grains when soaked overnight (see 'muesli').

CHROMIUM: Brewer's yeast; molasses; corn oil, whole-grain cereals; black pepper, beetroot, mushrooms; liver, beef; beer.

COBALT: Offal, e.g. heart, liver, kidneys, sweetbreads, brains; chicken, turkey; seafoods, especially oysters; milk; green leafy vegetables; nuts; wholegrains.

COPPER: Lamb's liver, calves' liver, organ meats; seafoods; soya beans, nuts, raisins, mushrooms, molasses; bone-meal*. (NB an excess is toxic.)

FLUORIDE: Tea; fish and seafoods; cheese and meats; bone-meal*; whole rye grains and rye bread; fluoridated water and fluoridated toothpaste. (NB an excess of fluoride is toxic.)

IODINE: Carageen moss, Gelozone, onions, garlic, watercress, carrots, potato skins, seafood, pears, pineapple, sea vegetables, kelp* and dulse*.

IRON: Organ meats, especially liver; lean meat; desiccated liver*; spirulina*; eggs; shellfish, fish; poultry; dried fruits, e.g. prunes, raisins, currants, apricots; pumpkin seeds; blackstrap molasses; leafy dark green vegetables, e.g. watercress, parsley, spinach; onions, garlic, raw cereal muesli grains when soaked overnight; iron cooking pots. (NB an excess of iron is toxic.)

MAGNESIUM: Milk, nuts; seafood; wholegrains, wheatgerm, wholegrain cereals; crude black molasses; dark green leafy vegetables; dolomite*.

MANGANESE: Wholegrains, e.g. wheat bran, corn germ, rice bran, oat bran, oats, brown rice; walnuts, chestnuts, almonds; cloves, cardamom, ginger; parsley, onions, watercress, spinach, lettuce, green beans, carrots, lima beans, dandelion leaves; egg yolks; apricots, pineapple.

* Denotes the supplemental form.

POTASSIUM: Lean meats; wholegrains, especially rye and maize; sesame seeds, millet, sunflower seeds, linseed; lentils, beans, peas; corn oil, safflower oil; walnuts, peanuts; spinach, sorrel; honey, molasses; Banbu, Pioneer and Postum coffee substitutes; molasses and Muscovado sugars; Ruthmol and Trufree salt replacers; vegetables.

SELENIUM: Herring, tuna; wheatgerm, wheatbran, wholegrains; broccoli brewer's yeast*; garlic; liver; eggs.

SILICA: Onions, garlic, chives, leeks, parsley; brown rice, pot barley, maize; kelp*; molasses; Pioneer coffee, equisetum herb tea (horsetail); figs, hard dates, prunes; lentils, beans; carob, caraway seeds.

SODIUM: Seafood, meat; seasalt, Biosalt, herbsalts; baking powder, bicarbonate of soda; processed foods; milk, milk products; sea vegetables, kelp*.

VANADIUM: Fish; fats and vegetable oils; black pepper; olives.

ZINC: Seafoods, all shellfish – especially oysters, herrings; pork, liver, beef liver, lamb, beef; wheat bran, wheatgerm, whole oatmeal, maize, plain 100% wholemeal flour, whole rye flour, brown rice; peas, carrots, beetroot, cabbage; prunes, sultanas, raisins, currants; egg, egg yolk, milk; whole nuts, peanut butter.

VITAMIN A (oil-soluble): Liver, eggs, herrings, mackerel, crab, butter, cheese; yellow and dark green fruits and vegetables – apricots, peaches, prunes, watermelon, corn, cornmeal, carrots, pumpkin, silver beet, cress, watercress, spinach, kale, broccoli, parsley, kombu and nori (sea vegetables); cod liver oil*, desiccated liver*, halibut liver oil*. (NB an excess is toxic.)

THE B COMPLEX: (these are water-soluble and heat sensitive)

VITAMIN B1 (THIAMINE): Rice polishings (rice bran), raw wheat germ, whole millet, barley, wheatbran, wholewheat, buckwheat, soya, brown rice; heart, brains, liver, pork, venison; Brazil nuts, sunflower seeds, mackerel, crab; chick peas, split peas, soya bean granules, black beans; brewer's yeast*.

VITAMIN B2 (RIBOFLAVIN) – also light sensitive: Beef heart, kidney, liver, brains, chicken liver, meat, venison; dried milk, yoghurt, milk; almonds, hazelnuts, whole millet, wholewheat pasta, wheatgerm, soya flour, cheese.

VITAMIN B5 (PANTOTHENIC ACID): Organ meats, e.g. liver, heart, kidney, brains; egg yolk, dried milk; wholegrains, especially buckwheat, wheat bran, wheatgerm; sesame seeds, sunflower seeds, cashew nuts, peanuts, soya beans, dried peas; brewer's yeast*.

VITAMIN B6 (PYRIDOXINE): Organ meats, especially beef liver, chicken liver; goose, mackerel, cod, crab, herring, trout, beef, chicken, lamb, rabbit; pot barley, wheatbran, buckwheat, brown rice, wheatgerm, soya.

VITAMIN B12 (CYANOCOBALAMINE): Organ meats, e.g. liver, kidney, heart; meat, mackerel, sardines; free range eggs; miso, shoyu; spirulina*; sea vegetables.

BIOTIN: Organ meats, e.g. beef heart, kidney, liver, brains, tongue, lamb's liver; sweetbreads; peanuts, soya, brown rice; almonds, egg yolk, dried milk; crab, mackerel; banana; brewer's yeast*. (NB Biotin is destroyed by the avidin in raw egg white: overcome this by immersing egg in very hot tap water, around 150°F, for 10 minutes.)

CHOLINE: Soya beans, peanuts, fish, beef liver, egg yolks, wheatgerm; lecithin granules*, brewer's yeast*.

* Denotes the supplemental form.

16

FOLIC ACID: Green leafy vegetables, e.g. spinach, silver beet, beetroot tops, kale, broccoli, endive, asparagus; turnips, potatoes (just beneath the skin); liver and kidney; almonds, pumpkin seeds, chick peas, fenugreek seed, wheat bran, wheatgerm, soya flour; brewer's yeast*.

INOSITOL: Beef brains and heart; wholegrains, e.g. bulgar wheat, wheatgerm, wholewheat, brown rice; nuts, citrus fruits, molasses; brewer's yeast*, lecithin granules*.

NIACIN (NICOTINAMIDE): Organ meats, e.g. beef heart, chicken liver, lamb liver; rabbit, dark turkey meat; halibut, mackerel, trout, herring, cod, haddock; rice polishings, wheat bran, wholewheat, wheatgerm, pot barley, brown rice.

P.A.B.A. (PARA-AMINOBENZOIC ACID): Liver, eggs, molasses, wheatgerm, yoghurt; green leafy vegetables; brewer's yeast*.

PANGAMIC ACID: Apricot kernels, pumpkin seeds, sesame seeds; organ meats; salmon; egg yolks; wholegrains, brown rice, wheatgerm, rice polishings; brewer's yeast*.

VITAMIN C (water-soluble; heat, light and oxygen sensitive): Rosehips, blackcurrants, citrus fruits, gooseberries, strawberries, parsley, raw cauliflower, sprouted alfalfa, other sprouted beans and grains, broccoli, Brussels sprouts, cabbage, spring greens, kale, kohl rabi, green pepper, Acerola cherries*.

VITAMIN D (oil-soluble): Oily fish, e.g. sardines, cod, tuna, herrings, mackerel; milk, cheese, butter, egg yolks, enriched margarine; desiccated liver*, cod liver oil*, halibut liver oil*. (NB the action of sunlight on the skin enables man to synthesize his own Vitamin D.)

VITAMIN E (oil-soluble): Cold-pressed vegetable oils, e.g. safflower, wheatgerm, corn, soya; peanuts; wholegrains, e.g. wholewheat, wheatgerm, brown rice, oats; green leafy vegetables, especially spinach, broccoli, cabbage; molasses; avocado; kelp*, dulse*; cottonseed oil*.

VITAMIN F (essential fatty acids – oil): Sunflower seeds, walnuts, sesame seeds; cold-pressed vegetable oils, e.g. sunflower seed, safflower, wheatgerm, soya, All-Blend; avocado; spirulina*, evening primrose*.

VITAMIN K (oil-soluble): Green leafy vegetables, especially spinach, cabbage, cauliflower; peas, carrots, tomatoes, potatoes, alfalfa sprouts; pork liver, lean meat; egg yolk, yoghurt, wheatgerm, soya beans; molasses; kelp.

VITAMIN P OR BIOFLAVONOIDS (water-soluble): Citrus fruit pith, skin and pulp; buckwheat; green peppers; apricots, cherries, grapes, blackcurrants, tomatoes, broccoli.

Remember that many minerals and vitamins are lost in food processing and preparation. See pages 6 and 17.

* Denotes the supplemental form.

Practical Knowhow

The enjoyment of a good meal starts with the eyes and the nose! To enhance the appetite and aid digestion the food should be attractive to look at, with a good contrast of colour and texture, and have an appealing aroma. Simple meals made from wholefoods are both satisfying and nourishing and can be delicious.

Every person is an individual and will vary in his or her dietary requirements, and from day to day. Only you know your exact needs and circumstances, likes and dislikes. Where you do not have the co-operation of your family, think out your plan of action carefully and make improvements where you can. Increasing vegetable and fresh fruit consumption, cutting back on frying, and using more wholegrains are all worthwhile changes to introduce gradually. Choose foods free from chemical additives, colourings, flavourings, anti-oxidants, flavour-enhancers, etc.

Savour the satisfaction of knowing that your careful food preparation and menu planning are making a positive contribution to the health of all the family.

Keeping the goodness in our foods

Vitamins are vital nutrients which can readily be lost en route to the table. The water-soluble vitamins C and B complex are most vulnerable, being also sensitive to heat. Here are some guidelines to help you:

- Avoid storage of perishable vegetables (greens especially). When necessary, store them in a cool, ventilated place. Wilted vegetables have lost much of their vitamin C.
- Avoid preparing in advance. Cut surfaces cause greater destruction of vitamins, and soaking leeches them out too. When prior preparation is necessary, leave in a closed container, in as large pieces as possible, in a cool place, out of the light, with just sufficient water to cover. Then use this water for cooking, and retain and use it for gravy, soup, as sauce or stock.
- Use the minimum amount of water when boiling vegetables and keep pot covered with a tightly fitting lid. Minerals as well as some vitamins are water-soluble and should not be poured down the sink. In some homes, the sink is the best fed mouth in the family! Nearly all stock is usable.
- Do not overcook. Most foods have a better colour and flavour when cooked to 'slightly rare', and food with a texture which encourages chewing will be better digested and more satisfying. Heat destroys most of the B complex vitamins and vitamin C as well as enzymes.
- Do not add bicarbonate of soda to greens. It destroys vitamins B_1 and C. For this reason, home-made bread made from yeast is more nutritious than quick breads made with sodium bicarbonate.
- Boil the water first before adding the prepared vegetables to minimize oxidation and loss of vitamin C.

- Serve all hot foods promptly. Keeping foods hot destroys further the vitamin C.
- Use stainless steel, enamelled or Pyrex cookware – copper and iron accelerate the destruction of vitamin C. Aluminium is a toxic mineral which reacts with foods and gradually accumulates in the body.

Comparison of cooking methods

Grilling is superior to frying from a nutritional point of view. The larger the proportion of cut surface, the greater the nutrient loss. Grilling also aids in extracting some of the animal fat present in most meats, whereas frying adds more fat. Deep frying seals in more nutrients, so is better than shallow frying. Sautéing is gentle frying in the minimum quantity of oil to bring out the flavour, without browning – as is 'sweating'. Use in strict moderation as it adds fat to the dish.

Steaming is better than boiling in a lot of water, though it may take a little longer in cooking vegetables. Fewer nutrients are dissolved into the steam than would be dissolved into surrounding water. When boiling vegetables till just tender in the minimum amount of water in a closed pan, most of them will be well above the water level, and virtually steamed. This is what we mean by 'conservative cooking'.

Stir-frying is another recommended method. Heat 2 tbsp vegetable oil in a wok or heavy-based frying pan. Fry the prepared vegetables quickly, on high heat stirring continuously to prevent burning. Cook 2 to 3 minutes – till softened a little and warmed through, but still crisp to eat. Suitable method for onions, young carrots and leeks (all finely sliced), for cabbage and Chinese leaves (shredded) or mung beansprouts.

Baking in the skin is the best way of retaining all the nutrients in potatoes. With baking and roasting, excess time or heat is destructive of thiamine (B_1).

Braising can be a method of cooking vegetables slowly, moistened with stock, in a closed, oiled casserole in the oven – e.g. marrow, courgettes, leeks. Some vegetables need softening with a little oil or butter as well, e.g. celery and onion. Braised meat is generally cooked on a platform of vegetables in the casserole after being sealed in hot oil.

Long slow heating, boiling dry, boiling in a lot of water, fast boiling with no lid (i.e. exposed to the air), and discarding of the cooking water are all causes of unnecessary nutrient loss from vegetables.

Long slow cooking is an effective way of tenderizing tough cuts of meat. Electric slow cookers are the modern equivalent of the old-fashioned 'hay-box' for producing the same effect.

When camping, we have brought stews or soups to the boil and then transferred them quickly to a well-heated wide-necked vacuum jar, so that they would cook slowly in our absence. When using a thermos jar, it is wisest to transfer the hot food to a saucepan and simmer it for five minutes before serving. Food left in a thermos flask or jar for more than 18 hours would be suspect for producing food poisoning. Pulses need to be cooked at a fast boil for ten minutes before transferring to a slow cooker.

Microwave cooking sounds appealing when you read the list of advantages claimed. But evidence is emerging that this cooking method shatters the life force of the food.

Pressure cooking is another way to save time, and, done in a stainless steel pressure cooker*, can also save valuable nutrients by:
- Cutting down on cooking time.
- Cooking in the absence of air.
- Using a steamer basket, fewer nutrients are dissolved out of the foods.
- The higher speed in reaching the cooking temperature again lessens the loss of vitamin C.

Other advantages are the savings in being able to use cheaper cuts of meat to produce good meals, lower fuel costs with shorter cooking times. Another economy note is that even old woody root vegetables become tender and retain their flavour well.

The disadvantages are minimal. Most necessary is the need to adhere to the cooking times exactly, or the food could be spoiled.

Alternatives

While it is better to use wholefoods rather than the refined foods to which we may be accustomed, it is useful to know which alternatives are practical, so here are some suggestions:

CORNFLOUR: for thickening, use half the quantity of arrowroot.

WHITE FLOUR: for thickening gravy, use 100% wholemeal flour, 85% wheatmeal flour, barley flour, fine oatmeal, yellow cornmeal, chick pea flour or brown rice flour. (Mix 2 tbsp of the wholegrain flour to a smooth paste with a little cold water. Boil ½ pt stock and stir in. Return to boil, stirring and simmer for 3 to 5 minutes.) Or avoid using flour altogether by liquidizing together a few potatoes, onions (or any other available suitable vegetable) together with the meat juices and vegetable stock to make a gluten-free gravy.

WHITE FLOUR: for baking, use 100% wholemeal flour. Or start by trying 85% brown flour until you are confident to change over to the 100% wholemeal. When substituting wholemeal for white flour in a recipe, be prepared to use about 20% more liquid, as the wheatgerm and bran in the wholemeal flour make it more absorptive, so the finished produce will be more moist as well as more full of flavour. Try also rye flour, barley flour, buckwheat flour, cornmeal, oatmeal, gram (chick pea) flour, potato flour, brown rice flour and soya flour.

WHITE SUGAR: substitute with genuine Demerara sugar (check the country of origin is Guyana; some apparent Demerara is white beet sugar, coloured!), light soft brown sugar, dark soft brown sugar, raw Muscovado sugar, molasses sugar, honey, malt and apple juice concentrate. The last five are the best of

---

* As with all cooking saucepans, stainless steel is recommended because it does not react with the food cooked, as does aluminium. Aluminium is a toxic metal and the tiny amount absorbed into the food is cumulative in the body, so do not use it for saucepans, frying pans, kettles, teapots or pressure cookers.

them all. Honey is sweeter than white sugar, so about 20% less is needed. Molasses and molasses sugar have a distinctive flavour which goes well with gingerbread and on porridge.

GOLDEN SYRUP: Substitute honey or a little black treacle, or honey and molasses mixed. Apple juice concentrate, maple syrup and malt are possibilities.

JAM AND MARMALADE: Whole Earth no sugar jams and marmalade, Pear 'n' Apple, and Sweet 'n' Fruity Spreads; Thursday Cottage reduced sugar jams and marmalade made with raw sugar; Infinity jams made with organically grown fruit; or make your own (p. 173).

COW'S MILK: try goat's milk, which is often tolerated where cow's milk is not – in cases of eczema for example. Otherwise soyabean milk, Plamil or nut milks, e.g. coconut, sesame, almond, etc. (See chapter on drinks.)

HARD CHEESE (high in fat and salt): prefer farmhouse to dyed or processed cheese. Better are low-fat soft cheeses (from cow's, goat's and ewe's milk), curd cheeses and quark. Otherwise tofu (low-fat high protein soya cheese) is the vegan alternative.

BUTTER for spreading: Butter Plus (p. 171), clarified butter, additive-free vegetable margarine (Alfonal Sunflower and Safflower margarines, Vitaquel, Vitasieg, Granose and Tomor), natural peanut butter (e.g. Harmony), Tahini, Sunflower and Tofu Spreads. Other possibilities, p. 170.

FRUIT SQUASH: use pure fruit juices (check the labels to ensure that no sugar, colourings, flavourings, or sugar substitutes are present), home-made lemon drink, water, apple drink made from apple juice concentrate etc.

COFFEE: decaffeinated coffee (if it is just the caffeine that is to be avoided). Otherwise roasted dandelion root coffee, Postum, Caro, Pioneer, Bambu or Barleycup – these last actually being good for you as well as tasting reasonably like coffee!

TEA: Japanese twig tea, 11 o'clock Rooibosch tea (a red tea from South Africa which has scarcely any tannin and no caffeine, but does taste like tea!), Luaka, Ceylon tea, herb teas, mint tea, weak China tea, green buckwheat tea.

SALT: Seasalt, Biosalt, Lane's Herb Salt, onion, garlic and celery salt; in cases of potassium deficiency, Ruthmol and Trufree (salt replacers). All these salty seasonings should be used sparingly. Vegit, Spike, garlic powder and kelp powder are other alternative seasonings.

VINEGAR: substitute lemon juice, natural yoghurt, whey.

MEAT: fish, eggs, cheese, cottage cheese, beans and pulses, soya beans, whole grain cereals, beansprouts, nuts and seeds; see chapter on proteins.

BREAD: corn on the cob, potatoes, yams, parsnips, beetroot, brown rice, tapioca, lentils, peas and beans, sprouted wheat, kasha and kruska.

GELATINE: Gelozone and Agar Agar (both made from seaweed) are good jelling agents. Agar Agar is tasteless – use 2 teaspoons to set one pint of liquid by sprinkling over the boiling liquid and stirring until dissolved. Gelozone has a stronger flavour and needs to be mixed with cold water first, then the hot liquid poured over, stirring, and the mixture simmered, stirring, for three minutes – in the same quantities as for Agar Agar.

PASTA: in place of the usual pastas made with white flour, wholewheat and buckwheat macaroni, spaghetti, etc., are available and have a good flavour.

TINNED FRUITS IN SYRUP: look for the fruits tinned in either their own or another natural fruit juice; better still, use fresh fruits, home stewed fruit sweetened with honey, raw brown sugar or dried fruits. (Choose tins with covered seams.)

STOCK CUBES: there are several alternatives available in good health food shops which contain no monosodium glutamate, artificial flavourings, colourings or anti-oxidants – e.g. Marigold Swiss Vegetable Bouillon Powder, Country Stock, Vecon, Morga's Vegetable Bouillon Cubes and Hugli's Clear Vegetable Stock Cubes. Other quick flavour enhancers are: Lea and Perrins Worcestershire Sauce, Whole Earth Kensington Sauce, tamari/shoyu, Tabasco, miso soya purée, and of course herbs and spices and good home-made stock. See chapter on stocks.

COCOA: use carob powder, (see page 155).

CHOCOLATE: use carob confectionery bar made with raw sugar.

Conversion tables

Solid Ingredients

25 gm	1 oz	275 gm	10 oz
50 gm	2 oz	300 gm	11 oz
75 gm	3 oz	350 gm	12 oz
100–125 gm	4 oz	375 gm	13 oz
150 gm	5 oz	400 gm	14 oz
175 gm	6 oz	425 gm	15 oz
200 gm	7 oz	450 gm	16 oz (1 lb)
225 gm	8 oz	900 gm	2 lb
250 gm	9 oz	1000 gm (1 kg)	2 lb 4 oz

Liquid Measurements

25 ml	1 fluid oz
50 ml	2 fluid oz
100–125 ml	4 fluid oz
150 ml	5 fluid oz (¼ pint)
300 ml	10 fluid oz (½ pint)
450 ml	15 fluid oz (¾ pint)
600 ml	20 fluid oz (1 pint)
1000 ml (1 litre)	35 fluid oz (1¾ pint)

Spoon Measurements

1 tbsp 15 ml approx
2 tsp 10 ml approx

1 tsp   5 ml approx
½ tsp 2.5 ml approx
Pinch = less than ⅛ teaspoon

1 cup = 7 fl oz = 200 ml

All spoon and cup measurements, whether for wet or dry ingredients, are for level spoons or cups in this book, unless otherwise indicated.

I find it more convenient, logical and time-saving to measure some ingtredients in cups (e.g. wholegrains, cereals, pulses, beansprouts etc).

Equivalent Oven Temperatures

Very, very cool	150°–175°F	70°– 80°C	
Very cool	200°–275°F	100°–140°C	¼–1 Gas
Cool	300°F	150°C	2 Gas
Warm	325°F	160°C	3 Gas
Moderate	350°F	180°C	4 Gas
Fairly hot	375°–400°F	190°–200°C	5–6 Gas
Hot	425°–450°F	220°–230°C	7–8 Gas
Very hot	475°–500°F	240°–260°C	9 Gas

Note: Use either all Imperial or all Metric measurements in following any recipe.

Key to symbols used in recipes

S = Suitable for slimmers
LF = Low fat
GF = Gluten-free
SF = Salt-free
A = Free from gluten, grain, sugar, milk and egg

Planning Balanced Meals

The exact proportions of foods in a balanced diet will depend on our metabolism, digestion and physical workload, as well as the climate. As a guide, our daily diet should include:

- 10–20% protein foods (see list on page 9)
- 45–65% vegetables, fruits and salads
- 20–40% natural wholegrains (in bread, baking, muesli, etc. – see page 117)
- 5–7% natural sugars (sweet fresh and dried fruits, honey and molasses)
- 25–30% total dietary fat* including 3–5% natural polyunsaturates for vitamin F

These proportions are for a diet including protein of animal origin.

Additionally, each day's meals should include all the water-soluble nutrients which cannot be stored by the body – vitamins C, P and the B complex, and trace minerals. Each week's menus should include the oil-soluble vitamins A, D, E and F, and a good source of iron – by the inclusion of organ meats, fish, nuts, seeds and cold-pressed vegetable oils. The wholegrains, vegetables and salads will also provide vital fibre to ensure efficient peristaltic action throughout the digestive tract and prevent constipation.

Plan your meals to contrast colours, flavours and textures. To complement a smooth food, serve one that is crisp and chewy (e.g. scrambled egg on wholemeal toast). Every meal should include something which needs thorough chewing – teeth and jaws need to be exercised in mastication as well as talking! Chewing mixes the food with the first digestive juices and triggers the preparation of later stages of digestion, as well as helping develop healthy well spaced teeth in our youngsters.

Try to include something raw at each meal and to finish with a food which will leave the teeth clean, such as raw fruit or celery.

The basic daily plan for an ideal balanced diet is as follows:

ON WAKING: Natural fruit juice, unsugared and diluted with water (orange, lemon, grapefruit, tomato, pineapple, grape or apple). Or drink of hot water with a slice of fresh lemon, or herb or Rooibosch tea (unsugared) with a vitamin C tablet (100–250 g).

---

* This diet is likely to include at least 20% total dietary fat before the addition of any butter, margarine or oil. Meat, oily fish, cheese, eggs, nuts, seeds, avocados and olives all contain a high proportion of dietary fat. Natural wholegrains, shellfish, white fish and pulses contain a smaller amount of hidden fat. Fried foods, the generous use of butter, margarine and oil, and the inclusion of rich foods (e.g. pastries, cakes, gravy, mayonnaise) quickly exceed the ideal of 30%. See chapter on nutrition.

BREAKFAST: A fresh fruit meal with non-flesh protein. Generous helping of fresh fruit muesli which includes mixed raw soaked cereal grains and sunflower seeds, nuts and lots of fruit. Or 4 tablespoons raw wheatgerm with milk and apples, and boiled, poached, scrambled or coddled free range egg with wholemeal toast.

(Growing children and those doing hard manual work can double up!)

MID MORNING: Drink of pure water, or fresh fruit, or fruit or vegetable juice, herb tea, Rooibosch tea or Barley cup or Pioneer. For hungry ones, a wholemeal sandwich.

LUNCH OR SUPPER: Principally a starch and vegetable meal, with a little protein. Ideally (digestion and climate allowing), this will consist of a large fresh salad of mostly raw ingredients, with cheese, nuts, egg (if not eaten for breakfast!) or little cold meat or vegetarian savoury. Wholemeal bread or baked jacket potatoes. Hot soup on cold days. Natural yoghurt with wheatgerm and honey as dessert if needed.

MID AFTERNOON: As mid morning.

MAIN MEAL: Principally a meal of protein and conservatively cooked vegetables. Include a green leafy vegetable and a root vegetable – or a raw green garnish of parsley, watercress, mustard and cress or beansprouts (to be eaten!). Raw fresh fruit for dessert, or cheese and apples or celery.

ON RETIRING: Bedtime drink (see chapter on health drinks).

DRINKS: Remember that the body needs pure water as well as good foods, and that fluid intake is best taken ½ hour before or 2 hours after a meal – not with it. Milk is the exception as it is a food requiring digestion.

Menu planning

In planning a week's menu, try to include fish once or twice, organ meat once, muscle meat or poultry 3–4 times and a vegetarian meal once or twice for the main meals. Try to avoid serving meat more than once a day.

It is even a good idea to have one day free from all animal produce, using pulses with wholegrains or nuts for protein (see page 9). This serves to boost our lecithin intake and give the body a rest from high cholesterol foods.

In the following sample weekly menus, desserts are included for those not yet accustomed to making a meal from a large salad or a one course meal where fresh vegetables predominate. Where puddings are part of your lifestyle, try these wholefood desserts. Vegetables should be steamed or boiled conservatively (pages 18 and 53) unless otherwise specified. The retained vegetable stocks should be used in the soups, sauces, gravy or casseroles. You can, of course, substitute grilled or roast meat for the suggested meat dishes, incorporate left-over vegetables and gravy in soups, serve soups and puddings a second day, and serve fresh fruit instead of dessert. Once you grasp the basic principles, you will enjoy being creative!

See also breakfast suggestions (page 29) and chapters on muesli and grain dishes (page 117), drinks (page 162) and packed lunches (page 169).

Menu Suggestions

SPRING

Monday

Casseroled Chicken
Baked Potatoes
Spring Greens, Leeks
Rhubarb Crumble

Cream of Leek Soup
Jewel Salad
Eggs in a Nest
Natural Yoghurt Enton Hall

Tuesday

Vegetarian Moussaka
Baked Potatoes
Sprouting Broccoli
Braised Leeks
Baked Apples

Chicken Broth
Creole Rice Salad
Green Salad
Banana Fluff

Wednesday

Fricandelles
Artichokes OR Carrots
Spring Greens
Steamed Mashed Potato
Orange Ice-cream

Quick Hazelnut Roast
Baked Potatoes
Watercress OR Mustard and Cress
Baked Bananas

Thursday

Watercress Soup
Grilled Plaice with lemon and
  tomato
Crunchy Mashed Potato
Apple and Orange Foam

Cream of Leek Soup
Waldorf Salad
Cheese and Herb Rolls
Hurry Crumble

Friday

Cassoulet
Baked Potatoes
Broccoli OR Spring Greens
Rhubarb Snow

Sardine Special Baked Potatoes
Green Salad
Coconut Custard

Saturday

Braised Lamb's Hearts with onions
Carrots OR Swede
Baked Potatoes
Sprouting Broccoli
Apple Sponge

Sustaining Salad
Green Salad OR
Carrot and Beansprout Salad
Baked Potatoes
Copenhagen Apple Pudding

Sunday

Foresight Rabbit
Spring Greens, Carrots
Gooseberry Pudding (using frozen
  gooseberries OR
Fresh Fruit Salad

Golden Pea Soup
Coleslaw with cold lamb's heart
Chicory and Orange Salad
Green Salad
Apple Cracknel

SUMMER

Monday

Wholemeal Spaghetti Bolognaise
New Peas, Carrots
Summer Lettuce
Strawberries with Orange Juice

Kedgeree
Banana Salad
Green Salad
Fruit Yoghurt

Tuesday

Speedy Cheesy Pie
Spinach
Courgettes
Raspberries with Cottage Cream

Spanish Summer Soup
Golden Salad
Green Salad
Steamed New Potatoes
Gooseberry Fool

Wednesday

Layered Liver
French Beans OR Runner Beans
Strawberries with Gran's Cream

Herring Roes on Toast
Bulgarian Salad
Green Salad
Banana Ice-cream

Thursday

Grilled Mackerel
Steamed New Potatoes
Raw Tomatoes and Watercress
Fresh Peaches

Cream of Runner Bean Soup
Lebanese Salad
Cheese
Pancakes with Strawberry
   or Orange Sauce

Friday

Beanburgers
Courgettes
Cauliflower
Carrots
Summer Pudding

Strawberry Shake OR
Salad Niçoise
Minted Orange Salad
Gooseberry Pudding

Saturday

Grilled Lamb Chops
Steamed New Potatoes
Ratatouille
Raspberries with Pineapple Juice

Chilled Raw Beetroot Soup
Courgette Salad
Cauliflower Salad
Cold Beanburgers
Trifle

Sunday

Super Spiced Chicken
Brown Rice
Cauliflower
French OR Runner Beans
Tomatoes – raw or oven-baked
Fresh Fruit Salad

Chilled Cucumber Soup
Black and White Salad
Orange Ice-cream OR Trifle

AUTUMN

Monday

Beefergine Loaf
Spinach Beet, Carrots
Melon OR
Banana Fluff

Sweetcorn
Beetroot and Pear Salad
Green Salad
Cheese OR Hard-boiled Egg
Stewed Blackberry and Apple

Tuesday

Sicilian Quiche
Leeks, Marrow, Cabbage
Peaches OR
Fruit Yoghurt

Picnic Lunch: Muesli in a jar
OR Avocado, cottage cheese and
    walnuts OR
Wholemeal Sandwiches
Apples

Wednesday

Irish Stew
Red Cabbage
Runner Beans
Apples OR Fruit Fluff

Rainbow Salad
Cold Sicilian Quiche OR
Beefergine Loaf
Blackberries with Gran's Cream

Thursday

Buckwheat Rissoles
Baked Potatoes
Carrots, Watercress
Pears OR Apple Crumble

Borsch
Chicory and Orange Salad
Tomato and Cauliflower Salad
Cottage Cheese
Old English Frumenty

Friday

Tomato Soup
Grilled Sprats
OR Sardine Specials
Mushroom and Beansprout Salad
Green Salad
Brown Bread Pudding

Golden Pea Soup
Liver Dumplings
Fresh Peaches or Pears

Saturday

Chicken Bermudan
Roast Potatoes, Swede
Spinach, Cauliflower
Rainbow Fruit Salad

Aubergine Pizza
Cauliflower Salad
Baked Bean and Celery Salad
Nut and Apple Pudding

Sunday

Pot Roast Brisket of Beef
Hot Beetroot
Brussels Sprouts, Pumpkin
Blackberry and Apple
    Crumble

Green Tomato Soup OR
Chicken Broth
Avocado and Crab Salad
Caraway Cabbage Slaw
Coconut Custard

WINTER

Monday

Casseroled Steak Jervaise
Baked Potatoes, Brussels Sprouts
Carrots OR Swede
Baked Bananas

Herring Roes on Toast
Coleslaw
Prune Salad
Cheese and Biscuits

Tuesday

Sweetbreads with Mushrooms
Mashed Parsnip and Potato
Brussels Sprouts OR Cabbage
Banana Fluff

Special Sea Green Soup
Savoury Brown Rice
Stuffed Marrow
Fruit Jelly

Wednesday

Chicken with Apricots
Mashed Swede
Spinach Beet, Cauliflower
Apple Cracknel

Mushroom Soup
Nut Case Potatoes
Green Salad
Carrot and Apple Salad
Christmas Custard

Thursday

Egg Cutlets OR Omelettes
  Jervaise
Spinach Beet OR Cabbage
Swede, Artichokes
Fluffin

Cream of Artichoke Soup
Brains on Wholemeal Toast
Mushroom and Beansprout Salad
Green Salad
Raspberry Duet

Friday

Baked Cod Supreme
Crunchy Mashed Potatoes
Peas, Tomatoes
Old English Frumenty

Simplicity Supper
Wholemeal Bread
Fruit Cake
Fresh Fruit and Yoghurt

Saturday – Dinner Party

Watercress Soup OR
Rollmop and Orange Salad
OR Fresh Grapefruit
Foresight Au Gratin Supreme
OR Chicken Imperial
Red Cabbage, Calabrese
Potato mashed with Celeriac OR
  with Parsnip
Foresight Fruit Salad
OR Pineapple Cheesecake

Quick Bean Supper Dish
Baked Potatoes
Watercress
Winter Fruit Salad

Sunday

Roast Lamb with Rosemary
Roast Potatoes and Parsnips
Sprouting Broccoli, Carrots
Fruit Salad

Cream of Fridge
Jewel Salad, Green Salad
Egg and Beetroot Salad
Pineapple Cheesecake

Breakfast suggestions
Fresh Fruit Muesli – large bowlful!
Cereal and dried fruit muesli with milk or apple juice. Fresh fruit.
Wholegrain unsugared cereals with milk or apple juice. Fresh or stewed fruit.
Wholegrain toast with free-range egg – boiled, poached, scrambled or coddled.
Fresh or stewed fruit.
Wholewheat toast with Butter Plus, Pease Spread or peanut butter; and Apricot
Marmalade, Houmous, Sunflower Spread, Tofu Spread, tahini or cheese; fruit.
Natural yoghurt with wheatgerm or oatgerm and honey, prunes or apricots.
Nuts and raisins with fresh fruit.
Meal in a Glass (see 'Drinks' page 165).
Oat, millet, barley or potato porridge with milk, molasses, molasses sugar, maple
syrup or Muscovado sugar or with apple juice.
Kruska or Kasha (page 123).
Cornflakes with wheatgerm or oatgerm, bran, or Linusit Gold, Frugrains or
Grapenuts and milk or apple juice. Fruit.
Ripe bananas, orange, sunflower seeds.
Wheatgerm with stewed fruit; fresh fruit.
Mushrooms, egg, tomato, ham, potato or brown rice.

Breakfast may be a quick meal, but it is an important start to the day. There is
evidence to suggest that omitting breakfast can make you less alert, giving you a
shorter attention span, slower reaction time and decreased efficiency. As it can
also reduce the blood sugar level, it encourages greater consumption of sugar-
laden snacks and caffeinated drinks. According to the Iowa Breakfast Study in
1976, it could even lead to poorer school results and more social and emotional
problems in school children.

Herbs & Spices for Flavour

Healthy foods should be full of flavour as well as goodness. Cutting back on salt and sugar should not leave tasteless foods, but open up the spectrum of the natural flavours in vegetables and herbs, grains, fruits and spices, meats, fish, poultry and dairy products.

Organically produced foods are the ideal but some may be unobtainable to many of us. Cutting down on meat and poultry is one economy which will help the budget stretch to include the wholegrains, free-range eggs and extra vegetables, fruit and salads that we recommend (see chapter on proteins).

In addition to using fresh wholesome produce, flavour in savoury dishes is improved by the use of good stocks and occasionally some wine. Read the ingredient list of most stock cubes, and you will realize why stock-making recipes are included in the soup chapter! As salt used in excess is a poison to the body, one answer to making foods tasty lies in the judicious use of herbs and spices. The accent is on the word judicious – too much spice (and some herbs) is not good for us either! Their use should be so subtle that the delighted eater cannot isolate the elusive fragrance or flavour which so enhances the dish.

The selective use of herbs and spices

As a general rule, when you wish to emphasize the sweetness of a dish, use: allspice, coriander, cinnamon, mace, cloves, nutmeg, cardamom, mint and curry. For well seasoned foods, experiment with: garlic, oregano, sage, basil, parsley, thyme, marjoram, dill, cumin, black pepper, mustard and bay leaves. Mixed spice may contain nutmeg, coriander, cinnamon, cassis, caraway, cloves, mace and ginger. Garam Masala is an Indian blend of spices specially selected for curries and savoury dishes. It is made from coriander, cumin, ginger, black pepper, cinnamon, pimento, cardamom, bay leaves, cloves and nutmeg. Using a pinch of this in a dish could be an easy introduction to the enhancement a little spice can add to a recipe.

Caution: Some herbs and spices are so very strong that they will irritate tender skin, so wash your hands very thoroughly before picking up a baby or rubbing your eyes.

While it is difficult to draw the line between some herbs and spices, here are lists of both, with suggestions for their use:

Herbs and their suggested uses

APPLE MINT: fruit sorbets
BASIL: liver, stews, soups, tomato, pasta, eggs, fish and salads
BAY LEAVES: good with sweet milk custards as well as most savoury dishes
BORAGE: salads, eggs, cucumber, and in cider or claret cup or lemonade

BOUQUET GARNI: contains parsley, thyme, marjoram and bay leaf tied in muslin. See page 33 also.

CHERVIL: fish and egg dishes, salads, as garnish on pork chops, steak, tomatoes, carrots and peas

CHIVES: (mild onion flavour) good with egg, attractive garnish; best used fresh

DILL WEED: the leaves are good in salads, meat, fish and in prawn sauces

DILL SEEDS: bruised (stronger flavour) with pork, boiled potatoes

FENNEL: (flavour like aniseed) use leaves with fish, soups and stuffings, fresh root in salads

GARLIC: strong onion flavour which helps many savoury dishes; also useful for its health-giving, blood-purifying properties

HORSERADISH: grated root used in sauce, vinegar, and egg sandwiches

LEMON BALM: salad dressings, soups, sauces, chicken dishes

LEMON THYME: stuffings, fish dishes

LOVAGE: (strong celery flavour); use in soups, stuffings, stews

MINT: salads, peas, sauce, jelly and tea – savoury and sweet recipes

MARJORAM: (similar but milder than oregano); use with game, chicken, beef

NASTURTIUM: leaves and flowers in salads

OREGANO: eggs, cheese, fish, mushrooms, tomatoes, minced pork and beef, pizzas and all Italian dishes

PARSLEY: all savoury dishes, hot and cold, salads, garnish, sauces (most flavour is in the stems for soups, stews, casseroles, etc.)

PEPPERMINT: tea, fruit cup, fruit salads

ROSEMARY: roast lamb, pork and chicken, casseroles, soups, marinades, and many Italian dishes

SAGE: stews and shepherd's pie, stuffings, pâtés, egg, pork, poultry, game

SUMMER SAVORY: stuffings, sausages, game

SWEET CICELY: fresh leaves cooked with sour fruit to lessen sugar needed

TARRAGON: fish, eggs, chicken, sauces, vinegar and herb butter

THYME: game stews, roasts, chicken, stuffings and tomato sauce

Spices and their suggested uses

ALLSPICE: marinades, pickling fruits and vegetables, curries, biscuits

ANISE (aniseed): sauces, breads, cakes and biscuits

BLACK PEPPER: best freshly ground in peppermill; good in all savoury dishes

CARAWAY: seeds for cabbage, salads, cakes and breads

CARDAMOM: seeds need to be bruised; use in casseroles, roasts, sauces, curries, also good in ice-cream (lemony flavour)

CAYENNE: (very hot) use sparingly in egg and cheese dishes

CHILLIES: if using the pods, remove the seeds, which are even hotter. Powdered, it is a hot pepper, good for curries. Wash hands *many* times after handling

CINNAMON: roast lamb and duck, in chicken and lamb casseroles, with apples or ground in cakes and biscuits

CLOVES: whole, for pickles, savoury and sweet dishes and with apples; powdered in baking

CORIANDER: ingredient of pickling spice; stews, soups, curries and fancy breads and biscuits

CUMIN: curry, lamb, meatballs

GINGER: ground, in cakes, curries, stews and dips. Fresh root (peel and chop finely) also in curries and savoury dishes

JUNIPER: crushed berries used in sauerkraut, game, marinades, stuffings

LEMON RIND (zest): fish, sauces, stuffings, cakes and sweet dishes

MACE: (husk of nutmeg) stews, chicken, chutneys; on swede, tomato soup

MUSTARD: pickling, salad dressings, sauces

NUTMEG: a gently flavoured spice, best freshly grated from a whole nutmeg; use in sauces, soups, creamed potato and swede, spinach and cream cheese, mushrooms; also sweet egg custard

PAPRIKA: (mildest of the peppers with good flavour and beautiful red colour); use with pork, chicken, egg and cheese dishes; a good garnish

TURMERIC: curries and pickles (has a lovely yellow colour which also stains fingers and work surfaces)

VANILLA: well-known flavour for sweet sauces, ice-cream (take care to buy pure vanilla pods or extract, not the imitation product, vanillin)

HERB BUTTERS

The basic proportion is 2 oz (50 g) of soft butter to one tablespoon of finely chopped fresh herbs (or substitute ½ teaspoon dried herbs) and 2 teaspoons fresh lemon juice.

Cream the butter, mix in the herb, add the lemon juice and beat well. Prepare several hours in advance for the herb flavour to be released. Chives, watercress, basil, chervil, rosemary, parsley, thyme, garlic, mint, marjoram, dill and fennel are all suitable for herb butter. Use for special sandwiches, in the preparation of egg dishes or for topping meat, savoury or vegetable dishes, just before serving and when grilling fish.

MAITRE D'HOTEL BUTTER

4 tbsp butter
4 tsp lemon juice
1 tbsp finely chopped parsley

⅛ tsp pepper
¼ tsp minced onion or shallot

Cream butter until very soft, add herbs and lemon juice very slowly, stirring constantly.

HERB STUFFING

1 onion, finely chopped
1 tbsp vegetable oil
2 oz (50 gm) fresh wholemeal breadcrumbs
2 tbsp fresh basil, chervil, tarragon or fennel, chopped, OR 1 tsp dried herbs OR 1 tsp mixed dried herbs

freshly ground black pepper
salty seasoning
1 egg, beaten

Sauté onion in hot oil. Remove from the heat and add the breadcrumbs, herbs, seasoning and egg. Stir to mix well. Use in grilled or baked fish. With appropriate choice of herbs, this stuffing is suitable for poultry, beef, lamb or tomatoes.

Suggested combinations for you to try:

Vegetable or Protein	*Herb and Spice*
Mushrooms	Nutmeg
Peas	Cook with mint or serve with mint or Maitre d'Hotel butter
Potato	Dill, nutmeg, parsley, mint, paprika
Broad Beans, French Beans and Runner Beans	Serve with parsley or Maitre d'Hotel butter or cook with summer savory
Swede	Mash the cooked swede with mace or nutmeg
Spinach	Grate on a little nutmeg just before serving or serve with butter and lemon juice
Tomatoes	Raw with basil or cooked with oregano or mace
Cucumber	Dill
Carrots	Raw with fresh chopped mint or cooked with rosemary
Courgettes	Cooked with garlic, or dill
Eggs	Basil, marjoram, chervil, savory, thyme, rosemary, chives, cayenne, paprika
Fish	Fennel, dill, bay leaves, basil, chervil, mint or tarragon, lemon peel
Soups	Rosemary, lavender, thyme, chervil, savory, marjoram or basil, lovage, garlic, celery seeds, cloves, paprika
Poultry	Bay leaves, basil, sage, thyme, tarragon, marjoram, rosemary, chervil, lovage, parsley, lemon rind, mace, cloves, cinnamon, ginger
Beef	Lovage, sage, thyme, garlic, basil, summer savory, savory, marjoram, celery seed, cumin
Lamb	Rosemary, garlic, spearmint, summer savory, chives, marjoram, tarragon, thyme, lovage, celery seed, oregano, bay leaves, cumin
Pork	Garlic, cumin seed, parsley, sage, bay leaves, lovage, rosemary, mustard

BOUQUET GARNI: This is a little bunch of fresh herbs tied together, or dried herbs tied in a muslin bag, cooked with the dish and removed before serving. Choose 3 or 4 from such herbs as parsley, thyme, tarragon, sage, celery stem, lovage, chervil, basil – according to the character of the dish. A piece of lemon rind and a few cloves or peppercorns may also be included.

SALTY SEASONING FOR FLAVOUR: For flavouring soups, casseroles, sauces, dressings, dips, cutlets, etc., my favourites are Lane's Herb Salt, Hugli's Vegetable Broth Granules, Vecon, Marigold's Vegetable Bouillon powder, Garlic Salt, Celery Salt, Onion Salt, Vegit and Spike (vegetable seasonings); and Tastex and Natex (yeast extracts). The fermented soya extracts – soysauce, shoyu, tamari and miso add a different savour. The well-known Worcester Sauce and Whole Earth's new Kensington Sauce are useful too. Keep a good selection with your herbs and spices. Taste and experiment to find the blends best suited to your palate.

For baking and cereal dishes (e.g. porridge and kruska), fine sea salt and Biosalt are more appropriate – or Ruthmol and Trufree if sodium is a problem. Season sparingly. More can be added later – but not subtracted!

THE FINAL TOUCH: 5-10 minutes before serving the finished hot dish or soup, stir in a tiny pinch of the appropriate herbs to add or renew their subtle aroma and delicate flavour.

Salads & Beansprouts

The best salad ingredients are those grown organically, locally, in their own season, picked fresh, washed and prepared just before eating. Never leave to soak in water; some of the water-soluble vitamins and minerals will be lost through cut edges.

Start with simple salads of four or five ingredients, twice weekly. Gradually increase the number of salad meals a week, and the diversification of ingredients as the digestion adapts to accept living foods. If troubled with 'wind', eat simpler salads with no dried or raw fruit at the same meal; toss salad in Vitality Dressing and chew it extra thoroughly. Do not rush a salad meal; sit down and enjoy it!

A salad is not just the usual lettuce, tomatoes, cucumber and beetroot; so many vegetables are delicious raw in salad. Be adventurous. Try to incorporate sprouted seeds into salads for their extra high vitamins B and C, amino acids (protein) content and their vital 'life force'. Vary dressings to add variety.

Thorough washing of salad ingredients and scrubbing of celery and root vegetables immediately before use goes without saying. Readers' attention is drawn to the added precaution for watercress, given below.

All the following can be used raw in salads:

ASPARAGUS: Choose young green spears.

AVOCADO: Cubed or sliced and dressed; ripen in a closed paper bag.

BEETROOT: Grate finely the young fresh beets; older stored beets can be cooked and dressed (see p. 54).

BROCCOLI LEAVES: Finely chopped.

BRUSSELS SPROUTS: Cut in thin slices; introduce gradually as they can be wind-provoking.

CABBAGE: Green, white and red, finely shredded.

CARROT: Grated or sliced or eaten whole when young.

CAULIFLOWER: In florets or chopped; delicious and very high in vitamin C.

CELERIAC: Slice thinly, blanch and marinate to prevent discoloration.

CELERY: By stalk or chopped; eat the leaves too.

CHICORY: Bitter flavour.

CHINESE LEAVES: Chopped.

CHIVES: Chopped, they are a wonderful addition to egg and tomato.

COURGETTES: Use sliced in ¼" slices or cubed.

CUCUMBER: Slice or cube; leave the peel on as it contains enzymes making it more easily digested.

DANDELION LEAVES: Chop for chlorophyll; use sparingly.

ENDIVE: Bitter flavour.

FENNEL: Use the 'head' of the root, thinly sliced; aniseed-like flavour.

FRENCH BEANS: Eat young.

JERUSALEM ARTICHOKES: Deliciously nutty; scrub, dice and marinate in a dressing.

KALE LEAVES: Finely chopped.

KHOL RABI: Young, cubed.

LEEKS: Finely sliced or chopped and used sparingly at first as they can repeat.

LETTUCE: Whole leaves or chopped in large pieces.

MUSHROOMS: Cultivated ones, preferably; wash well and slice.

MUSTARD AND CRESS: Leave growing till the last moment.

NASTURTIUM LEAVES: Flowers and seeds are all edible and hot!

ONIONS: Finely sliced or chopped; use sparingly until appreciation grows. Becomes very bitter if grated.

PARSLEY: Chopped or in sprigs.

PEAS: Eat young.

PEPPER (RED, GREEN & YELLOW): Slice, saving seeds for stockpot.

RADISH: Whole, made into flowers or sliced.

RUNNER BEANS: Eat young; delicious straight off the plant.

SPINACH LEAVES: Chop for chlorophyll; use sparingly (see page 62).

SPRING ONION: Whole or chopped.

SPROUTED GRAINS: Seeds and legumes, whole or chopped; see section on sprouting seeds.

TOMATOES: Keep their flavour best uncut; wash well if bought.

TURNIP AND SWEDE: Eat young; cubed or grated.

WATERCRESS: Chop as little as possible – it is such a nutritious food. Soak for 10 minutes in cold salted water to kill any river flukes, then rinse thoroughly in fresh water. Store loosely covered.

Salad quantities are flexible. Vary the proportions according to availability and preference, starting with the ingredients you like.

SIDE SALADS

Salad combinations to enjoy

Avocado. Toss peeled, cubed avocado in orange juice.

Baked Beans & Celery. Tinned baked beans (free from additives) and chopped celery, sprouted mung beans or alfalfa sprouts.

Banana Salad. Finely shredded white cabbage, sliced ripe banana, chopped mint, in pineapple juice.

Beetroot and Apple. Finely grated raw beetroot, coarsely grated apple, little lemon juice.

Beetroot and Pear. Finely grated raw beetroot, chopped fresh pears, little lemon or orange juice.

Carrot and Apple. Grated carrot, coarsely grated or chopped apple, raisins and a little lemon or orange juice.

Carrot and Beansprout. Grated carrot, alfalfa sprouts, mung beansprouts and sliced raw mushroom in French Dressing.

Carrot and Celery. Grated carrot, chopped celery, coarsely grated or chopped apple, chopped mint, lemon or orange juice.

Carrot and Orange. Grated carrot, zest and juice of an orange.

Celeriac. Thinly sliced or cut in matchsticks, in Slimmer's Herb Dressing.

Cheesey Carrot. Grated carrot and grated cheese.

Chicory and Orange. Chicory leaves arranged with slices of peeled orange.

Cucumber. Diced cucumber in Slimmer's Garlic Dressing or natural yoghurt, decorated with mint sprigs and paprika.

Herbed Tomato. Sliced tomato with chopped fresh basil and parsley and a sprinkling of cider vinegar and salty seasoning.

Jerusalem Artichoke. Diced raw artichoke in Tahini or Vinaigrette dressing.

Kohl Rabi. Diced raw kohl rabi in Slimmer's Herb Dressing or French Dressing.

Minted Beetroot. Grated raw beetroot, chopped mint, a little lemon or orange juice.

Minted Orange. Shredded white cabbage, chopped mint, chopped fresh peeled orange slices in Yoghurt and Honey Dressing or pineapple juice.

Mushroom and Beansprout. Sliced raw mushrooms, sliced tomato, beansprouts and chopped parsley in French Dressing.

Provençal. Raw diced courgettes, quartered tomatoes, sliced green peppers, little thinly sliced raw onion, in French Dressing with garlic or Slimmer's Garlic Dressing.

Ratatouille. Cold left-over ratatouille with green salad.

Sweet Onion. Slice ½ lb Spanish onions, sprinkle with 1 tbsp Muscovado sugar and pour on boiling water to just cover. Stir and leave for 5 minutes. Pour off water. Cover with Slimmer's Apple Dressing and refrigerate till needed.

Tomato and cauliflower. Sliced tomato, raw cauliflower florets, bulgar wheat (or sprouted wheat) and chopped parsley in Yoghurt and Honey Dressing.

Tomato and Onion. Sliced tomatoes and sliced mild onion rings, sprinkled with chopped basil and freshly ground black pepper, with French lemon dressing.

Tropical Slaw. Shredded white cabbage, whole or grated nuts, pineapple pieces, sultanas and raisins in Green Cucumber Dressing, Coleslaw Dressing or French Dressing.

Green Salads

Crisp Iceberg lettuce, chopped coarsely, watercress and sliced cucumber.

Rough chopped soft lettuce, finely chopped celery (including leaves), mustard and cress or alfalfa sprouts.

Shredded Chinese leaves, mustard and cress, sliced cucumber, finely chopped spring onions or chives.

Cos lettuce, diced cucumber, mung or other beansprouts.

Watercress, shredded white cabbage, alfalfa sprouts.

Shredded green cabbage, chopped celery, coarsely chopped parsley.

Cauliflower florets, sliced green pepper, alfalfa sprouts or mustard and cress.

Webbs Wonderful lettuce, fresh chopped mint and/or chives, cubed cucumber.

Endive, cucumber, sliced green pepper.

Finely shredded white cabbage, chopped green celery (including leaves), chopped parsley and mint.

Chicory, finely sliced courgette, chopped parsley.

Spinach leaves shredded with cucumber, celery and green pepper.

BULGARIAN SALAD

1 lb (450 gm) new young carrots
1 tsp honey
1 clove garlic, pressed
¼ pint (150 ml) natural yoghurt

2 tsp chopped parsley
2 tsp chopped chives
salty seasoning and paprika

Simmer carrots whole in a very little water with the honey, until just tender. Cool and cut into cubes. Cream the pressed garlic with a little of the yoghurt to blend evenly, and add herbs, seasonings and a little of the carrot stock. Marinate the carrots in the herb dressing in the refrigerator for 1–2 hours before serving cold.

CARAWAY CABBAGE SLAW

½ lb (225 gm) white cabbage, finely
    shredded
1 Bramley apple, peeled and diced
1 tsp caraway seeds

1 stick celery, finely chopped
½ Coleslaw Dressing (see page 49)
sprouted fenugreek

Mix first 4 ingredients with the dressing and decorate with fenugreek.

CAULIFLOWER SALAD

2 tsp thin honey
1 cup natural yoghurt
2 cups chopped cabbage
2 tbsp chopped red pepper
4 tbsp chopped spring onion

2 cups chopped cauliflower
4 tbsp chopped parsley
½ avocado, cut in strips into lemon
    juice

Dissolve honey in yoghurt. Mix all chopped ingredients into the yoghurt and decorate with the avocado.

COLESLAW

6 oz (175 gm) finely shredded white
    cabbage
3 oz (75 gm) grated carrot

1 tbsp finely chopped onion
½ Coleslaw Dressing (page 48)

Mix together. Vary by adding sliced banana, chopped orange segments, chopped celery, chopped mint or parsley, chives in place of the onion, or beansprouts.

COURGETTE SALAD

2-3 courgettes, sliced thinly
½ small red pepper, sliced thinly
6-8 fresh radishes, sliced thinly
¼ pint (150 ml) natural yoghurt

2 tsp chopped parsley
2 tsp chopped chives
1 tsp chopped mint
salty seasoning to taste

Arrange vegetables decoratively. Mix yoghurt and herb dressing and sprinkle over.

FENNEL SALAD

1 fennel root
1 hard-boiled egg, chopped

2 tbsp chopped parsley
French lemon dressing

Chill fennel root in ice water for ½-1 hour to crisp it. Slice finely and combine with egg and parsley. Sprinkle with French lemon dressing and serve.

JEWEL SALAD

1 lettuce
½ cup diced raw apple
¼-½ cup chopped red and green
   peppers

½ cup carrot, finely sliced or grated
1 cup chopped celery
2 tbsp raisins
½ cup orange juice

Line dish with lettuce leaves, mix other ingredients in the orange juice and arrange in the centre.

LEBANESE SALAD

1 bunch spring onions, chopped
½-1 lb (225-450 gm) tomatoes, diced
½ cucumber, diced

1 tbsp chopped mint
1 tbsp chopped parsley
¼ pint (150 ml) natural yoghurt
freshly ground black pepper to taste

Mix vegetables and herbs in yoghurt. Season.

PRUNE SALAD

1 cup prunes, soaked for 24 hours
½ cup grated carrot

1 cup diced raw apple
1 cup finely shredded cabbage

Chop prunes (removing stones) and combine ingredients.

RAINBOW SALAD

3 cups finely sliced cabbage
½-1 cup chopped red and green
  pepper
chopped hard dates to taste

1 cup chopped celery
1 cup coarsely grated cooking apple
lemon juice dressing

Combine ingredients and mix in lemon juice dressing.

QUICK SNACK SALAD MEALS OR HORS D'OEUVRES

FRENCH BEAN SALAD

1 lb (450 gm) young French beans
French dressing
1 small onion, chopped finely

1-4 hard-boiled eggs
Smokey Snaps
chopped parsley

Steam the beans till they are barely cooked. Pour over the dressing and chopped onion, stir well and cool. When cold, decorate with hard-boiled egg slices, Smokey Snaps and parsley. (4)

TABBOULEH

Tabbouleh garlic dressing:
3 tbsp fresh lemon juice
6 tbsp sunflower oil
2 cloves garlic, crushed
seasoning (optional)

4-5 spring onions, chives, 1 shallot
  OR 1 small onion, finely chopped
8 oz (225 gm) tomatoes, diced
½ cucumber, diced
4-8 oz (125-225 gm) sprouted wheat
2 bunches parsley, chopped
1 bunch fresh mint, chopped
1 large cos lettuce

Shake 4 dressing ingredients together in screw-top jar. Mix spring onions, tomato, cucumber, wheat and herbs. Arrange whole lettuce leaves around large shallow dish. Pile tabbouleh in the centre and pour over the dressing. A traditional Lebanese dish. (4)

PEAR AND GRAPE SALAD

3 oranges
1-3 ripe raw pears
1 tbsp sunflower seeds
8 oz (225 gm) cottage cheese

1 crisp lettuce
3-4 oz (75-100 gm) black grapes
1 cup alfalfa sprouts
1 bunch watercress (see page 36)

Squeeze ½ orange for juice. Peel and cut pears into slices and toss in orange juice. Peel and slice remaining oranges. Mix sunflower seeds into cottage cheese. With the lettuce as a base, put the cottage cheese in the centre, with the sliced pears, orange, grapes, alfalfa sprouts and watercress arranged around it. (4-6)

BLACKBERRY AND APPLE SALAD

2-3 tsp honey
3 tbsp natural yoghurt
3 tbsp orange juice
½ cup diced cooking apple

½ cup blackberries, uncooked
2 tbsp coconut flakes
1 cup cold cooked brown rice
lettuce leaves

Blend honey, yoghurt and orange juice together in a basin. Add diced apple and blackberries and coconut and stir well. Stir in brown rice and serve on a bed of lettuce leaves. (4)

GOLDEN SALAD

lettuce or endive
4 bananas, sliced
juice of 1 orange
½ cup walnuts, cashws or pecan
    nuts

1 small ripe pineapple, chopped
2 oranges, sliced
½ cup coconut flakes

Arrange crisp lettuce or endive to cover the plate. Toss the sliced banana in the orange juice, add all other ingredients and arrange on green base. (4-6)

TROPICANA SALAD

3 parts adzuki beansprouts
1 part dried apricots, soaked and
    chopped

1 part raisins
1 part peanuts or cashew nuts

Mix together in given proportions and serve with a green salad.

WALDORF SALAD

1 red sweet apple
1 green Bramley apple
½ pint (300 ml) yoghurt dressing
1-2 sticks celery
½ lb (225 gm) white cabbage

2 tbsp chopped walnuts
2 tbsp raisins, well washed
2 oz (50 gm) black grapes
1 cup alfalfa sprouts

Core the apples, retaining the skins and cut them in neat wedges or cubes, covering with dressing to prevent oxidation. Coarsely chop the celery, finely shred the cabbage and add to the apples, together with the nuts and raisins. Stir well. Halve and de-pip the grapes and use to decorate the top of the salad. Arrange the alfalfa sprouts around the edge of the dish. (4-6)

EGG AND BEETROOT SALAD

Chinese leaves, sliced
4 tbsp mayonnaise
1 tsp horseradish sauce, or to taste
8 oz (225 gm) cold steamed
  potatoes, diced

3 boiled eggs, sliced
½-1 bunch spring onions, chopped
8 oz (225 gm) dressed salad beetroot

Make a base with the Chinese leaves. Combine mayonnaise with horseradish sauce to taste. Mix potato, half the egg and spring onions with mayonnaise and spoon on to base. Arrange beetroot slices around edge and decorate with remaining egg and spring onions. (3-4)

DATE AND WALNUT SALAD

1 small lettuce
2 sweet red apples
yoghurt and honey dressing
3 sticks celery, chopped finely

4 oz (100 gm) stoned dates, chopped
2 oz (50 gm) walnut pieces
1 cup mung beansprouts

Arrange lettuce leaves as a base. Cut apple into cubes, dropping straight into the yoghurt dressing. Add celery, chopped dates, walnuts and beansprouts and mix well. Pile on to the lettuce and serve. (4)

ROLLMOP AND ORANGE SALAD

1 large orange
2 cups alfalfa sprouts
8 rollmops (pickled herrings)

6 tomatoes, quartered
½ bunch watercress (see p. 36)
1 onion, sliced in rings

Peel the orange and cut into eight halfmoons. Make a base of the alfalfa sprouts and arrange the drained rollmops, orange and tomato sections and watercress in a satisfying pattern. Garnish with the onion rings. (4)

HEARTY SALADS

BLACK AND WHITE SALAD

1 lb (450 gm) potatoes (waxy
  varieties are best)
OR finely shredded white cabbage
¾ lb (350 gm) cold cooked chicken
OR broken cashew nuts or almonds
2 oz (50 gm) black olives (optional)
8 oz (225 gm) black grapes

1 ripe cooking apple, diced
6 fl oz (175 ml) home-made
  mayonnaise
freshly ground black pepper
2 oz (50 gm) raisins (seedless,
  washed)
1 bunch spring onions

Steam or boil the scrubbed potatoes till just cooked. Then peel, cool and dice them. Cut the chicken into bite-sized pieces, halve and remove stones from olives. Halve and remove pips from grapes. Mix apple, potato and chicken (or apple, cabbage and nuts) with mayonnaise and black pepper to taste, and spread over serving dish. Arrange remaining ingredients decoratively across the top. (6)

CREOLE RICE SALAD

Creole Dressing:
1 tsp garam masala
1 tsp tamari (soy sauce)
2 tsp thin honey
4 tbsp lemon juice

¾ cup vegetable oil
3 tbsp chopped parsley
herb salt to taste

Rice Salad:
3 cups cooked brown rice
1 green pepper, finely chopped
½ cup raisins or sultanas
1 cup finely chopped celery
1 onion, finely chopped

½ cup sunflower seeds (soaked overnight) or slivers of cooked chicken
3 fresh peaches (skinned) or nectarines, sliced

Dressing: Mix garam masala to a paste with tamari, honey and lemon juice, then blend in oil, herbs and seasoning. Shake well in screw-top jar. Mix salad ingredients together, reserving one peach for decoration. Combine with dressing and decorate. (6)

BANANA AND NUT SALAD

6 oz (175 gm) brown rice, long grain
2 bananas
zest and juice of 1 small lemon
½-1 cucumber, sliced
2 tbsp sunflower oil or safflower oil
1 tsp honey

¼ tsp garam masala
4 tbsp washed sultanas or seedless raisins
3-4 oz (75-100 gm) broken cashews, walnuts or almonds

Cook the brown rice for 40–50 minutes till tender (see page 123) and drain and cool. Slice the peeled bananas into the lemon juice. Add cucumber. Drain off the lemon juice and whisk with the oil, honey and spices. Add all other ingredients and leave in cool place for one hour for flavours to mix before serving. (6)

SEAFOOD SALAD SPECIAL

1 lb (450 gm) white fish
home-made mayonnaise
6 hard-boiled eggs
1 tin crabmeat
1 lb (450 gm) cooked prawns
2 tbsp chopped chives

1 cos lettuce
½ cucumber, sliced or cubed
6 tomatoes, sliced
1 bunch watercress (see page 36)
1 cup alfalfa sprouts
1 bunch spring onions

Steam or poach the white fish (page 74). Cool and remove skin and bones. Thin the mayonnaise with a little of the fish stock and add to the flaked fish, with the chopped egg, crab pieces, prawns and chives. Mix well. Arrange the lettuce as a base around a large shallow platter, with the seafood mixture in the centre. Add the other ingredients, arranging them attractively. (8-12)

AVOCADO AND CRAB SALAD

1 lb (450 gm) cooked crabmeat
1 lettuce
2 ripe avocados, peeled & sliced
lemon juice

1 cup alfalfa sprouts
6 tomatoes, quartered
black grapes, halved and de-pipped
Herb Mayonnaise (page 47)

Remove any shell from the crabmeat. Arrange lettuce leaves as base on large serving platter, with the prepared crabmeat in the centre. Peel the avocados and cut into long slices, gently applying lemon juice to every cut surface to prevent discoloration. Arrange the avocado slices, alfalfa sprouts, tomato quarters and halved grapes to look attractive. Serve with Herb Mayonnaise. (4-5)

SALAD NIÇOISE

1 tin tuna fish (200 gm)
juice of 1 lemon
4 tbsp chopped parsley OR chives
4 hard-boiled eggs, sliced
1 cos lettuce or Chinese Leaves

1 lb (450 gm) small tomatoes,
    quartered
12 oz (350 gm) cooked French beans
1 bunch watercress
2 oz (50 gm) black olives OR grapes

Flake fish and mix with fish oil, lemon juice, parsley and half the egg. Arrange coarsely chopped lettuce as base on serving plate. Spoon fish mixture in centre and arrange other ingredients decoratively. (4-6)

SUSTAINING SALAD

1 cup sprouted wheat
1 cup sprouted sunflower seeds
4 tbsp natural yoghurt
½ cup orange juice

3 sharp ripe apples, diced
½ cup washed raisins OR sultanas
pinch of paprika
½ bunch watercress

Sprout the wheat and sunflower seeds (page 51). Combine the yoghurt and orange juice in a bowl. Mix apples into the dressing. Add sprouts and raisins with paprika to taste. Arrange in serving bowl with border of watercress. (4-6)

SALAD DRESSINGS

BLUE CHEESE DRESSING   S

¼ pint (150 ml) natural yoghurt
½ tsp Worcester sauce
tamari OR shoyu

2-4 oz (50-100 gm) crumbled blue
  cheese
1 clove garlic, pressed

Liquidize all ingredients. If too thick, add a little water, whey or rejuvelac.

HERB VINAIGRETTE

½ pint (300 ml) safflower oil
2 tbsp lemon juice
1 tsp dried oregano
½ tsp dried marjoram
1 tsp kelp powder OR
½ tsp Lane's Herb Salt

¼ pint (150 ml) apple cider vinegar
2 tbsp tamari OR shoyu
1 tsp dried thyme
½ tsp rosemary
2 tbsp sesame seeds

Shake all the ingredients together in a screw-top jar with a secure lid, or liquidize
in a blender.

GREEN CUCUMBER DRESSING   S

1 cucumber
6-10 fl oz (175-300 ml) natural
  yoghurt
¾ tsp kelp powder

¼ tsp dried basil
juice of 1 lemon
1 clove garlic, pressed
¼ tsp dried dillweed

Discard ends of cucumber. Chop coarsely and put in blender with other ingredients. Liquidize. Substitute fresh herbs if available.

TAHINI DRESSING

4 tbsp tahini
6 tbsp mayonnaise
1 clove garlic, pressed
pinch oregano

4 tbsp natural yoghurt
½ tsp Worcester sauce
½ tsp salty seasoning

Mix all ingredients together adding a little whey if too thick.

S SLIMMER'S HERB DRESSING

¼ tsp honey
2 tbsp natural yoghurt
2 tbsp safflower oil
2 tsp cider OR white wine vinegar

1 tbsp fresh dill, chopped
1 tbsp chopped chives
1 tbsp fresh tarragon, chopped
black pepper and salty seasoning

Blend the honey into the yoghurt. Add other ingredients in a screw-top jar and shake all together (or liquidize). Good for a mixed green salad, or on raw cubed kohl rabi or celeriac salad.

S SLIMMER'S APPLE DRESSING

¼ cup cider vinegar
¼ tsp garlic powder
pinch garam masala OR powdered
   mustard

¼-½ cup water
1 tsp apple juice concentrate

Whisk all together.

S TOMATO DRESSING (OR SAUCE)

1 tin of peeled tomatoes (14 oz)
2 tsp cider vinegar
¼ tsp basil OR oregano

1 shallot OR small onion
pinch cayenne
2 ripe tomatoes, peeled

Finely chop the raw and tinned tomatoes and the onion and mix in other ingredients. Good with salads, pasta, rice, fish or baked potatoes.

YOGHURT AND HONEY DRESSING

2 tbsp plain yoghurt
thin honey to taste

2 tbsp orange juice

Mix together.

SALT-FREE VINAIGRETTE DRESSING

¼ tsp dry mustard
1 tsp honey
5 tbsp apple cider vinegar

10 tbsp sunflower oil
½ tsp kelp powder, Spike OR Vegit
¼ tsp paprika

Blend mustard in honey. Place all ingredients in screw-top jar with efficient lid. Shake to combine well.

S SLIMMER'S GARLIC DRESSING

2 cloves garlic
½ pint (300 ml) natural yoghurt

4 sprigs fresh mint
salty seasoning

Crush the garlic into the yoghurt and blend with finely chopped mint. Season to taste.

MAYONNAISE

1 small pickling onion OR shallot OR
  ½ clove garlic
1 tbsp raw brown sugar
1 tsp dry mustard
1 tsp paprika

1 tsp salty seasoning
1 large egg
½ pint (300 ml) sunflower oil
2 tbsp lemon juice
1 tbsp cider vinegar

Chop the onion or garlic and put in blender with sugar, spices and seasonings. Liquidize at slow speed with egg. Add oil very slowly until thick again. Stir in the vinegar and lemon juice. Store in screw-top jars in refrigerator.

HERB MAYONNAISE

½ pint (300 ml) home-made
  mayonnaise
2 tsp finely chopped fresh tarragon
  OR ¼ tsp dried tarragon

1 hard-boiled egg, chopped
1 tbsp finely chopped parsley
1 clove garlic, pressed (optional)

Stir ingredients together.

QUICK FRENCH DRESSING

½ tsp French mustard
½ tsp clear honey
6 tbsp sunflower/safflower/soya oil

¼ tsp salty seasoning
3 tbsp apple cider vinegar

Put all ingredients into a screw-top jar. Replace lid firmly and shake vigorously to mix the ingredients thoroughly. Add to a green salad just before serving.

VARIATIONS TO FRENCH DRESSING

1. Add a small clove of garlic, whole or crushed.
2. Add 1 tsp of salad herbs to the dressing.
3. Use lemon juice in place of cider vinegar.
4. Add 2 tsp of chopped parsley.
5. Add 2 tsp of chopped mint.
6. Add 2 tsp of chopped chives.
7. Use half quantity of powdered mustard in place of French mustard.
8. Add a few drops of Worcester or Kensington Sauce.
9. Add a little fresh ginger, very finely chopped.
10. Season with garam masala.

AVOCADO DRESSING

3 tbsp mashed ripe avocado
3 tbsp water
4 tsp lemon juice

½ tsp bouillon powder
3 drops Worcester Sauce

Whisk all ingredients together and use promptly.

DRESSING FOR AVOCADO

1 tsp clear honey
¼ tsp French mustard
¼ tsp salty seasoning
1 tbsp hot water

2 tbsp lemon juice OR apple cider vinegar
5 tbsp sunflower/safflower/soya oil

Mix together honey, mustard and salt and dissolve in hot water. Add lemon juice and oil and whisk briskly. This dressing is milder and more suited to the delicate flavour of a ripe avocado.

MILD DRESSING

2 tbsp cider vinegar
3 tbsp lemon juice
2 tbsp water or apple juice
4 tbsp sunflower or safflower oil

pinch salty seasoning
pinch paprika
pinch dried tarragon, basil & marjoram (OR steeped fresh herbs)

Blend in liquidizer or shake well together in a screw-top jar. If fresh herbs are available, steep them in the prepared dressing for 24 hours before serving. Use for salads with fruits.

S ENTON HALL SALAD CREAM

2 tbsp cornflower
2 tsp raw Barbados sugar
1 tsp dry mustard

1 pint (600 ml) milk
4 fl oz (125 ml) cider vinegar
salty seasoning

Mix the dry ingredients to a creamy paste with a little of the cold milk. Heat the remaining milk in a double saucepan. Whisk the boiling milk into cornflour mixture and return to double boiler to cook for 8–10 minutes, stirring occasionally. Cool. Beat in vinegar and add seasoning to taste.

(This tasty salad dressing contains very little fat or gluten, if gluten-free cornflour and mustard are used.)

FORESIGHT COLESLAW DRESSING

1 tbsp raw Barbados sugar
¼ tsp French mustard
¼ tsp bouillon powder

2 tsp sunflower oil
1 cup natural yoghurt
1 tbsp lemon juice

Mix the dry ingredients to a smooth paste with the oil, then whisk in all the other ingredients – or use liquidizer.

VITALITY DRESSING

⅛ tsp miso
2 tbsp rejuvelac (page 165)

1 tsp clear honey
1 tbsp freshly squeezed lemon juice

Cream miso with a little rejuvelac. Whisk in remaining ingredients. This enzyme-rich dressing may help the digestion of raw salads.

BEANSPROUTS

Sprouted beans, seeds and grains are the most nutritious foods you can possibly prepare and eat – the only food you can readily eat every day while it is alive and still growing. Think of the natural foods wild animals eat. The most intelligent animals that work for man include the horse, the donkey, the ox and the elephant. Do they need bacon and eggs for breakfast? Where do they find their protein? Their protein comes from living vegetation, and from dried grains. For optimum health man also needs living food and sprouted seeds are ideal for his different digestive system.

Buy fresh seeds, beans and grains, organically produced where possible, and check that they are suitable for human consumption (i.e. that they are not treated with fungicides). Besides health food shops, more and more supermarkets are now stocking the more popular seeds. Try the following:

Triticale (a wheat-rye hybrid)	Corn (maize)
Organic wheat	Alfalfa seeds
Organic brown rice	Sunflower seeds (hulled)
Buckwheat (unroasted)	Sesame seeds
Mung beans (the usual Chinese beansprouts)	Radish seeds
Adzuki beans (red Japanese beans)	Chinese lettuce seeds
Chick peas (garbanzos)	Spinach seeds
Brown lentils	Fenugreek

Successful sprouting can be achieved without any special sprouting equipment. All you need is:
- Wide-necked clean glass jar – coffee jars are excellent.
- Piece of cheesecloth, muttoncloth, net or buttermuslin large enough to clamp over the open neck of the jar with a rubber band (double thickness if necessary).

BASIC METHOD:
1. Take about 2 tablespoons of the selected grain or pulse (more of the larger chick peas, or less – say 2 teaspoons – of the fine seeds, like alfalfa). Wash well in cold water in a sieve.
2. Put to soak in a basin well covered with cold water, for 8–10 hours for seeds and grains, 10–24 hours for pulses – until softened and almost doubled in size. Strain off the soaking water and rinse.
3. Transfer soaked seeds to the sprouting jar, cover with the net or cheesecloth, and secure with the rubber band.
4. Pour cold water *through* the net or muslin, into the jar to fill it, and then immediately drain it *all* off through the muslin. This is to humidify the air in the jar. Drain thoroughly – any excess water left after the initial soaking period is liable to cause rotting of the seeds.
5. Leave the jar in a relatively warm place (below blood heat); the kitchen windowsill is fine. (Or it could be left in a warm dark cupboard for the first day or two, during the germination period – as is done for bought beansprouts. Mung beans can be bitter if sprouted in the light.)
6. Rinse the growing seeds twice daily (wheat and triticale are the exceptions – see below) with cool water, *gently*, as the newly emerging shoots are very soft and vulnerable. The cool water washes away any waste products, prevents the seeds from sticking together, and re-humidifies the air.

Depending on the variety and the temperature, the sprouts will be ready to eat in 2 to 7 days.

Chick peas are the fastest legume, adzuki beans one of the slowest. Bought Chinese beansprouts are grown in the dark in a very warm atmosphere. But light is advisable for the later stage of growth to enable the sprouts to develop chlorophyll in their green shoots. Generally, the sprouts are ready to eat when the root is 2–5 times the length of the seed, and any uneaten then should be stored in a closed container in the refrigerator, to retard the growth rate – otherwise the food-store of the seed would be exhausted, and the sprouts would spoil. Poor germination rate indicates old seed, drying out or waterlogging. Some beansprouts prefer pure filtered water to tapwater.

All these sprouted foods are an excellent source of vitamins A, B complex, C and K, minerals, amino acids, and vital 'life-force.'

SUNFLOWER SEEDS are best eaten after being soaked in the minimum of water overnight (as suggested in the muesli recipes). They will not grow large sprouts satisfactorily after being hulled – and are very irksome to detach from their shells if sprouted whole. Soaked overnight, they are a useful source of vitamin D, B6 and B12 and all the essential amino acids. As they are so rich in protein, do not eat more than 2 oz a day.

SESAME SEEDS are especially rich in calcium, iron, phosphorus and methionine. Sprout for 1 day only.

ALFALFA SEEDS after seven days' growth in sunlight are an excellent source of chlorophyll, and rich in iron, calcium and phosphorus – nutrients needed to help rebuild decaying teeth.

BUCKWHEAT SPROUTS are rich in rutin and lecithin, helpful for healthy blood circulation.

WHEAT SPROUTS are much more nutritious and health-giving than cooked wheat (bread). Much of the starch is transformed into simple sugars (i.e. 'predigested'), the vitamin C content is increased by 600% and the vitamin B complex shows increases of from 20%–1200%. Wheat sprouts can grow long and tough, so eat while the sprouts are tiny, chew well – or mince the young wheatsprouts just before eating.

To sprout organic wheat and triticale, soak first in cold water overnight; drain, rinse, and transfer to sprouting jar, muslin-covered, for the daytime. Rinse and put to soak again the next night. (This and subsequent soaking water is weak rejuvelac – see p. 165.) Repeat the sequence of days in the sprouting jar, drained, and nights soaking in cold water, until the sprout is ¼" (2 mm) long, when it is ready to eat. Then refrigerate, drained, to retard further growth.

PULSES OR LEGUMES cooked traditionally are sometimes difficult to digest, and raw (soaked but unsprouted) or inadequately cooked tend to be poisonous but sprouting transforms them into first class nourishment. They are natural protectors from toxic metals.

MUNG BEANSPROUTS are now a well-known and generally accepted salad ingredient and are very easy and economical to grow yourself so they are recommended for your first adventure in sprouting.

The maximum nutritional value from your sprouted seeds, beans and grains is obtained only when you eat them raw and freshly grown. Heating destroys many of the B vitamins and vitamin C and kills the vital life-force in the enzymes and amino acids, which have multiplied up to 1300 times during the germination and sprouting period. If you want them hot for a change, try the Chinese stir-fry method of cooking till hot but still crisp, which is less destructive of their nutrient content.

Use beansprouts in salads, sandwiches, omelettes, pancakes and as a raw garnish.

Vegetables and Vegetable Dishes

Raw and cooked vegetables, with fruits, are 'protective' foods, which should form 45% to 65% of our daily diet. It may be impossible to choose produce not subject to toxic fall-out (as acid rain) during growth. But we can refuse to buy fruit and vegetables displayed close to traffic-laden roads. To obtain the maximum nutritional value from vegetables:

- Buy as fresh as possible those vegetables in season, locally grown and store in a cool, shady, ventilated place. Choose organically grown produce whenever possible. Next best are those grown without pesticides.
- Prepare vegetables just before cooking (except whole root vegetables, which can be cleaned ahead) and do not leave cut vegetables soaking in water for long.
- Use the minimum amount of water in the saucepan, and boil it before adding the prepared vegetables. (Remember that steam is just as hot as boiling water and cooks equally efficiently!)
- Conservative Cooking: boil till just tender – don't overcook. Strain off the cooking liquid and retain it. Most of the water-soluble minerals and vitamins are in this stock. Use it in gravy, sauce and soup or drink it.
- Vitamins of the B complex group are lost by heating (and in refining). Vitamin C is lost in storage, wilting, by oxidation when cut up and exposed to air, by bruising and cutting with blunt knives, by cooking and keeping hot. No wonder so many of us are short of these vitamins – the little left at the end of the cooking process is often tipped down the sink!
- When preparing root vegetables, wash them thoroughly (or scrub) rather than peel them. It saves time as well as nutrients. New potatoes boiled or steamed in their skins have much better flavour, and the skin alone is easily discarded when eating by those who object. Potatoes retain most nutrients when baked in their jackets either in the oven or in a 'Gourmette' type pan which uses a low gas flame to produce a 'mini-oven'.
- Succulent vegetables like spring greens, cos lettuce, celery and watercress keep fresh longer if just the tips of their stems stand in fresh water – pretend they are cut flowers! Similarly freshly dug carrots, spring onions and beetroot benefit from giving their tip roots a drink of fresh water.

ASPARAGUS. When very young, try a little in your salad, raw. Cook by steaming or boiling, after washing thoroughly and tying up in bundles. Eat alone with Butter Plus. Also good in soufflés, quiches, pancakes, omelettes and salads.

ARTICHOKES, JERUSALEM. Scrub well. Steamed or boiled, they have a subtle flavour. Cook till barely tender, so that they do not mush. Any left-overs make a delicious soup base with its own stock.

AUBERGINES. (Eggplant.) Wash and slice in ¼" slices, retaining the purple skin, and (to reduce bitterness) sprinkle slices with salt, leave ½ hour, then wipe off salt and excess moisture. Sweat in a little oil.

RATATOUILLE

2 onions, sliced
1 aubergine, sliced
3 tbsp olive OR soya oil
4 tomatoes, skinned and chopped
2 green peppers, de-seeded and
   sliced

2 cloves garlic, crushed or finely
   chopped
4 courgettes, sliced
salty seasoning to taste
little fresh ground black pepper

Sweat the onions and aubergine in the hot oil. Add the tomatoes, green peppers, garlic and courgettes, and cook gently in a covered saucepan for about 15 minutes, giving an occasional stir to prevent sticking – if necessary, add a very little water. Adjust seasoning to taste. Serve hot or cold. Ratatouille may also be made by omitting either the courgettes or the green peppers, according to preference or availability. Omission of the aubergine also gives a delicious dish, though this should no longer truly be called a 'ratatouille'. (4-6)

BEANS. Being legumes, they contain more protein than other vegetables. Traditionally, beans were often served with a little bacon. See also Pulses.
BEANS, FRENCH. Best picked young, when they need only topping and tailing, and conservative cooking till just tender.

QUICK BEAN SUPPER DISH

1½ lb (700 gm) French beans
little summer savory
2 hard-boiled eggs, sliced
vegetable oil OR French dressing

4 oz (100 gm) mild ham slices OR 4 oz
(100 gm) prepared ham-flavoured
TVP

Simmer the prepared beans with the summer savory. Combine with eggs and ham and heat through if required hot, serving with a little vegetable oil to glaze. OR drain the beans, cool, and toss in French dressing before adding the egg slices and ham. Serve with wholemeal bread and butter.

BEANS, RUNNER. Need stringing, and retain more flavour if chopped into half inch slices instead of shredding finely in a bean slicer. This is a vital point when preparing them for freezing, too. Young beans are good eaten raw.

HERBED BEANS WITH RICE

1 lb (450 gm) runner or French beans
4 oz (100 gm) cooked brown rice
4 tbsp oil OR butter
1 clove garlic, pressed

½ tsp marjoram
½ tsp summer savory
shoyu OR tamari to taste

Conservatively cook the prepared green beans, adding the cooked rice for the final five minutes cooking time. Heat the oil. Add garlic, herbs, drained beans and rice. Cook gently for few minutes. Add shoyu or tamari to taste, and serve.

BEANS, BROAD. If you grow your own, cook the broad bean tops snipped off when fully flowering – they have a flavour between spinach and asparagus. When the earlier beans appear and the pods are only 3–4 inches long, the whole bean, pod and all, can be cooked and eaten with parsley sauce. Normally, broad beans are nicer if individually peeled after podding, before being cooked conservatively.

BEETROOT. Young tender beetroots are good to eat raw when grated – they are good blood-builders. Young beetroot leaves, cooked, are like beautiful spinach and very nutritious. Russian Borsch soups are different and good. To cook beetroot, wash very carefully, taking care not to puncture the skin or cut the root. Leave stubs when cutting the leaves – beetroots 'bleed' when the skin is broken, leaking out colour, flavour and nutrients. Cover with water and simmer for 1–3 hours, or pressure cook for 20–45 minutes (depending on age and size) till slightly soft when pressed. After cooking, the stock needs to be strained through a sieve lined with kitchen paper, to remove all the grit. The cooked beetroot are easy to peel – and stain! (Be forewarned; eaten in excess beetroot may also colour urine and stools!) Beetroot may be served hot with a glaze made from its own stock thickened with arrowroot, with a little lemon juice or cider vinegar added to taste. Beetroot may also be roasted in hot fat. For salad use, marinate in dressing.

DRESSED SALAD BEETROOT

2 tbsp honey OR dark Muscovado sugar

1½ cups strained beetroot stock
½ cup cider vinegar

Dissolve honey or raw sugar in the warm beetroot stock, add vinegar and pour over 2 lbs sliced cooked beetroot.

BROCCOLI OR CALABRESE. Conservatively cooked and served with a little butter, these make a delectable dish on their own, eaten like asparagus. Or stir fry. High in vitamin C.

BRUSSELS SPROUTS. Rich in vitamin C. Conservatively cooked and served immediately, they are completely different from the foul smelling khaki-coloured mush which can result from over-cooking and long waiting! Finely sliced raw Brussels sprouts provide useful greens in a winter salad – introduce them slowly, as they tend to be 'windy'.

CABBAGE. Also is high in vitamin C. Like Brussels sprouts, cabbage can be delicious or detestable, depending on how it is cooked! The greener the leaves, the more nutritious, so be sparing to the waste bucket! The chopped outer leaves can be cooked longer by putting them in the boiling water a few minutes before the rest. Cook conservatively till just done – or stir fry, so that they are not mushy. Raw outer green cabbage leaves are helpful as a poultice too (see Maurice Mességué's 'Of Men and Plants').

SAUERKRAUT

Sauerkraut is traditionally made from just white cabbage and salt, with a few juniper berries, relying on the salt to preserve it. Here is a healthier alternative. It is a slow process which is made worthwhile when all the vegetables and herbs have been organically grown and freshly picked.

1 tbsp dill seed
1 tbsp celery seed
1 tbsp caraway seed
1 tbsp juniper berries
fresh herbs as available – parsley, tarragon, marjoram, basil, bay leaves

8 lb (4 kg) white cabbage
2 tsp fine salty seasoning
1 lb (450 gm) fresh carrots
1 lb (450 gm) fresh beetroot

These quantities will vary depending upon availability and the size of your chosen container, which should be a large glass, china, earthenware or stainless steel jar, at least 8″ deep, with neck wide enough to permit your fist to reach comfortably to the bottom. If pottery, make sure that it has a safe glaze unaffected by acid. Under no circumstances use aluminium. Wash the jar thoroughly and sterilize it with boiling water. An old (shop) glass sweet jar (6 pint capacity) is ideal.

Enlist a friend to help you and choose a time when you need not be hurried, as the long operation must be completed at one go! If possible, secure mechanical help in the form of an electric shredder and mincer, or, better still, an electric juicer.

Crush the spice seeds in a pestle and mortar, and bruise the juniper berries. (Do not put in a liquidizer with a plastic container, or the flavour will permanently impregnate the container!) Wash the herbs and dry in a cloth. Wash the vegetables and drain well.

Finely mince or grate some white cabbage and pack it tightly into the jar, to form a layer about 1½″ (4 cm) deep. OR juice the cabbage in small batches, as needed to provide each 1½″ layer, using the juice mixed with all its fibrous pulp. Punch it down so that no air bubbles remain and it becomes covered with its own juice. Sprinkle over with a little of the salty seasoning. Finely chop some of the mixed herbs (but use bay leaves whole) and sprinkle right across the cabbage layer, pressing down firmly again. Finely grate some carrot and beetroot (beetroot could be juiced and reconstituted) and add a layer to bring the total depth up to 2″, again punching down firmly to remove all air. Then sprinkle over juniper berries and about half a teaspoon of the mixed spices.

Continue with these layers in the same order, adjusting the depth so that the final layer is of cabbage sprinkled with salt, and add a few spices as well. Check that all is thoroughly punched down and no air bubbles are trapped.

Cover with a large cabbage leaf, then a clean cotton cloth, weighted down by a large clean oval stone. Stand the jar in a large clean basin to catch any overspill, and put in a warm place where the temperature will not fall below 70°F (possibly an airing cupboard). Fermentation will soon start and continue for some weeks and the juice may overflow. Check the top regularly, washing the cloth and stone, and removing foam and possible mildew from the top. Leave the sauerkraut in this warm environment for 3–4 weeks, then transfer to a cool, dry, dark, airy storage place. It will be ready for eating within a week, or will store untouched for several months. Once a jar is started, the top layer may spoil and need to be discarded (as with opened jam).

Sauerkraut is a very nutritious food, which should be eaten raw in order to enjoy its full health-giving potential, high in natural lactic acid and enzymes which aid the digestion of grains and counteract cravings for sugar.

CARROTS. When cooking carrots, scrub rather than peel them, and cut lengthwise rather than in rounds, as this helps speed the cooking time. High in vitamin A.

56

CAULIFLOWER. When steaming or boiling, cut the cauliflower into serving size pieces to aid faster cooking of the stem. A crust of bread on top of the cauliflower will minimize the cooking smell.

CELERIAC. Celeriac makes a good alternative to celery, having a similar flavour, but no strings. Cut off the fibrous skin and chop into dice for cooking, putting straight into cold water and then boiling when ready (as it oxidizes). It is good as a vegetable on its own or in soups, stuffings and stews. Celeriac looks better served with a white sauce made from some of its own stock – or mash it with potato.

CELERY. The tougher outer stems are delicious cooked and greatly enhance casseroles and stews. Scub well and cut into short lengths. Sweat in a little oil before adding water and simmer till tender. Do not discard the celery leaves – they add flavour to the stockpot and casserole, or to a salad. Also good braised.

CORN ON THE COB, SWEETCORN OR MAIZE. Best when young and pale yellow in colour, needing only 5 minutes cooking. Remove only the dirty outer husks and wash well. Trim back the stems to fit your widest saucepan. Boil or steam 5–10 minutes, turning once. Allow to drain for a minute or two before removing leaves and silk (use a tea-towel to protect your fingers). Serve alone or with a little Butter Plus.

COURGETTES. Young courgettes do not need peeling. Slice and cook conservatively either in a little water, diluted wine or grape juice; or braise them in a little butter in a tightly closed saucepan or casserole.

FENNEL. Leaf fronds are used as a herb for flavouring fish. The root, finely sliced raw, is useful in salads, and for cooking.

COOKED FENNEL

2 heads of fennel
1-2 tbsp vegetable oil
½ lb (225 gm) small tomatoes

salty seasoning
freshly ground black pepper
1 tbsp chopped fresh dill

Thinly slice the fennel and sweat in the hot oil, until nearly tender. Slice the tomatoes and carefully cook them with the fennel. Season and sprinkle with dill. Serve cold several hours after preparing to allow the flavours to blend.

KOHL RABI. A mild flavoured root vegetable. Remove the tough skin, dice and cook conservatively till tender. May be served with parsley or cheese sauce.

LEEKS. A gently onion flavoured vegetable. They need careful washing to remove any trapped grit. Discard outer damaged leaves, but use as much of the green part as you can – or reserve it for the stockpot. Conservatively cook about 10–20 minutes till tender. Or sweat in a little butter in a tightly lidded saucepan or casserole. Leeks are also good braised: put prepared leeks in a closed oiled casserole with a little stock for 1–2 hours in cool to moderate oven.

LEEKS PROVENÇAL

2 tbsp butter OR oil
2 cloves garlic
1 lb (450 gm) leeks

2 tomatoes, skinned and chopped
3 oz (75 gm) mushrooms

Melt butter and add crushed garlic. Add leeks cut in ½″ slices, placing separately over base of the pan. Cover and cook for 3–4 minutes. Turn each piece and add tomatoes. Slice mushrooms finely and add. Simmer for further 8–10 minutes, covered. Carefully transfer leeks to a serving dish and pour over the Provençal sauce.

LEEKS VINAIGRETTE

1 lb (450 gm) fresh leeks	1 tsp wine vinegar
1 tbsp vegetable oil	Vinaigrette or French Dressing
¼ pt (150 ml) water	1-2 tbsp chopped parsley

Cut leeks in 2″ (5 cm) lengths and halve lengthwise. Sauté gently in oil, shaking to glaze all over. Add water and vinegar, and simmer till barely tender. Cool. Pour over dressing and sprinkle with parsley.

LETTUCE. If you grow your own lettuce and so know it is pesticide-free (bought lettuce may have been sprayed up to fourteen times, and so are not recommended in this book!) you may have a surplus. This is Norman's way of using them at Enton Hall:

SUMMER LETTUCE

2-4 lettuce	1 small onion, finely chopped
1 tbsp vegetable oil	2-6 ripe tomatoes, skinned &
1 clove garlic, pressed	chopped

Wash lettuce and drain. Blanch (i.e. dip in boiling water for 10 seconds). Heat oil and sweat the garlic and onion. Add tomato. Cut lettuces in half and add, cut side down. Put on lid and simmer for 10–12 minutes, till tender. Serve hot covered with its tomato stock poured over.

MARROW. When young they can be peeled and cooked like courgettes, including the seeds. Being a watery vegetable which readily loses its flavour into the cooking water, steaming or braising is advisable: grease a covered casserole and lay the peeled pieces of marrow across, season lightly, and bake till tender. Alternatively, remove the seeds only, cut and bake or roast the marrow in its skin.

STUFFED MARROW

5 oz (150 gm) lotus TVP mince (beef-like flavoured soya granules)	1 clove garlic, pressed
	1 tbsp vegetable oil
	2-3 tbsp chopped parsley
or 8 oz (225 gm) cooked adzuki beans	sprig rosemary
	4 oz (125 gm) soft wholemeal breadcrumbs
or brown lentils, well flavoured	
½ pint (300 ml) vegetable stock	½ tsp Tastex or bouillon powder
1 onion, finely chopped	1 marrow, washed

Soak the TVP in cold stock for ten minutes. Bring to boil and simmer for ten minutes. Sweat the onion and garlic in the oil. Combine and add herbs, breadcrumbs, and Tastex to taste. Cut marrow in half lengthwise, remove seeds and fill with the stuffing. Place in baking tin with very little water. (As a variation you could use 12 oz (350 gm) cooked minced meat in place of the TVP or cooked beans and left-over gravy instead of all or part of the stock. Or substitute 12 oz (350 gm) raw minced beef for the TVP or beans, browning mince in the pan after removing sautéed onion and garlic; drain off the fat before adding to other stuffing ingredients.) Bake 1–1½ hours in moderate oven till marrow is tender. (4-6)

MUSHROOMS. The large open dark gilled mushrooms have more flavour than button mushrooms. Field mushrooms excel in flavour, need several washings to remove grit from the gills, and should always be cooked. To serve as a vegetable: chop the mushroom stems and place in a saucepan with half an inch depth of water. Place the largest mushrooms in a layer over these, cup side uppermost. Pour a little melted dripping, butter or oil into each 'cup'. Sprinkle with fine seasalt, and a little grated nutmeg. Continue the mushroom layers in this way, cover and cook. They will steam from below while cooking in the fat; you will have a delicious mushroom stock for making soup with the stems and any left-over mushrooms – and mushrooms which are neither too fatty nor shrunken as your vegetable. Alternatively grill them with a drizzle of oil in the 'cup' or simmer in milk.

ONIONS. The most useful of vegetables. Conservatively cooked onions are delicious as a vegetable on their own, or with a sauce made partly with their own stock. Braised onions are tasty. Onion slices placed over fish or meat before grilling add to the dish. Stuffings, stews, soup, stock, casseroles – all gain from the inclusion of onions. If properly washed, the outer brown skins will add colour to the stock before discarding.

PARSNIPS. Combine well with carrots, conservatively cooked together, or mashed together. For roasting, par-boil the parsnips for five minutes before putting to roast. As I prefer to roast meat 'long and slow', I put the par-boiled parsnips and potatoes in a baking tin with dripping at the top of the oven when the joint is put to roast at the bottom; the oven set at 300–325°F, 150–160°C, Gas 2–3. Turn the parsnips and potatoes once during cooking, and drain off the fat twenty minutes before end of cooking time, for a crisp golden finish.

PEAS. Let the children eat the youngest raw peas as they help you pod them; raw baby peas are a real delicacy. Cook peas conservatively with a sprig of bruised mint, or simmer in milk. Fresh peas are better nutritionally than commercially frozen peas which are chemically treated to retain their bright colour. Cold cooked peas are good in salads with seafoods. Like beans, peas contain more protein than many other vegetables.

PEPPERS, RED AND GREEN. Very high in vitamin C. Steam, bake or sauté green peppers, reserving the seeds to add to stock or recipes to boost their vitamin C content. Peppers lend themselves to baking, filled with your favourite stuffing, and add unique flavour to many dishes.

POTATOES. Cooked whole they are a good, satisfying, alkaline food and not particularly fattening if cooked and served without fat (only 24 calories per ounce compared with 93 calories per ounce for pasta). They are an excellent source of complex carbohydrate and especially nutritious when oven baked in their jackets, so no nutrients are leaked out. Otherwise steam or boil them in their skins, removing skin after cooking if preferred. The skins contain fibre, so deserve to be eaten too. Folic acid is present immediately beneath the skin and is readily lost in peeling. They also contain vitamin C, some B vitamins and trace minerals, including iron. For jacket potatoes, scrub potatoes well, remove blemishes and prick whole skins to prevent bursting. Bake at 375°F, 190°C, Gas 5 until soft in centre (1–2 hours depending on size and variety – reds take longer). Serve with Butter Plus, cottage cheese, salad dressings, gravy etc., or use for delicious easy snack meals.

POMMES DAUPHINOISE

1 lb (450 gm) waxy potatoes (reds)   6 oz (150 gm) Edam cheese
3-6 cloves garlic, finely chopped   ¼ pint (150 ml) milk

Par-boil the scrubbed potatoes in their skins. Peel and slice. Arrange layers of potato and garlic in a greased casserole with the grated cheese. Pour over the milk and bake in a moderate oven till golden brown, about 1–1¼ hours. A delicious and rich dish.

CRUNCHY MASHED POTATOES WITH BEANSPROUTS

hot boiled potato (unpeeled)   grated cheese – Lancashire,
butter OR vegetable margarine OR oil   Parmesan, Edam OR Cheddar
hot milk OR potato stock   sprouted mung OR adzuki beans OR
paprika   lentilsprouts (fresh and raw)

Remove the skins and mash hot cooked potato with the butter, hot fluid and paprika until smooth and creamy. Add grated cheese to taste and incorporate well. Keep hot. When serving, add a heaped tbsp of raw beansprouts to each portion of hot potato and fold in. Thus the beansprouts are not cooked and retain their high nutritional value, while adding flavour and texture to the dish.

SMOKED COD'S ROE POTATOES

2 oz (50 gm) smoked cod's roe   4 large freshly baked potatoes
3 tbsp home-made mayonnaise   watercress (see page 36)
3 tbsp tomato purée

Skin and mash the cod's roe with mayonnaise and tomato purée. Cut potato in half and remove pulp into a basin. Mash in the tomato mixture and pile back into the potato skins. Reheat and serve with fresh watercress. (4)

POTATO EGGS

large freshly baked potatoes
butter OR vegetable margarine OR oil
salty seasoning and paprika

chopped chives
free-range eggs
alfalfa sprouts

Halve the large baked potatoes and scoop out egg-sized indentations in each half. Into each hollow put butter, a little seasoning and chopped chives and break in a raw egg. Return to the oven until just nicely set. Decorate with more chopped chives and a sprinkling of paprika on the egg. Serve with alfalfa sprouts and a tomato.

NUTCASE POTATOES

1 tsp Tastex
2 tbsp vegetable stock
4 freshly baked potatoes
2 tbsp Harmony crunchy peanut
   butter

1 tsp sesame seeds, roasted
tossed green salad

Dissolve the Tastex in the hot stock. Halve potatoes and mash the flesh with the stock, peanut butter and sesame seeds. Pile back in skins and reheat. Serve with a tossed green salad. (4)

SARDINE SPECIALS

tinned sardines in olive oil
natural yoghurt
tomato purée
freshly ground black pepper
mung bean sprouts

freshly baked potatoes
salty seasoning
wedges of lemon
crisp green salad

Blend the sardine oil with the yoghurt, tomato pureé and black pepper. Flake the sardines and add. Rough chop the bean sprouts if longer than ¾", and mix in with the scooped out potato and yoghurt mixture. Correct seasoning, pile back into skins and reheat. Garnish with lemon wedges and serve with crisp green salad.

HORSERADISH SCRAMBLE POTATOES

vegetable stock or milk
freshly baked potatoes
horseradish cream

scrambled egg
parsley sprigs
tomato and onion salad

Mash a little hot vegetable stock or milk into the potato flesh and add a little horseradish cream. Reheat. Scramble the egg and pile over. Serve with parsley garnish, and tomato and onion salad.

GARLIC AND CHEESE POTATOES

freshly baked potatoes
curd cheese
sea salt and paprika
garlic cloves, pressed

fresh parsley, chives, mint, basil as
  available
parsley sprigs
mushroom and beansprout salad

Cut potatoes in half and mash flesh with the curd cheese, blended with the seasonings, crushed garlic and chopped fresh herbs. Pile back into skins, reheat and served garnished with parsley sprigs and mushroom and beansprout salad.

CHUTNEY CHEESE POTATOES

freshly baked potatoes
natural yoghurt
home-made chutney

grated cheddar cheese
watercress (see page 36)
golden salad

Halve the potatoes. Mash the flesh with natural yoghurt blended with chutney to taste. Refill skins with alternating layers of enriched potato and grated cheese, finishing with the cheese. Reheat until the cheese melts and browns on top. Garnish with watercress and serve with golden salad.

FRENCH BEAN BAKES

8 oz (225 gm) French beans
4 oz (100 gm) grilled streaky bacon
4 freshly baked potoatoes

vegetable stock
vinaigrette dressing
8 tomatoes

Conservatively cook small French beans until just tender. Grill the bacon and cut in strips. Mash the potato with a little hot stock and the bacon fat. Put back in skins. Toss the beans and bacon in vinaigrette dressing and pile on top. Reheat and serve with whole tomatoes. (4)

PUMPKIN. Wash the skin. Cut into portion size pieces (use an axe on the toughest skins). Leave the skin on and steam, bake or roast.
RED CABBAGE. A delicious vegetable cooked as in the recipe below.

RED CABBAGE

1 lb (450 gm) red cabbage, coarsely
  sliced
1-2 tsp Muscovado sugar
1/4 tsp allspice
1/4 tsp paprika

1 large cooking apple, chopped
juice of 1/2 lemon OR 1 tsp apple cider
  vinegar
1 small onion, finely chopped

Add all ingredients to just sufficient water to cook conservatively without boiling dry. Cook about 20 minutes, until just tender; don't allow it to become mushy.

SEAWEEDS OR SEA VEGETABLES. Very high in trace minerals and a good source of iodine. Valuable for their protective value, sea vegetables deserve greater use in soups, stews and pulse dishes (see page 187).

KOMBU (VEGETABLE)

Boil the kombu in water for about five minutes, reserving stock for soup if the kombu is served as a vegetable. Include when cooking pulses to enhance flavour and digestibility.

ARAME OR HIZIKI (VEGETABLE)

Wash well in cold water and then soak for 20–30 minutes (reserve the soaking water). Cut into strips and sweat in a little hot vegetable oil. Add tamari and the reserved water and simmer for about one hour.

NORI (GARNISH)

Toast the thin sheets briefly in a hot oven or above a gas flame. Crumble them for use in soups or with salads.

SPINACH. Rich in vitamin A, E and folic acid, but also contains oxalic acid. For this reason it is an exception to the conservative cooking rule. After thorough washing to remove all grit, cook spinach leaves in plenty of boiling water till tender. Drain well in colander or sieve. Serve with little butter or squeeze of lemon juice, or little grated nutmeg. Good with poached egg, in quiches, or 'creamed' by liquidizing with a little white sauce.

TOMATOES. Good raw, grilled, baked, stewed or stuffed; used in grills, soups, stews, casseroles or with fish. Juice and purée are useful too. Freeze whole for winter cooking use. Tomatoes contain some vitamin C. (Unsuitable for those with arthritis, skin problems and digestive disorders.)

WATERCRESS. Especially nutritious – high in iron, vitamins C, A and folic acid. Use as garnish and in hot and cold soups. (See page 36.)

Soups and Stocks

Soups can be a warming starter to a winter salad meal, a flavourful blend of nutritious vegetables subtly enhanced with herbs and spices. They are useful in bringing good nutrients to reluctant vegetable eaters and are economical in using up left-overs. Hearty thick soups and broths can be a meal on their own with wholemeal bread or dumplings, followed by fresh fruit or celery and cheese.

Herbs and *bouquet garni* can add a subtle aroma to soups. When sautéing vegetables sweat them carefully in the oil or butter without browning them, to extract the flavour into the fat and soften the vegetables. Root vegetables take longer to cook and should be added before garlic, leeks, mushrooms, etc.

When a soup is to be liquidized, the vegetables need only be cooked till just tender, and all their own stock incorporated. To conserve vitamins, avoid over-long simmering when the soup is ready. If milk, yoghurt or cream is included, add it at the end and reheat without boiling, or it may curdle. Add chopped parsley or chives when serving.

To thicken soup, remember extra cooked vegetables liquidized with the soup are a good alternative to the use of cornflour or wholemeal flour: or use left-over cooked wholegrains – brown rice, oats, barley, millet, etc. For slimmers, sprinkle in rice, oat or soya bran flakes, or Linusit Gold occasionally.

Norman's secret ingredient in soup-making is butter. While not strictly health food cookery, using extra butter in which to sweat the vegetables imparts an epicurean touch to a smooth liquidized soup.

Soups freeze well (before addition of cream or yoghurt), so we sometimes make large quantities to keep our frozen selection for rushed days. To speed thawing, lay block of soup in large saucepan, with a little compatible stock, over moderate heat. Turn block frequently and pierce it with kitchen fork to break up the ice, stirring occasionally. Freezing alters the texture of some puréed soups – re-liquidizing soon remedies this.

Vegetable stocks

Vegetable stock gives more flavour and goodness than water in soups, sauces, pastas and wholegrain dishes. All stock in which vegetables have been cooked (except sprouts and savoys, which, though nutritious, really smell unpleasant) should be saved and used – even potato stock, though this does not keep so long.

Starting from scratch, a good vegetable stock can easily be produced from chosen root and leafy green vegetables: carrots, onions, leeks, lettuce, celery, potato, parsnip, parsley, spinach, broccoli, watercress, spring onions, spring greens, pea pods, turnip, swede, young dandelion leaves, nettletops and leek greens. Choose smaller quantities of these last five, stronger-flavoured vegetables, so that they do not predominate. Beetroot, carrot and turnip tops can also be used – and the blemish-free peelings and outer coarser leaves of vegetables that would normally be discarded. Wash and finely chop them and immerse immediately in cold water in a saucepan with a tight lid. Green pepper seeds add flavour and vitamins. Bring to the boil, then simmer slowly for ¾–1¾ hours (depending on woodiness), till the flavour is extracted into the liquid. Strain, cool and refrigerate the stock until needed (will keep for 4 days). Enhance flavour with fresh or dried herbs and careful seasoning (see page 30) when preparing final dish.

SUMMER VEGETABLE STOCK

If you need a brown stock, sauté ½ cup finely chopped onion in 2 tablespoons oil till brown OR add brown onions skins and remove them later. Transfer to large saucepan and add:

2 cups diced celery and yellow leaves	mushroom or tomato skins
1 cup shredded lettuce	a dash of white pepper
1 small onion, studded with 2 cloves	½ tsp salty seasoning
1 carrot, chopped	a dash of cayenne
1 leek, chopped	a bouquet garni (3 sprigs
1 slice of turnip or parsnip, chopped	parsley/chervil, ½ bay leaf, 2
cold water to cover	sprigs fresh thyme)

Bring to the boil, cover and simmer until the vegetables are very tender. Strain and chill till needed.

RECOVERY BROTH

2-2½ lb (1 kg) old potatoes	3 celery stalks, chopped
2 pt (1,200 ml) water	1 clove garlic, crushed or chopped
2-4 parsley stems or sprigs	sweet basil OR bay leaf
1 carrot, chopped	paprika
1-2 onions, chopped	salty seasoning

Scrub potatoes and peel *thickly*. It is the peel needed for this recipe – use the potatoes separately. Put into cold water and add other ingredients. Cover and simmer for 1 hour. Strain for use as stock, or liquidize for soup. Good for those feeling 'off their food' or with 'acidity'. This is the traditional 'Potassium Broth' renowned at many health hydros – alkalinizing and high in potassium.

WINTER VEGETABLE STOCKPOT

1 large onion	2 Jerusalem artichokes
2 carrots	1 turnip, swede or parsnip
outer stalks celery	green part of leeks
parsley stems	salty seasoning

Into a large heavy enamel or stainless steel saucepan put 2 pints (1,200 ml) of cold water, adding the vegetables as prepared. Scrub the root vegetables well and remove blight but do not peel. Chop finely all the vegetables to allow maximum release of flavour to the water. Add more water if necessary to cover the vegetables well. Simmer for 1–2 hours. Strain. Cool and refrigerate till needed (within 5 days).

CHICKEN STOCK

necks, wings, giblets of 2 chickens
  OR raw carcass, neck, wings,
  giblets from 1 bird
1 carrot, scrubbed and sliced
outer stalks of celery, scrubbed and
  sliced

2-3 onions, sliced
parsley (stems if possible)
1 bay leaf
freshly ground black pepper
salty seasoning

Cover the chicken pieces with cold water and bring to the boil, skimming off the scum as necessary. Add the other ingredients and simmer, covered, for 2–3 hours (longer for an older bird). Strain the stock, and use as required. Any surplus can be cooled and then deep frozen for later use. For babies, omit seasoning.

BEEF STOCK

3-4 lbs (1¼-1¾ kg) beef marrow
  bones
water
2 carrots, scrubbed and sliced

2-3 large onions, sliced
outer stalks of celery, chopped
parsley (stems if possible)
salty seasoning and black pepper

Buy the marrow bones sawn into 1–2″ slices, if possible. Cover these with cold water in a large saucepan. Bring to the boil, skimming off the scum as it forms on the surface. Simmer for 2½–3 hours, then add remaining ingredients and simmer for further hour. Strain the stock and use as required. Any surplus can be cooled then deep frozen for later use. For babies, omit seasoning, to give a nourishing bone broth.

MUSHROOM SOUP

1 small onion, chopped
1 stick celery, finely sliced
1 oz (25 gm) butter
1 carrot, sliced
8 oz (225 gm) large mushrooms
1½ pt (900 ml) water

2 tsp yeast extract
freshly ground nutmeg
salty seasoning
freshly ground black pepper
4 tbsp double cream, whipped
pinch paprika

Gently sauté onion and celery in hot butter. Add carrot, mushrooms, water and yeast extract and bring to boil. Simmer till vegetables are tender. Liquidize and reheat, adding a miserly pinch of finely grated nutmeg, and season to taste. Just before serving, stir in half the cream. Float remaining cream in dabs on each serving, sprinkled with paprika. (4)

GREEN TOMATO SOUP   S

1 large onion, sliced
2 tbsp butter or vegetable oil
1 lb (450 gm) green tomatoes,
  quartered
1½ pt (900 ml) stock OR water
1 tsp oregano

1 small potato, scrubbed and sliced
¼ pt (150 ml) natural yoghurt
honey to taste
salty seasoning and black pepper
2-3 tbsp chopped chives OR parsley

Sweat onion in hot butter. Add tomatoes and cook for 5 minutes. Add stock, oregano and potato. Cook till potato is done. Liquidize. Stir in yoghurt. Add honey and seasoning to taste. Reheat without boiling and serve, garnished with chives or parsley. An interestingly different soup. (4–6)

S CREAM OF LEEK SOUP

3 leeks
1½ pt (900 ml) water OR stock
1 large potato, scrubbed & sliced
2 bay leaves

¼-½ pt (150-300 ml) milk
vegetable bouillon powder
freshly ground black pepper
2 tbsp chopped chives OR parsley

Chop leeks, using as much of the green as possible. Cook in the stock with potato and bay leaves. Remove bay leaves and liquidize. Add milk and adjust seasoning. Reheat and serve garnished with chives or parsley. (4–6)

S GREEN LEEK-TOP SOUP

When using up the top, dark green part of leeks for soup, cook with parsnip (to counterbalance the bitterness of the leeks) in place of the potato and proceed as for cream of leek soup.

TOMATO SOUP

2 tbsp butter OR vegetable oil
½ lb (225 gm) onion, chopped
2 sticks celery, finely chopped
2 lb (900 gm) good-flavoured
    tomatoes OR 2 × 14 oz tins
    tomatoes
½ lb (225 gm) carrots, chopped

½ tsp dried basil OR oregano
1½ pt (900 ml) water OR stock
2 tsp vegetable bouillon powder
freshly ground black pepper
paprika
½ tsp honey (optional)

Gently sauté onion and celery. Add other ingredients except honey, and simmer till tender. Liquidize and adjust seasoning, adding honey if needed, and reheat. (4–6)

S ARTICHOKE SOUP

1 lb (450 gm) Jerusalem artichokes
½ lb (225 gm) potatoes
1½ pt (900 ml) water or stock
2 tsp vegetable bouillon powder

paprika
¼-½ pt (150-300 ml) milk
chopped parsley

Cook the sliced artichokes and potatoes in water with seasoning until tender. Liquidize with the milk. Heat and serve with chopped parsley to garnish. (4–6)

S CREAM OF RUNNER BEAN SOUP

1 lb (450 gm) runner beans
1 lb (450 gm) potatoes
2 pints (1,200 ml) water
2 tbsp butter OR vegetable margarine

2 tsp vegetable bouillon powder
2-4 cloves garlic, chopped
½ pint (300 ml) natural yoghurt

String the beans and slice. Cut potatoes into 2–3 slices. Boil together in the water with the butter, seasoning and garlic till tender. Remove potato skins when cooked, if preferred. Liquidize and add yoghurt. Adjust seasoning. Reheat without boiling and serve. **(6)**

SPECIAL SEA GREEN SOUP

2 tbsp hiziki (dried sea vegetable)
1¾ pt (1 litre) cold water
1-2 onions, chopped
1-2 carrots, chopped
2 tbsp vegetable oil
1 small cooking apple, chopped
1 tbsp raisins

1 oz (25 gm) almonds
2 oz (50 gm) wholegrain macaroni
¾ tsp bouillon powder
1 bunch watercress, chopped
2 tsp miso (soya paste)
3 tbsp chopped parsley
2 tbsp toasted sesame seeds

Soak the hiziki in 1 pint of the water for 10 minutes. Sauté onion and carrot in the hot oil till softened a little, then add hiziki water, apple, raisins and almonds. Cook till tender. Boil the pasta in the ¾ pint water with the bouillon powder till tender, then add watercress and cook one minute more. Mix miso with a little cool stock and add all together. Reheat without boiling, adjusting seasoning to taste. Garnish with chopped parsley and sesame seeds. Full of goodness! **(4–6)**

FRENCH ONION SOUP

1½ lb (675 gm) onions, sliced
2-4 cloves garlic, pressed
2 tbsp butter or vegetable oil
2 pt (1,200 ml) water OR stock
¼ tsp paprika
pinch grated nutmeg

freshly ground black pepper
shoyu or tamari to taste
1 tbsp Muscovado sugar (optional)
Parmesan cheese
2-3 slices wholemeal toast, diced or
   'croutons' (p. 71)

Sweat the onions and garlic in hot butter till transparent. Add water, spices, shoyu and sugar and boil for a few minutes. Serve very hot with the wholemeal toast ('croutons') and a sprinkling of Parmesan cheese. **(4–6)**

SWEDE AND PARSNIP SOUP   S

2 onions, chopped
2 tbsp butter OR vegetable oil
2 pt (1,200 ml) water OR stock
1 swede, sliced

1 parsnip, sliced
tiny pinch powdered mace
2 tsp bouillon powder

Sweat the onion in oil. Add the stock and other vegetables and simmer until just cooked. Liquidize, add mace and correct seasoning. **(6)**

S SAUERKRAUT AND MUSHROOM SOUP

12 oz (350 gm) mushrooms, sliced
3 tbsp butter OR vegetable margarine
1½ pt (900 ml) meat OR vegetable
  stock

8 oz (225 gm) sauerkraut
freshly ground black pepper
2 pt (1,200 ml) tomato juice

Sweat mushrooms in butter for a few minutes. Add to the stock with sauerkraut and seasoning. Simmer for one hour, without allowing to boil. Add the tomato juice, stir, reheat, and serve piping hot. (8–10)

S SPANISH SUMMER SOUP

1 pt (600 ml) tomato juice
½ pt (300 ml) chicken stock
2-3 tbsp cider vinegar
1 tsp chopped onion
¼ tsp oregano (approx)

2-4 tomatoes, diced
¼ cucumber, diced
yellow and/or green pepper, diced
spring onions, chopped

Mix together the tomato juice, stock and vinegar, blending with chopped onion and oregano to taste. Chill. Prepare separate dishes of diced tomatoes, cucumber, pepper and spring onions and chill. Serve the chilled soup and hand the salad garnishes separately. (4–6)

PROVENÇAL SUMMER VEGETABLE SOUP

6 oz (175 gm) courgettes, cut in ½″
  slices
3 tbsp olive OR sunflower oil
1 onion, chopped
2 small leeks, chopped
2 pt (1,200 ml) water OR stock
6 oz (175 gm) French beans, cut in
  ½″ slices
2 young carrots, chopped

1-3 cloves garlic, pressed
2 tbsp fresh basil, finely chopped
sea salt and black pepper
10 oz (275 gm) tomatoes, skinned
  and quartered
2 oz (50 gm) wholewheat or
  buckwheat macaroni
2 oz (50 gm) grated Parmesan cheese

Prepare the vegetables, leaving the courgettes unpeeled. In the hot oil, sweat the onion and leeks until soft. Add the water, French beans, carrots, garlic, basil and seasoning and simmer about ¼ hour. Add the tomatoes, courgettes and macaroni and continue cooking for 15–20 minutes. Adjust seasoning. Serve with grated Parmesan cheese. (8)

CHICKEN BROTH

3-4 pt (2 litre) water
2 tbsp Worcester sauce
1 boiling fowl (including feet)
½ cup pot barley, OR brown rice OR
  soup mixture OR lentils, etc
outer celery leaves, finely chopped

3 large onions, chopped
1 leek, chopped
2-3 large carrots, chopped
fresh or dried herbs as available:
  (see page 30)

Into a large preserving pan put the cold water, Worcester sauce, cleaned fowl and giblets. Bring to the boil and skim. Add barley or soup mixture and simmer for 1 hour. Add celery, onions, leek and carrots with rice or lentils. Return to boil, then simmer with half of the mixed herbs (left whole if fresh). Cover and cook till all is tender. Remove cooked fresh herbs and replace with remaining herbs finely chopped, or add a few more dried herbs. Remove chicken for using for a separate meal (perhaps with supreme sauce made from some of the strained soup). Chop any left-over chicken and add to soup, adjust seasoning, heat and serve. (8–10)

TURKEY BROTH

Make in the same way from the cooked turkey carcass. Soup in excess of immediate requirements can be frozen for later use.

LENTIL SOUP   S

2 carrots, chopped
2 onions, chopped
2 tbsp vegetable oil
2 pt (1,200 ml) stock OR water + 1 tsp
  Tastex

2 bay leaves
4 oz (100 gm) lentils
2-3 tsp lemon juice (optional)
salty seasoning

Sweat the carrot and onion in hot oil. Add the stock, bay leaves and washed lentils and simmer until cooked, about ¾ hour. Sieve or liquidize and add a little lemon juice and adjust seasoning.

GOLDEN PEA SOUP   A

8 oz (225 gm) split peas, soaked
  overnight
1 large onion, chopped
1 small parsnip, chopped
1 stick celery, chopped finely
1 large carrot, chopped
1-2 tomatoes, halved

1 leaf fresh lovage, chopped
3 pt (1,800 ml) unseasoned stock OR
  water
½ tsp salty seasoning
chives or parsley, chopped
  (optional)
½ tsp paprika

Add vegetables, rinsed split peas and lovage to stock and boil rapidly for 10 minutes. Simmer with lid just ajar till peas are cooked, about 1 hour. Add seasoning. Liquidize. Serve with chopped chives or parsley, or sprinkling of paprika. A nourishing soup, free from oil, grains, milk and meat. (6–8)

BLACK BEAN SOUP

10 oz (275 gm) black beans
4-6" Kombu (sea vegetable)
3 pt (1,800 ml) unseasoned stock OR
  water
1 tsp dried lovage
freshly ground black pepper
1 bay leaf

2 onions, chopped
3 sticks celery, chopped finely
2 tbsp vegetable oil
1 large potato, sliced
1 lemon, grated zest & juice
salty seasoning
chopped parsley

Soak beans overnight and rinse. (see p. 101). Soak kombu in the cold stock or water for 10 minutes. Add beans, lovage, black pepper and bay leaf. Boil rapidly then simmer 1½ hours. Sweat onion and celery in hot oil. Add potato and sautéed vegetables to beanpot and continue cooking till everything is tender. Discard bay leaf and remove a few black beans for garnish. Liquidize soup with lemon juice and zest. Reheat soup, thinning with more stock or water if needed, and season to taste. Garnish with reserved black beans and parsley. (6–8)

S WAKAME SOUP

2 tbsp dried wakame
2 pints (1,200 ml) water
2 carrots, chopped

½ lb (225 gm) onions, chopped
tamari OR miso to taste
freshly ground black pepper

Soak the dried wakame in the cold water for 15 minutes. Add carrot and onion. Simmer till tender. Add tamari or miso and black pepper to taste. (4–6)

S CHILLED RAW BEETROOT SOUP

4-5 oz (100-130 gm) young beetroot,
  raw
1¼ pt (750 ml) natural yoghurt
2 tbsp chopped chives

lemon juice to taste
salty seasoning to taste
pinch paprika

Grate the scrubbed beetroot into a pint of yoghurt and liquidize with half the chives (or use food processor). Add lemon juice and seasoning to taste. Chill. Serve with a swirl of yoghurt, sprinkling of paprika and the remaining chives. An eye-catching and concentrated soup – use small servings. (6)

S CHILLED CUCUMBER SOUP

S2 large cucumbers
1 large onion, chopped
1 clove garlic, chopped
2 tbsp butter OR oil
1½ pt (900 ml) vegetable OR meat
  stock

1 small potato, scrubbed & sliced
bouillon powder
1-2 tbsp fresh dill
zest of 1 lemon
¼ pt (150 ml) natural yoghurt

Reserve thin slices of cucumber for decoration; peel and chop remainder. Sweat the onion and garlic in the hot butter till transparent. Add to the stock with the cucumber, potato, seasoning, and half the fresh dill. Simmer till tender. Remove dill and liquidize. Stir in the remaining fresh dill, finely chopped, the lemon zest and yoghurt. Check seasoning and chill. Decorate with cucumber slices. (4–6)

WATERCRESS SOUP   S

½-¾ lb (225-350 gm) potatoes, sliced
½-¾ lb (225-350 gm) onions, sliced
1 pt (600 ml) water OR stock

salty seasoning & paprika
½ tsp dried dill or marjoram
1-2 bunches watercress (see p. 36)
½ pt (300 ml) milk (optional)

Cook potatoes and onions in stock with seasoning and herbs. Reserve a few sprigs of watercress for garnish. Liquidize remaining watercress in the soup with the milk. Heat through. Check seasoning. Serve with the watercress garnish. Also good served chilled. (4–6)

BORSCHT   S

1¼ lb (550 gm) raw beetroot, chopped
2 sticks celery, finely chopped
¼ lb (100 gm) tomatoes, halved
¾ lb (350 gm) carrots, chopped
1 large onion, chopped

2 pt (1,200 ml) good vegetable stock
salty seasoning to taste
½ pt (300 ml) natural yoghurt
1 tsp honey, or to taste
pinch paprika

Put vegetables in cold stock with a little seasoning. Simmer for ¾ hour, adding a little more water if necessary. Liquidize. Stir in half the yoghurt. Reheat without boiling. Taste and add honey if needed. Serve with blobs of yoghurt and sparse sprinkling of paprika. (6–8)

CROUTONS

slices of wholemeal bread
garlic powder

sunflower or soya oil

Use stale bread cut into cubes and leave to dry out at room temperature for 2–3 days or put into cool oven (250°F) till dry. Sprinkle with garlic powder and oil and heat in oven, or deep fry and drain thoroughly.

BAVARIAN DUMPLINGS

2 oz (50 gm) vegetable margarine OR
  butter
6 oz (175 gm) SR 100% wholemeal
  flour
½ tsp salty seasoning

¼ tsp freshly ground black pepper
2 tbsp grated cheese
2 tbsp chopped chives OR onion
vegetable stock OR soup

Rub the fat into the seasoned flour. Add cheese and chives, moisten with stock or soup to make a soft dough. Roll into balls about 1″ diameter. Cook in boiling soup (or wet casserole dish) for about ½ hour, till done (test by removing one and cutting in half). Dumplings add wholesome wholegrain body to a soup – turn a soup into a meal!

LIVER DUMPLINGS

12 oz (350 gm) minced liver
8 oz (225 gm) wholemeal
  breadcrumbs
4 eggs
½ tsp nutmeg
2-3 onions, finely chopped

1-6 cloves garlic, pressed or finely
  chopped
3 tbsp vegetable oil
salty seasoning
wholemeal flour
vegetable soup

Mix the first eight ingredients, adding sufficient flour to make the mixture quite stiff. Form into balls and drop into fast boiling vegetable soup. Cook for 10–15 minutes until cooked – check by cutting one in half. Serve with the soup. (4–6)

'CREAM OF FRIDGE'

This is a common title given when guests ask what soup we are serving! Contrary to the expectations of traditional cooks, imaginative vegetable soups can be easy to prepare and quickly and economically made. Use left-over vegetables with their own stock, remains of savoury dishes, casseroles and sauces, and liquidize them. When brought to the boil and simmered together, check the taste and exercise your creativity. Select from your range of salty seasonings, and add herbs, tomato juice, a little grated cheese or grated lemon rind to enhance the flavour. Remember, a little macaroni cheese does delicious things to a mixture of vegetables.

Fish Dishes

Fresh fish deserves greater popularity, being one of the most nourishing and most easily digested of foods. Its protein value is higher than meat, yet it contains none of the antibiotics or hormones which may be fed to farm animals. Fish has a high proportion of good polyunsaturated fat including EPA and DHA which help protect from heart disease and are good for the brain. It contains a wide range of trace minerals, including iodine.

Whole fresh fish has round, bright eyes, scales unloosened, a firm body almost stiff, and leaves no imprint when prodded with a finger. It should smell pleasantly of fish. Fish steaks or fillets should exhibit firm flesh with a close grain, and not be watery.

Cooking methods are important. There are better dishes than fried fish and fish fingers. Frying renders fish less digestible, overloads with fat and lessens the nutritional value of the natural fish oil content. Poaching, grilling, baking and steaming are all recommended. Fish is cooked when it becomes opaque, flakes easily with a fork, and comes away from the bone. Overcooking dries out the succulent flesh and destroys the delicate flavour. As fish contains no fibre, include vegetables, salad or wholegrains in some form at the same meal – eat the garnish!

FISH STOCK

Any white fish trimmings (except the 'guts'), i.e. the bones, heads, tails, fins and skins, are suitable for making a well-flavoured fish stock, which will greatly enhance the flavour of the cooked fish or its sauce – or make a good base for a fish soup. Ask your fishmonger for these trimmings when you buy the fish filleted or cut into steaks. Oily fish is unsuitable. A cod's head is particularly valuable, but use whatever is available.

white fish trimmings
water to cover
2 tbsp lemon juice OR little white
   wine vinegar or wine
bouquet garni (optional)

1 onion, sliced
6 peppercorns
salty seasoning
parsley stems or sprigs

Wash the fish trimmings and break the bones a little. Just cover with water and add other ingredients. Simmer 30 minutes. Strain.

COURT BOUILLON

1-2 carrots, finely chopped
1 stick celery, finely chopped
1 onion, chopped
1½ pt (900 ml) water

bouquet garni
12 peppercorns
salty seasoning
½ pt (300 ml) dry white wine

Simmer all ingredients for 30 minutes to make a mild stock for poaching fish.

POACHED FISH STEAKS

4-6 fish steaks (cod, halibut, hake,
  haddock, turbot or salmon)
butter OR oil
¼ pt (150 ml) fish stock OR Court
  bouillon
¼ pt (150 ml) dry white wine

OR 2 tbsp lemon juice
salty seasoning
freshly ground black pepper
natural yoghurt
lemon wedges
parsley sprigs

Choose a casserole which will just accommodate the steaks, lying flat and closely packed, and grease it well. Arrange fish and pour over the blended fish stock and wine to just cover. Season. Cover with buttered paper and lid. Bake in hot oven, 425–450°F, 220–230°C, Gas 7–8, about 10–15 minutes, till fish is tender and will come away from the bone. Blend cooking liquid with yoghurt to taste and reheat without boiling, adjusting seasoning. Serve with the fish, decorated with lemon wedges and parsley. (4–6)

TASTY STEAMED FISH

Steaming is practical for cooking small fish and fillets in small quantities. Choose two matching plates or shallow casserole which will accommodate the fish and either fit inside your steamer or over a large saucepan. Fillets may be folded over. Most suitable fish are whiting, slip soles, lemon soles or dabs, or plaice fillets.

butter OR oil
2 small fish OR 4 fillets plaice
salty seasoning
freshly ground black pepper

2 tsp lemon juice
1 tsp shoyu OR tamari
1 tbsp finely chopped spring onion
arrowroot (optional)

Butter lower plate and arrange fish on it. Season and add lemon juice, shoyu and onion. Cover with buttered greaseproof paper and lid (or inverted second plate). Lower into steamer, or put over saucepan of boiling water. Steam 20–30 minutes, till just cooked. Serve the fish with its own liquor poured over, or thicken liquor with arrowroot or 85% flour to make a tasty sauce. For babies omit seasoning and shoyu – or steam in milk with herbs. (2)

GRILLED HERRINGS OR MACKEREL

4 herrings OR mackerel
vegetable oil
salty seasoning

freshly ground black pepper
finely chopped or dried parsley
lemon wedges

Choose herrings with soft roes for preference. Cut off heads and fins and clean without splitting them open. Scrape off the scales, wash and dry the fish. Score the skin diagonally 3 or 4 times on each side and paint with a little oil. Sprinkle with seasoning and parsley. Grease the grillpan to prevent sticking. Grill, turning once or twice, till just tender. Serve with lemon wedges, or Maitre d'hotel butter. Mackerel spoils faster than most fish, so buy extra fresh and eat it the same day. (4)

SALMON OR SALMON TROUT

For special occasions treat yourselves to these most delectable of fish, which may be baked or poached, served hot or cold. Salmon, the king of fish, has the better flavour, especially if really fresh. But salmon trout bought at a trout farm and cooked within an hour or two will also be superb. The larger fish have the most flavour, are easier to serve attractively, and make it easier to serve without bones. Whether to be served hot or cold, remove the skin while hot and baste with own liquor. Cover with the greased paper while cooling.

POACHED SALMON OR SALMON TROUT

whole salmon, 3-4 lb (1½-1¾ kg)
2 pt (1 litre) court bouillon (approx)
¼ pt (150 ml) white wine
salty seasoning and black pepper
bouquet garni or parsley stems

arrowroot
2 lemons
mayonnaise
tomato slices
cucumber slices

Wipe the cleaned fish and place in greased baking dish which will accommodate the whole fish – or use a fish kettle. Pour over sufficient court bouillon and wine to just cover and add seasoning and bouquet garni or parsley stems. Cover and poach gently, simmering till just tender (about ¾–1 hour on the hob, probably a little longer in a moderate oven). Do not overcook. Serve hot with a sauce made from a little of its cooking liquor, reduced by fast boiling (uncovered), then thickened with arrowroot and flavoured with lemon juice. Decorate the salmon with piped mayonnaise, tomato and cucumber slices and lemon 'butterflies', on its hot plate. If to be served cold, cool before decorating and serve with mayonnaise or Herb Mayonnaise (p. 47), omitting the garlic. (6–8)

BAKED SALMON OR SALMON TROUT

butter OR vegetable oil
whole salmon trout, 2½-3 lb
  (1.1-1.4 kg)
salty seasoning
freshly ground black pepper

parsley stems OR chopped parsley
2 tbsp white wine
lemon, cucumber, tomato slices
mayonnaise

Put two large sheets of greaseproof paper over a sheet of foil on a baking tray. Butter the paper and place the cleaned fish on it. Sprinkle all over with seasoning and parsley, and drizzle over the wine. Wrap up carefully, folding over the paper on top to seal in the juices. (The foil is to strengthen the parcel, but should not make contact with the fish.) Bake in oven, 325–350°F, 160–180°C, Gas 3–4 till just cooked (about an hour). Unwrap greaseproof paper and carefully slide fish, with its juices, on to hot serving dish. Skin and decorate as for poached salmon. (4–5)

STUFFED COD

1½-2 lb (¾-1 kg) cod
Herb Stuffing (p. 32)
2 tbsp vegetable oil
salty seasoning and black pepper
wholemeal breadcrumbs

1 tsp lemon juice
1 tsp shoyu or tamari
parsley sprigs
lemon wedges

Choose a piece from the head end of the cod (in steaks or in one piece). Wipe the cleaned fish and stuff the opening, securing the stuffing with wooden toothpicks or skewer. Grease a shallow oval casserole and place the prepared cod in it. Brush the fish all over with oil. Sprinkle over seasoning and breadcrumbs. Pour in the lemon juice and shoyu. Cover with oiled greaseproof paper and lid to seal the dish. Bake ½–¾ hour at 350°F, 180°C, Gas 4. After ½ hour, baste and leave uncovered, to crispen the breadcrumbs. Remove toothpicks before serving on hot plate, garnished with parsley and lemon. Could be served with Tomato Sauce (p. 46). Haddock fillets may be substituted, rolling up the fish around the stuffing. (4–5)

FISH CAKES OR PIE

Any left-over cooked fish, or mixed fish scraps including 1–2 sardines, is suitable, provided it is fresh enough (i.e. not more than 48 hours in the refrigerator). Carefully remove every single bone and the skin before weighing.

8 oz (225 gm) steamed potatoes
8 oz (225 gm) flaked cooked fish
¼ tsp celery seed
2 eggs, beaten (optional)
wholemeal flour

salty seasoning and black pepper
few drops Worcester or Kensington
  Sauce
dry wholemeal breadcrumbs

Mash the hot potato with the flaked fish and celery seed. Mix in half the egg and sufficient flour to give a firm consistency. Add seasoning to taste. Shape into flattened cakes. Dip in beaten egg and coat with breadcrumbs. Grill or oven bake till cooked through and nicely browned. Serve hot with Tomato Sauce (p. 46) or cold with salad. You could also make Fish Pie by mixing together the potatoes, fish, celery seed and seasonings. Bake in a greased casserole, sprinkled with breadcrumbs (or topped with more mashed potato – which would make it free from egg, milk and gluten). (4)

GRILLED WHOLE PLAICE

4 small whole plaice
3 tbsp wholewheat flour OR brown
  rice flour
½ tsp salty seasoning
freshly ground black pepper
1 tsp dried basil or marjoram

butter OR vegetable margarine
1 large onion, finely chopped
2 tomatoes, sliced
parsley sprigs
1 lemon, cut in wedges

Wash, trim and gut the fish and dry with kitchen paper. Mix flour, seasoning and herbs and coat fish with it. Remove the rack from the grill pan and generously grease the bottom. Sprinkle half the chopped onion on this, where the fish is to lie, and cover with the plaice, again sprinkled with chopped onion. Dot with small dabs of butter and put under medium hot grill to cook. Add a smear of butter as necessary while cooking and grill until just tender, turning to grill second side. Serve decorated with tomato, parsley, and lemon. (4)

BAKED HADDOCK   S

2 lb (900 gm) haddock, hake or cod
¼ pt (150 ml) fish stock
1 onion, chopped finely
¼-½ green pepper, chopped finely
1 tbsp vegetable oil
1 large tomato

freshly ground black pepper
¼ tsp dried oregano
salty seasoning
1 lemon, cut in wedges
parsley sprigs

Clean and gut the fish. Remove the backbone system. Use trimmings for fish stock. Sweat onion and pepper in the hot oil. Remove from heat and add the tomato and seasoning. Grease a casserole, lay in the fish and cover with the vegetable mixture. Pour over the fish stock. Cover tightly and bake until just done – about 20 minutes at 300–325°F, 150–160°C, Gas 2–3. Serve with lemon and parsley. (4)

BAKED COD SUPREME   S

1 bunch spring onions, chopped
2 tomatoes, chopped
1 carrot, scrubbed and grated
1 tbsp fresh parsley OR dill

black pepper
salty seasoning
4 cod steaks OR halibut
1 lemon, cut in wedges

Mix spring onions with the prepared vegetables, herbs and seasoning. Line a greased casserole with half the mixture. Wipe the cod and arrange as second layer, with remaining vegetable mixture over the top. Add 2 tbsp water, cover and bake till just done, about 20 minutes at 350°F, 180°C, Gas 4. Serve with lemon. (4)

GRILLED SPRATS OR SARDINES

Buy really fresh sprats or sardines to use the same day. Wash thoroughly but leave whole. Place in large grill tray, top to tail and grill under moderately hot grill for 6–10 minutes. They need no seasoning or fat and will cook in their own juices. Serve 6–12 per portion, depending on size and appetite, with paper squares and finger bowls, and eat them Spanish 'tapas' style – holding them in the fingers by the head and the tail, gently pulling off the soft flesh with the lips, so all the bones and the 'guts' remain; they can be enjoyed without the difficulty of coping with tiny bones. A squeeze of lemon juice is all that is needed to enhance the delicious flavour. Serve with wholemeal bread and butter and salad.

HERRING ROES ON TOAST

wholemeal flour OR soya flour
salty seasoning
paprika
½ lb (225 gm) herring roes

vegetable oil
4 slices wholemeal toast
lemon wedges
4-8 tomatoes

Season the flour. Wash and dry the roes, cutting the dark line on the underside skin to help even cooking. Fry on both sides until golden. Drain well and serve on hot toast with lemon and tomato. (2)

S MOULES MARINIÈRES

2 lb (900 gm) fresh mussels
1 large onion, chopped
2 tbsp butter OR oil

bunch of parsley
glass dry white wine
freshly ground black pepper

Wash the mussels thoroughly to remove grit and beards, discarding those with broken shells and any that float. Sweat onion in hot butter. Add the chopped parsley stems, wine, pepper and the mussels and add enough water to just cover. Cook over a steady heat until they open (about 7–10 minutes). Serve in large soup bowls, with the liquor poured over, sprinkled with chopped parsley, with wholemeal bread and butter. (4)

KEDGEREE

8-12 oz (225-350 gm) smoked
   haddock
1 cup brown rice
2½ cups haddock stock
pinch saffron, turmeric or paprika

2 tbsp butter, margarine OR oil
2 eggs, freshly hard-boiled
2-3 tbsp chopped parsley
parsley sprigs
lemon wedges

Poach haddock in water to cover for 10 minutes. Drain, reserving stock. Remove bones and skin. Boil the rice in the stock with the haddock skins, spice and half the butter, about 40 minutes. Remove skin. Flake the fish. Shell and chop the eggs. Add remaining butter to the rice and stir in flaked haddock, egg and chopped parsley. Heat through carefully. Check seasoning and serve decorated with parsley sprigs and lemon wedges. (4)

Meat Dishes

Meat is the most popular protein food, and a good source of zinc. Yet we tend to eat more than is good for our health. The protein value of any meat is independent of its cost; so the protein present in the cheapest cuts of beef will be equal to that in sirloin steak. Older, harder-working muscle meat (e.g. shin of beef) has more flavour than young tender cuts (e.g. veal fillet). Marinating and long slow cooking methods can tenderize tough meat and produce delicious cheap dishes.

The best meats to eat, from a nutritional and health viewpoint, are (in descending order):

- Lean dark meats of 'free range' wild animals – rabbit, pigeon, venison, hare, pheasant, etc. (free from any danger of hormone or drug residue).
- Organ meats – heart, brains, sweetbreads, tongue – which contain less cholesterol than muscle meats, so providing healthier (and more economical) meat protein. Liver and kidneys are also very high in nutritive value, but as organs of purification may contain contaminants also.
- Butcher's meat. Animals may have been treated with antibiotics or steroids, and been intensively reared on pelleted food. Lamb is more naturally produced than beef, veal or pork. Choose 'free range' fresh poultry whenever possible.
- Delicatessen meats, sausages, smoked foods, fish fingers etc. There are now many processed foods containing chemical additives. They are likely to be the least nutritious, are not suitable for young children and are not recommended.

Research into heart disease has highlighted the advisability of cutting down on animal fat (which occurs, hidden, in even the leanest of meats). This means eating a lower proportion of meat in our diet. So extended meat dishes like Spaghetti Bolognaise, Beefergine Loaf, Irish Stew and Stuffed Marrow are recommended.

For better health and vitality, eat meat less frequently and in smaller quantities. Fish and vegetarian dishes can be delicious too.

POT ROAST OF BEEF   S

2½-3½ lb (1-1½ kg) brisket of beef
2 cloves garlic (optional)
wholemeal OR soya flour
salty seasoning

vegetable oil
1 large onion, sliced thickly
¼ pt (150 ml) water OR stock

Wipe the meat. Make small knife slits in the joint and push in slivers of fresh garlic. Coat joint with seasoned flour. Heat a little oil and fry the joint on all sides to seal it. Drain off any surplus fat. Place the beef on onion slices in the saucepan and add stock. Simmer gently with lid tightly closed until tender (about 3-4 hours) or pressure cook for 1 hour at 15 lb pressure (with more stock). Remove beef and turn under hot grill to dry out the surface before serving. **(6-8)**

GF
SF
LF
POT ROAST BRISKET OF BEEF

3-4 lb (1¼-1¾ kg) fresh brisket of
   beef
1-2 cloves garlic
¼ tsp freshly ground black pepper
½ tsp freshly ground allspice

3 tbsp brown rice flour
1 lb (450 gm) onions, sliced
2 fl oz (50 ml) water OR stock
1 stick celery, chopped
1 tsp marjoram

Wipe the meat and trim off the excess fat. Melt this fat in a large heavy-based saucepan while you prepare the brisket by making small knife jabs in the surface and pushing in slivers of fresh garlic. Mix half the ground spices with the flour and dust over the brisket joint. Then brown the beef on all sides in its own fat. Remove joint and pour off the fat. Put prepared onions, water and celery in the bottom of the pan (or use Romertopf). Replace brisket on top and sprinkle over remaining spices and dried marjoram. Cover and simmer for about 4 hours, turning and basting occasionally. When tender, remove the joint and strain the stock from the vegetables. Separate off the fat and liquidize the remaining juices with the strained vegetables to make a delicious gravy. **(6-8)**

S # CASSEROLED STEAK WITH CELERY JERVAISE

12 oz (350 gm) stewing steak
soya OR wholewheat flour
1 tsp marjoram
4 tbsp tomato purée

1 tbsp Worcester sauce OR shoyu
½ pt (300 ml) stock OR water
4 oz (100 gm) lean bacon, chopped
8-12 celery sticks, chopped finely

Wipe the beef, cut into inch cubes and coat in the flour mixed with the marjoram. Grease a deep casserole and mix in it the tomato purée, Worcester sauce and water. Stir in the meats and celery. Heat gently to just bring to the boil, then cook in very slow oven (250°F, 120°C, Gas ½) for 2-3 hours. A delicious unfatty dish without the usual onion and garlic flavour. **(4-5)**

SPAGHETTI BOLOGNAISE

2 tbsp vegetable oil
1 stick celery, chopped
1 clove garlic, pressed (optional)
1 large onion, chopped
8 oz (225 gm) minced beef
salty seasoning
freshly ground black pepper
oregano
bay leaf
1 small cooking apple, peeled and
   finely sliced

½ lb (225 gm) tomatoes, skinned
   and chopped
2 tbsp tomato purée
8-10 oz (225-275 gm) wholewheat
   spaghetti OR buckwheat pasta
stock OR water
2 oz (50 gm) grated cheese
1 extra tomato for garnish

To the hot oil in a pan, add the celery, garlic, onion and beef and fry for a few minutes until beef browns. Add the seasoning, herbs, apple, tomatoes and purée and a little water if too thick. Simmer gently, covered. Boil the pasta in seasoned stock until just tender. Drain and reserve stock for other use. Add half the spaghetti to the cooked Bolognaise sauce and correct seasoning. Serve on a large hot dish surrounded by the extra spaghetti. Sprinkle with grated cheese and decorate with the final sliced tomato. Serve with a green vegetable or side salad. **(5-6)**

ROAST LAMB WITH ROSEMARY   S

leg OR shoulder of lamb
wholemeal flour
salty seasoning and black pepper

1-4 cloves garlic
stem fresh rosemary
1 large onion, chopped coarsely

Wipe the joint. Season the flour and rub all over the surface of the meat. Cut the garlic into long slivers. Make jab cuts into the joint with a pointed knife, inserting a garlic sliver into each, with a small sprig of rosemary to plug the top. Place onions in base of covered baking dish with the lamb on top. Add 3 tablespoons water and cover. Bake at 300-325°F, 150-160°C, Gas 2-3 till tender, removing lid to baste and then crisp surface for the last half hour.

A clay baking 'Romertopf' is helpful in roasting with this method, as the lamb will roast in its own fat, the juices later being poured into a gravy separator to remove the fat and separate the meat juices for the gravy. The onion beneath the joint is a good addition, liquidized, to the gravy. **(6-8 for shoulder, 8-10 for leg)**

IRISH STEW

2 lb (900 gm) neck of mutton OR lamb
¼ lb (100 gm) pot barley OR pearl
  barley
1 tbsp cider vinegar
stock OR water
1 turnip, cubed
1 lb (450 gm) carrots, chopped

2 large onions, chopped
1 lb (450 gm) potatoes, scrubbed and
  halved
2 bouquet garni
salty seasoning
freshly ground black pepper

Put meat, barley and vinegar into a large pan with a tight-fitting lid with sufficient stock to cover. Bring to boil and remove scum. Simmer 1¾ hours. Add vegetables, one bouquet garni and seasoning. Continue to simmer till all is tender. Leave to go cold and refrigerate. Remove fat from the top and discard. Take meat off the bones and replace. Remove used bouquet garni and renew. Reheat, check seasoning and serve hot with greens. **(6)**

BOILED BEEF ROLL

1 lb (450 gm) minced beef
4 oz (100 gm) soft wholemeal
  breadcrumbs
1 large onion, chopped finely
1 egg, beaten
a little marjoram

1 tbsp chopped parsley
1 tsp Worcester sauce OR shoyu
½ tsp salty seasoning
¼ tsp freshly ground black pepper
1 tbsp tomato purée

Mix all ingredients. Turn on to a floured work surface and shape into a long roll. Place on floured pudding cloth and roll up, securing the ends. Boil gently but steadily for 2 hours in stock. Serve hot or cold. (**4**)

S FRICANDELLES

1 large egg	1 clove garlic, crushed
3 tbsp stock OR water	grated rind of 1 lemon
1 tsp Worcester sauce OR shoyu	1 tbsp chopped parsley
1 lb (450 gm) minced beef	½ tsp dried thyme
5 oz (150 gm) fresh wholemeal breadcrumbs	black pepper and salty seasoning
	a little wholemeal flour
1-2 onions, finely chopped	

In a large bowl whisk together the egg, stock and Worcester sauce. Add mince, breadcrumbs, onions, garlic, lemon zest, parsley, thyme seasoning and mix to blend thoroughly. Roll into balls and coat with a little flour. Grill, oven bake or fry in barely greased non-stick pan. Serve with tomato sauce. (**4**)

S BEEFERGINE LOAF

1 large aubergine	2 cloves garlic, crushed
1 tbsp tamari OR shoyu	½ tsp salty seasoning
1 egg, beaten	black pepper
1 lb (450 gm) minced beef	¼ tsp garam masala
3 tbsp fine bran OR oatflakes	½ tsp dried thyme
1 tbsp chopped parsley	garnish: tomato and parsley

First cook the aubergine: prick it thoroughly, place in greased casserole, bake in oven, 350-375°F, 180-190°C, Gas 4-5 till tender (½-¾ hour). Cut open, remove and chop aubergine flesh and mix with all remaining ingredients. Transfer to a greased loaf tin, cover with greased butterpapers and bake for a further 1¼-1½ hours. Turn out before serving and decorate with tomato slices and parsley. (**4-6**)

TASTY TENDER STEAK CASSEROLE

1 lb (450 gm) stewing steak	¼ inch ginger root, finely chopped
4 tbsp tomato purée	2-3 cloves garlic, finely sliced
¼ pt (150 ml) red wine	black pepper
3 tbsp vegetable oil	3-4 sticks celery, finely chopped
¼ tsp ground coriander	salty seasoning

Wipe and cube the stewing steak, removing fatty connective tissue. Mix tomato purée, wine, oil, spices, garlic and pepper. Stir in the steak so that each piece is well coated. Leave soaking in this marinade 4-24 hours, covered, in refrigerator. Add celery and salt. Transfer to casserole with tight-fitting lid (clay baking pot is ideal) and bake slowly 275°F, 140°C, Gas 1 for about 3 hours, till tender. If the excess fat is spooned off this dish, it is suitable for slimmers. Also suitable for cooking in a slow cooker. (**4**)

POULTRY

SUPER SPICED CHICKEN

GF
SF
LF

1 roasting chicken
½ inch ginger root
1-2 cloves garlic
1 tsp coriander seeds
½ tsp cumin seeds
½-3 dried chillies
½ tsp ground ginger

zest and juice of ½ lemon
3 tbsp natural yoghurt
3 tbsp vegetable oil
brown rice flour for coating
1-1½ cups brown long grain rice
lemon for garnish
parsley sprigs

For stock and sauce:
carcass, neck and giblets from
    chicken
1 large onion
1 carrot
2 scrubbed potatoes

reserved chilli seeds
stems from the parsley
1-1½ pts (600-900 ml) water
¼ pt (150 ml) natural yoghurt

4-12 hours before cooking: Wipe and cut the chicken into serving pieces and slash the skin. To make the marinade, first crush the sliced ginger root, garlic, coriander and cumin seeds (splitting open the seeds). Use a pestle and mortar or place between greaseproof paper and press hard with a flat heavy knife blade. Carefully remove all seeds from the chillies (reserving a third for the chicken stockpot) and grind red flesh with the other spices. Add ground ginger, lemon juice and yoghurt and mix. Coat chicken pieces with the mixture. Leave to marinate, refrigerated, for several hours, preferably overnight.

Make chicken stock: Cook the chicken carcass, neck and giblets with prepared onion, carrots and potatoes, reserved chilli seeds, parsley stems and water. Use strained stock for cooking the accompanying brown rice without salt.

Cooking: Drain the chicken joints from the marinade, coat in the rice flour and seal all over in the hot oil till golden brown. Transfer to a greased casserole, add the marinade, cover and bake 1-1¼ hours at 300-325°F, 150-160°C, Gas 2-3 till tender. Drain off the liquid from the chicken, strain out the spices and separate off the fat with a saucière (for low fat dish) or simply pour off excess fat, keeping chicken warm. Add the extra yoghurt to the de-fatted cooking liquor and liquidize with sufficient peeled potato to produce a coating consistency. Add the reserved spices to the sauce in the pan before reheating without boiling. Arrange chicken on serving dish with the sauce and garnish with lemon slices and parsley.
(6)

SWEET CHICKEN WITH COCONUT

2 tbsp sultanas
8 fl oz (250 ml) stock OR water
2 tbsp desiccated coconut
4 fl oz (125 ml) boiling milk
4 chicken winglets

wholemeal flour OR soya flour
salty seasoning
2 tbsp vegetable oil
1 large onion, sliced
1 tsp garam masala

Soak sultanas in stock, coconut in milk, for ½ hour. Dust winglets with seasoned flour and seal in hot oil. Drain. Sauté onion till transparent. Add garam masala and 2 tbsp flour and cook, stirring. Stir in stock, sultanas, coconut milk and chicken. Transfer to closed casserole and bake 1-1½ hours at 325°F, 160°C, Gas 3. Serve accompanied by brown rice or lightly cooked (i.e. stir-fried) white cabbage. (You can substitute curry powder for garam masala.) (2)

CASSEROLED CHICKEN

1 boiling fowl, prepared
wholemeal flour
salty seasoning
vegetable oil
½ lb (225 gm) carrots, sliced

½ pt (300 ml) tomato juice OR 1 (14 oz)
  can tomatoes
1 lb (450 gm) small onions
1 clove garlic, finely chopped
2 stalks celery, finely chopped

Cut chicken into joints and portions, reserving carcass and giblets for making chicken stock or soup. Coat the chicken portions in seasoned flour and seal in the hot oil until nicely browned. Into a deep casserole, pour the carrots, tomatoes, whole prepared onions, garlic, celery and chicken pieces. Cover tightly and bake in cool oven 275°F, 140°C, Gas 1 for 3-4 hours until tender. Check seasoning. (6-8)

OLD TIMER'S CHICKEN CASSEROLE

1 boiling fowl, prepared
salty seasoning
freshly ground black pepper
pinch mace
little sage (if fowl is rather fat)
1 eating apple, studded with cloves

2 large onions, peeled and thickly
  sliced and 1 small onion
1 clove garlic (optional)
1 bay leaf
1 cup brown rice, long grain
1 pt (600 ml) milk

This method involves cooking all day in a casserole with a close fitting lid, so prepare it at breakfast time for the evening meal. Wipe the fowl inside and out and dust with mixed seasoning and herbs. Fill the cavity with the clove-studded apple, small onion, garlic and bay leaf. Into the greased casserole put the washed brown rice, milk, sliced onions and the prepared chicken. Sprinkle with seasoning and cover tightly. Bake in a very slow oven all day or use slow cooker. It should not need attention but check that the oven is cool enough to prevent the chicken from becoming dry. This is also a good method for cooking a tough, elderly 'boiling duck' with appropriate changes of herbs. (6-8)

CHICKEN IMPERIAL

1 roasting chicken, portioned
3 oz (75 gm) butter OR beaten egg
1 large onion, finely chopped
large bunch fresh parsley, chopped
4 oz (100 gm) Edam cheese, grated

4 oz (100 gm) soft wholemeal
  breadcrumbs
freshly ground black pepper
2 oranges, sliced
parsley sprigs

Wipe the chicken and cut into joints, separating thighs from drums. Melt the butter. Mix together the finely chopped onion, parsley, cheese and breadcrumbs. Coat the chicken pieces in melted butter or beaten egg, then press a layer of the stuffing mixture all round them. Into a large greased casserole dish arrange the coated chicken and sprinkle any remaining stuffing and black pepper over the top. Bake 325-350°F, 160-180°C, Gas 3-4 for about 1¼-1¾ hours until tender. This rich dish is a party favourite and needs no gravy or added seasoning, if prepared with salted butter. Strain off fat before serving. Garnish with orange slices and parsley sprigs. (6)

CARIBBEAN CHICKEN   GF

1 free-range chicken for roasting
½ tsp dried tarragon
soya flour
salty seasoning
2 onions, sliced
vegetable margarine OR oil
1 tin pineapple in own juice OR fresh
  pineapple

2 cups natural yoghurt
pineapple or lemon juice to taste
thin honey, to taste
2-3 cups cooked brown rice
2 tbsp green pepper, sliced
2 tbsp red pepper, sliced
flaked almonds OR flaked coconut,
  toasted

Wash and dry the chicken. Sprinkle cavity with mixed tarragon, flour and seasoning and rub over the exterior. Put half onions in the cavity and remainder in the base of a Romertopf or covered roasting tin with the margarine. Roast the chicken slowly till tender. Let cool. Cut into fork sized pieces when ready to assemble dish. Cut pineapple into small pieces.
Dressing:
Blend the yoghurt with pineapple or lemon juice and honey to taste. Mix together the cold cooked rice, chicken pieces, dressing and ⅔ of the pineapple and pepper pieces. Spread on a serving dish and decorate the dish with the remaining pineapple and pepper and flaked almonds. Serve cold. (8)

CHICKEN BERMUDAN   GF

3 oz (75 gm) sultanas
¼ tsp cinnamon
¼ tsp allspice
1 tbsp rice flour

1 roasting chicken
1 eating apple, quartered
1 small onion, quartered
2 bananas

Wash sultanas and soak in water several hours. Mix spices and rice flour and use to sprinkle inside the cavity and rub all over the surface of the bird. Push apple and onion pieces into the cavity. Roast the chicken slowly till tender. Simmer the sultanas for 5 minutes in their soaking water and then liquidize to make the sauce. Cut the peeled bananas in half lengthwise and into halves again, dipping each quarter into the sauce to prevent oxidation. Serve the chicken with the hot sauce, garnished with the banana slices. (5-6)

CHICKEN WITH APRICOTS

1 roasting chicken
salty seasoning
freshly ground black pepper
pinch mace
2-4 rashers bacon (optional)
2 onions, sliced

3-4 tbsp cooked brown rice
½ pt (300 ml) vegetable stock
1 bay leaf
4 oz (100 gm) dried apricots, soaked
    for 24 hours
parsley sprigs

Cut the chicken into portions and season with the herb salt, pepper and mace. Line the bottom of a casserole with the bacon and place the chicken joints on them. Cover with the sliced onions and rice and pour over the stock with the bay leaf. Cover tightly and cook for 1½ hours at 300°F, 150°C, Gas 2 until tender. Gently simmer apricots in their soaking liquid for 5 minutes. Serve the chicken on its bed of rice, decorated with the apricots and parsley. (6)

S BRAISED DUCK

1 large duck, oven ready
½ tsp ground ginger
⅛ tsp ground mace
salty seasoning
freshly ground black pepper
1 eating apple, quartered

4 cloves
3 onions, sliced
2 lb (900 gm) ripe tomatoes, halved
bay leaf
2 oranges, sliced
parsley sprigs

Wipe duck and dust cavity with a little of the mixed seasoning and spices. Stud the apple pieces with cloves and place in the cavity. Choose a suitable casserole with a tight fitting lid and nestle the bird in it, with the onions, tomatoes and bay leaf. Sprinkle over remaining seasoning. Add no fat or liquid. Bake in moderate oven 350°F, 180°C, Gas 4 for 2-4 hours until tender. After removing fat with saucière use the tomato liquid to make an accompanying sauce or a delicious soup. Serve decorated with orange slices and parsley. (Also suitable for a boiling fowl.) (4)

GAME

Game from wild, free-ranging birds and animals, provides meat of excellent flavour and the highest nutritional value, with very little saturated fat, but expect the harder working muscles to provide tough meat. As it is exceptionally lean, it would readily dry out if roasted in the usual way. With venison, the haunch (leg and loin together) is the most suitable joint for roasting.

Other venison cuts, game birds, hare and wild rabbit, are best casseroled or stewed, and marinating helps tenderize and moisturize them. Marinate the prepared meat before cooking: Use 2 parts red wine to 1 part vegetable oil (OR 2 parts oil to 1 part lemon juice). Make sufficient marinade to just cover the prepared meat, and give it an occasional stir. Leave covered in a cool place for 8-48 hours – the longer time for a tougher cut and/or older animal. After draining the marinade from the meat, separate the oil with a saucière. Then the oil can be used for sealing the meat and sweating the onions, and the wine or lemon juice incorporated into the stock used for cooking.

ROAST VENISON   S

3½-5½ lb (1½-2½ kg) haunch of venison
vegetable oil
4 tbsp wholemeal flour
¼ tsp dried thyme
¼ tsp dried marjoram

1-3 cloves garlic, crushed
sprig rosemary
½ tsp salty seasoning
4-8 oz (100-225 gm) fat salt pork OR unsmoked bacon slices (optional)
¼ tsp freshly ground black pepper

Rub oil into joint. Coat with flour seasoned with herbs, salt and pepper. Cover joint with thin layer of salt pork to provide larding fat while roasting – or baste frequently. Roast with oil in covered self-basting dish OR cover joint with greaseproof paper over fat pork and use Romertopf or clay baking pot. Roast slowly at 250-300°F, 120-150°C, Gas ½-2, for 2-5 hours, depending on age and size, until tender. (8-12)

CASSEROLE OF VENISON

1¼ lb (550 gm) venison steak
4 fl oz (100 ml) red wine
2 fl oz (50 ml) vegetable oil
2 bay leaves, crumbled
salty seasoning
freshly ground black pepper

wholemeal flour
1 lb (450 gm) onions, sliced
bouquet garni (parsley, thyme, lemon rind)
¾ pt (450 ml) stock OR water
2-3 tbsp chopped parsley

Cut venison into 1 inch cubes. Mix wine, oil and bay leaves for marinade. Stir in meat. Marinate, covered, in refrigerator. Drain meat and strain marinade. Coat meat in seasoned flour and seal in hot oil (from marinade). Sauté onions. Add bouquet garni, meat, wine, stock and seasoning. Bake in closed casserole 2-3 hours at 300-325°F, 150-160°C, Gas 2-3, till tender. Remove bouquet garni. Thicken gravy with wholemeal flour. Serve sprinkled with parsley. (5)

s FORESIGHT RABBIT

4 joints of young rabbit, OR 1 lb (450 gm) raw boned rabbit
wholemeal, soya OR rice flour
salty seasoning and black pepper
vegetable oil
2 large onions, chopped
2-4 sticks celery, chopped

1 carrot, sliced
4 soaked prunes
½ tsp dried marjoram OR basil
fresh sage, parsley and thyme OR pinch dried
¼ pt (150 ml) stock OR water
½ tsp Worcester sauce OR shoyu

Coat rabbit pieces in seasoned flour and seal in hot oil. Drain. Mix the vegetables and put a third in the bottom of a casserole. Cover with rabbit, prunes and remaining vegetables. Sprinkle over dried herbs and nestle fresh herbs among the top vegetables to facilitate their easy removal before serving. Mix water with Worcester sauce and pour over. Bake in slow oven tightly covered till rabbit is tender, about 1¾-2 hours. (4)

s RABBIT FRICASSEE

6 young rabbit joints
1 turnip, sliced thickly
2 onions, sliced thickly
1 carrot, sliced thickly
2 tbsp brown rice, washed

bouquet garni
salty seasoning
freshly ground black pepper
chopped parsley
wholemeal toast

Cover rabbit with cold water, bring quickly to the boil then discard the water. Add vegetables, rice, herbs, seasoning and fresh water to cover the rabbit, bring to boil and simmer until tender (about 1-2 hours). Make a good white sauce from the stock, either traditionally or by liquidizing sufficient rabbit stock with the cooked onions and rice and reheating. Serve rabbit covered in its sauce, decorated with carrot slices and chopped parsley sprinkled over. Surround by triangles of wholemeal toast. (6)

POTTED RABBIT

1 rabbit
2 tsp capers
2 onions, sliced
2 carrots, sliced
herb salt

1 tsp cider vinegar
freshly ground black pepper
1 tsp zest of lemon
2 tbsp parsley, finely chopped
melted butter

Cover rabbit with cold water, bring quickly to the boil and discard the water. Cover rabbit with fresh water, add capers, onions, carrots, herb salt and cider vinegar. Bring to boil and simmer for 1½-3 hours, until quite tender. Cool. Strip the meat off the bones and mince finely. Season to taste with black pepper, freshly grated lemon rind, parsley and herb salt. Mix in sufficient of its own strained stock to wet it well and transfer to clean, dry frying pan. Heat, stirring constantly to evaporate the excess water and give a good spreading consistency. Pot into small sterilized jars, press down well and leave to get cold. Run the melted butter over the top to seal out the air. Refrigerate.

RABBIT CASSEROLE

1 young rabbit, jointed
salty seasoning
sage and thyme
wholemeal flour
vegetable oil
2 large onions, sliced

4 oz (100 gm) open mushrooms,
  sliced
½ cup pot barley, washed
1 bay leaf
vegetable stock OR water

Coat the rabbit pieces with seasoned flour. Seal in hot oil. Drain and transfer to large casserole. Sauté onions and mushrooms for five minutes. Drain and add to casserole with the other ingredients, with sufficient stock just to cover. Cover tightly and cook slowly for about 2½ hours until the rabbit and barley are tender. (4-5)

OFFAL

Liver, kidney, brains, heart and sweetbreads are very high in nutritional value and deserve more popularity.

GRILLED CALVES' LIVER

1 lb (450 gm) calves' liver, sliced
freshly ground black pepper

1 large onion, sliced in rings
butter OR vegetable oil

Season the wiped liver with pepper and place on grill pan, cover with the onion rings and brush with butter or oil. Grill 5 minutes, turn, placing onion slices on the second side. Cook a few minutes more until done. (4)

LAYERED LIVER

2 onions, chopped
1 lb (450 gm) sliced liver
½ lb (225 gm) ripe tomatoes, halved
  (or tinned tomatoes)
1½ lb (675 gm) potatoes, scrubbed
  and sliced
sage, thyme and basil

freshly ground black pepper
½ pt (300 ml) stock OR water
salty seasoning
wholemeal flour for thickening
½ lb (225 gm) streaky bacon rashers
  (optional)

Into a deep greased casserole, put layers of onion, liver, tomato and potato, seasoning with the herbs judiciously as you go and finishing with a potato layer. Pour over the seasoned stock. Bake covered in a moderate oven, 350°F, 180°C, Gas 4 for 1 hour. Then thicken stock if necessary and cover top with bacon rashers and cook for a further half hour. (6)

REALLY TENDER LIVER

4 oz (100 gm) wholemeal flour
6 fl oz (150 ml) water
1 lb (450 gm) pig's liver, cut in ¼"
  slices

3-4 tbsp vegetable oil
Tomato and Onion Sauce (p. 92)
salty seasoning
2-3 tbsp chopped parsley

Mix flour and water to thick 'batter'. Dry liver with kitchen paper, coat with batter and fry briefly in hot oil, turning once (about 2 minutes altogether). Transfer to saucepan of hot tomato sauce and barely simmer for 10-15 minutes. Check seasoning. Serve sprinkled with parsley. **(4-5)**

BRAISED LAMBS' HEARTS

2 lambs' hearts
Mushroom Stuffing:
4 oz (100 gm) mushrooms, sliced
1 tbsp onions, sliced
3 tbsp vegetable oil
4 oz (100 gm) wholemeal
  breadcrumbs

pinch mace
1 egg, beaten
salty seasoning
1 lb (450 gm) onions, sliced
a little wholemeal flour
½ pt (300 ml) stock OR water
½ tsp dried marjoram

Wash hearts, removing tubes. Make stuffing: Sauté mushrooms and 1 tbsp onion in hot oil. Drain and mix with breadcrumbs, mace, egg and seasoning. Use for filling hearts. Sprinkle hearts with seasoned flour and seal in oil. Place on bed of onions in casserole, adding stock, marjoram and seasoning. Cover and bake about 2 hours at 300°F, 150°C, Gas 2, turning after one hour. When tender, thicken stock and correct seasoning. **(4-6)**

S GRILLED SWEETBREADS

8 oz (225 gm) sweetbreads
¼ tsp salty seasoning
½ tsp lemon juice

little vegetable oil
2 slices wholemeal toast

Soak sweetbreads in cold water 1 hour. Drain and discard water. Simmer barely covered with salted water with lemon juice for 20-25 minutes. Drain, reserving stock for sauce, etc., and slit lengthwise. Brush with oil and grill under medium heat for about 5 minutes, turning, till golden. Serve on slices of wholemeal toast. **(2)**

S SWEETBREADS WITH MUSHROOMS

1 lb (450 gm) sweetbreads
salty seasoning
½ tsp lemon juice
2-3 sprigs parsley
½ lb (225 gm) mushrooms, sliced
¼ pt (150 ml) milk

2-3 tbsp wholemeal flour
2-3 tbsp chopped chives OR spring
  onions
2 egg yolks, beaten
4 fl oz (120 ml) natural yoghurt
4-6 slices wholemeal toast

Soak sweetbreads in cold water 1 hour. Drain. Simmer in ¾ pt (450 ml) seasoned water with lemon juice and parsley stems for 20-25 minutes, till firmed. Drain, reserving stock and slice neatly. Cook mushrooms in milk 5 minutes. Mix stock with milk, slightly thicken with wholemeal flour. Stir in sweetbreads, mushrooms, chives, check seasoning and simmer 10 minutes. Just before serving, mix yolks with yoghurt and stir in. Heat through, stirring, without boiling. Serve decorated with toast triangles and sprinkled with chopped parsley. (5-6)

KIDNEY STEW

¾-1 lb (350-450 gm) kidneys
salty seasoning
3 tbsp butter OR oil
¾-1 lb (350-450 gm) onions, sliced
4 oz (100 gm) mushrooms, sliced

4 tbsp wholemeal or rice flour
1 pt (600 ml) stock
lemon juice to taste
celery seed OR lovage, to taste
1 carrot, sliced

Scald kidneys by plunging into boiling water; remove skin, then soak in cold salted water for half an hour, to remove urates. Halve. Remove the hard tissue and tubes. Cut into slices, season, then sauté in oil for 5-7 minutes. Remove kidney from pan. Add prepared onion and mushroom. Brown them in the oil, then remove. Add flour and stock, blending into a sauce with a little lemon juice and celery seed or chopped lovage. Transfer all to casserole with carrots and cook slowly till tender. (4-6)

BRAINS ON TOAST

1 calf's brain
¼ tsp salty seasoning
2 oz (50 gm) mushrooms, sliced
1 tbsp butter
2 eggs, beaten

2-3 tbsp chopped parsley
1 tsp shoyu OR tamari
wholemeal toast
1 large tomato, sliced

Wash brain thoroughly; remove membranes and blood vessels. Soak in cold water for 1 hour. Drain and cover with fresh water, add salt, bring to boil and simmer slowly for about ½ hour. Cut into slices and keep hot in its stock. Sweat mushrooms in the butter, add the mixed egg, parsley and shoyu, and stir over low heat until beginning to scramble. Then add the hot, drained brains, and serve immediately on wholemeal toast. Garnish with tomato. (2-3)

Vegetarian Dishes

All protein is manufactured by plants from the nitrogen in the soil and the carbon dioxide in the air. Animals can obtain their protein by eating plant protein or other animals, as can man. Only 10% of the food given to animals appears as flesh, eggs or milk – 90% is used by the animals for energy. So meat protein is very wasteful of the earth's resources.

There are other reasons, too, for recommending non-meat dishes in the weekly eating plan – nourishment, economy and variety of flavour. Pulse dishes also provide a rest from cholesterol and protection from toxic metals (see chapter on Allergies), so are positive contributors to good health.

Good quality protein is not confined to meat. The only perfectly constituted protein food for man is human protein – as found in breast milk! Meat does not even rate second or third best (see Proteins, page 8).

Nuts and seeds are nature's convenience foods. These are good protein foods which may be tastier and more digestible when lightly toasted in the oven, or under the grill, or dry pot-roasted. Dairy products provide excellent nourishment too – see also chapters on Milk Recipes and Health Drinks.

NUT ROAST FOR CHRISTMAS

6 oz (175 gm) mixed nuts (excluding
 peanuts)
3 oz (75 gm) wholemeal
 breadcrumbs
3 oz (75 gm) grated Cheddar cheese
1 tsp mixed herbs
2 onions, chopped

2 tbsp vegetable oil
3 oz (75 gm) chopped mushrooms
½-1 tsp Tastex
4 fl oz (100 ml) vegetable stock OR
 water
1 egg, beaten

Mix roughly chopped nuts with breadcrumbs, cheese and herbs. Sweat the onions in hot oil. Add mushrooms and cook a few minutes longer. Dissolve Tastex in warm water or stock. Mix all ingredients together. Check seasoning. Bake in greased casserole for 30-40 minutes at 350°F, 180°C, Gas 4. Delicious hot or cold. (4-5)

TOMATO AND ONION SAUCE

2 sticks celery, finely chopped
1 tbsp vegetable oil
½ pt (300 ml) water
14 oz tin tomatoes OR 1 lb tomatoes
1 large onion, chopped
½ cooking apple, chopped

1 bay leaf
1 tsp vegetable bouillon powder
¼ tsp celery seed
¼-½ tsp oregano
¼ tsp nutmeg
1 tsp honey (optional)

Sauté celery in hot oil. Simmer all but last 3 ingredients together till tender – about 20 minutes. Remove bay leaf. Liquidize. Add oregano, nutmeg and honey to taste. Reheat, stirring. Makes 1¼ pt (750 ml).

PERSIAN NUT SAVOURY   GF

1 cup organic brown rice
3 cups stock OR water
Vecon OR Tastex
1 egg
1 cup natural yoghurt

pinch grated nutmeg
freshly ground black pepper
1 tbsp butter
1 cup chopped nuts

Cook rice in boiling stock or water with Vecon till tender, 35-45 minutes. Drain. Beat egg with yoghurt and nutmeg. Stir in rice. Season to taste. Grease a casserole and put in layers of rice, then nuts, finishing with nuts. Dot with butter and bake for about 1 hour at 300°F, 150°C, Gas 2 or in a bain-marie. (See 'Cooking Wholegrains', page 123.) (3-4)

QUICK HAZELNUT ROAST   GF

1 large onion, chopped
1 tbsp vegetable oil
10 oz (300 gm) tomatoes, sliced
3 oz (75 gm) grated cheese

5 oz (150 gm) grated hazelnuts
5 oz (150 gm) cooked mashed potato
2 tbsp chopped parsley
salty seasoning and black pepper

Sauté onion in hot oil. Add tomatoes. Mix in half the cheese with the other ingredients and put in greased casserole. Sprinkle remaining cheese on top. Bake 30-40 minutes at 375°F, 190°C, Gas 5. (3-4)

NUT RISSOLES OR ROAST   S

4 oz (100 gm) wholemeal bread OR
   oatflakes
7 fl oz (200 ml) vegetable stock OR
   water
Tastex OR Vecon to taste
1 large onion, sliced

1 tsp vegetable oil
5 oz (150 gm) grated nuts
½ tsp tarragon
beaten egg
wholemeal breadcrumbs

Soak bread in hot stock with Tastex. Sauté onion. Add nuts and herbs and check seasoning. Bake in greased casserole for ¾ hour at 375°F, 190°C, Gas 5. OR shape into rissoles, egg and breadcrumb them, and grill or bake till brown. (3-4)

GF AUBERGINE PIZZA

1 aubergine, cut in ⅛" (4 mm) slices
1 egg, beaten
salty seasoning
1 large onion, finely sliced
1 tbsp vegetable oil

4 oz (100 gm) Edam OR Lancashire
   cheese, grated
2 tbsp tomato purée OR 4-6 fresh
   tomatoes, sliced

Dip aubergine slices in egg and arrange overlapping to cover base and sides of oiled pie-dish. Pour remaining egg over and season. Sauté onion until transparent. Drain. Spread ⅔ of cheese over aubergine base. Add layer of onions, tomato paste or sliced tomatoes and remaining cheese. Bake for about 30-45 minutes at 350°F, 180°C, Gas 4 until the aubergine is tender and the cheese lightly browned. Extra ingredients for the topping could include 2 oz (50 gm) sautéed mushrooms OR anchovy fillets OR mashed sardines OR black and green olives OR use crushed clove of garlic in place of the chopped onion. (2)

VEGETARIAN PIZZA

1 lb (450 gm) wholemeal bread
   dough (after the first proving)
vegetable oil
1 large onion, finely chopped

tomato paste OR sliced tomatoes
6 oz (175 gm) grated Edam cheese
½-1 tsp oregano, basil OR majoram
black olives, extra sliced tomato

Divide dough and knead into 2 balls. Roll out into two very thin circles to fit small sandwich tins. Brush tops with oil. Put to rise, covered, in a warm place, till doubled in size. Scatter onion over the bases. Cover with tomato and cheese. Sprinkle with herbs. Decorate with olives and slices of tomato. Bake at 375°F, 190°C, Gas 5 for about 20 minutes. (4-6)

CHESTNUT SAVOURY

1 lb (450 gm) sweet chestnuts
2 large onions, chopped
3 sticks celery, chopped
2 oz (50 gm) mushrooms
2 tbsp vegetable oil
1 egg

6-8 oz (175-225 gm) fresh
   wholemeal breadcrumbs OR
   rolled oats
a little grated nutmeg
salty seasoning

Boil chestnuts for 15 minutes, cool and scoop out the flesh with a teaspoon. Reserve a few whole peeled chestnuts for decoration. Sweat onions, celery and mushrooms in the oil. Rough chop chestnuts and mix with all other ingredients. Adjust seasoning. Put into a greased casserole and decorate top with reserved chestnuts. Bake at 325-350°F, 160-180°C, Gas 3-4 for about 1 hour. Serve with peas or beans to increase protein value of the meal. (4-6)

FORESIGHT VEGETARIAN CASSEROLE   A

2 large potatoes, sliced
8 oz (225 gm) cooked black eye
  beans OR 3 oz (75 gm) protoveg
  TVP chunks
1 vegetable bouillon cube
½ tsp marjoram
3 tbsp vegetable oil
tomato purée

2-3 large onions, sliced
2 cloves garlic, sliced
6 oz (175 gm) mushrooms, sliced
4 eggs, beaten
3 oz (75 gm) grated cheese
2 tomatoes, sliced
parsley sprigs

Parboil the potatoes. Hydrate TVP with water as directed and simmer with bouillon cube, marjoram and 1 tsp oil till water is absorbed OR season beans similarly and drain. Add tomato purée to taste. Sweat onions and garlic in hot oil and transfer to greased casserole. Cover with layers of beans OR TVP, mushrooms and potatoes. Bake, covered, for 45 minutes at 350°F, 180°C, Gas 4. Combine eggs and cheese and pour over the casserole. Decorate with tomatoes. Return to oven, uncovered, till cheese melts on the top (about 10 minutes). Garnish with parsley. A delicious party dish. (6)

BUCKWHEAT RISSOLES   S

1 tsp Tastex OR Vecon
2 cups water
1 cup buckwheat
1-2 onions, chopped
1 tbsp oil

½ tsp basil
½ tsp marjoram
4 oz (100 gm) grated cheese
2 eggs, beaten
buckwheat flour

Dissolve Tastex in the water and boil buckwheat for 2 minutes. Then cover tightly and leave standing for 20 minutes. Sweat onion in hot oil. Add the buckwheat, herbs, grated cheese and half egg to bind. Shape into rissoles, dip into beaten egg and buckwheat flour. Grill or oven bake. Serve with tomato and onion sauce. (4)

VEGETARIAN MOUSSAKA   S

1 lb (450 gm) hydrated protoveg
  mince (TVP) OR cooked brown
  lentils
2-3 onions, chopped
2 cloves garlic, finely chopped
2 tbsp vegetable oil
1 large aubergine, sliced

3 tbsp tomato purée
1 tsp Tastex OR Vecon
½ tsp basil
4-6 tbsp vegetable OR lentil stock
2 bay leaves
2 oz (50 gm) grated cheese

Hydrate the protoveg as directed. Sweat onion and garlic in hot oil, brown aubergine and drain. Mix tomato purée, Tastex and basil with vegetable stock in the pan. Add the onion, bay leaves and protoveg OR lentils and simmer for 10 minutes. In a deep greased casserole, assemble layers of aubergine, mince mixture and grated cheese. Bake until cheese melts and all is heated through. (6)

OMELETTES JERVAISE

Favourite among recipes demonstrated by Norman at Enton Hall were his omelettes. His secret is a good heavy pan used exclusively for omelettes, and *never washed*. After use, wipe clean with kitchen paper and store in a dust-proof paper bag.

2 tsp vegetable oil   **salty seasoning**
2 eggs

Heat oil. Whisk eggs and season. Using fork, put a little egg into pan to check oil is hot enough to set egg without burning. Pour beaten egg into pan, stirring immediately with fork to allow mixture to reach hot base. When egg starts to set (20-30 seconds), add filling of choice. Place pan on large wooden chopping board and jerk pan to and fro quickly to produce a 'bolster' shape. Holding pan in right hand, hit right forearm firmly with left fist, to throw the omelette to far edge of pan. Slide on to hot plate, decorate and serve immediately. **(1)**

Suggested omelette fillings:
1. Choice of sliced cooked mushrooms, carrots, peas, beans, asparagus, cauliflower florets.
2. Spanish – hot sliced boiled potato with sautéed onion.
3. Herbs of choice, chopped fresh or dried; chives are particularly good.
4. Stir-fried sliced red peppers, onions and beansprouts.
5. Grated cheese with chopped spring onions or diced raw tomato.
6. Hot tomato purée with cooked onion or leeks.
7. Warm prawns and peas.

EGG CUTLETS

2 oz (50 gm) butter or margarine   **4 hard-boiled eggs, chopped**
3 tbsp cornflour   **1 tbsp onion, finely chopped**
½ pt (300 ml) milk   **2 tbsp chopped parsley**
½ tsp Tastex OR Vecon   **salty seasoning and black pepper**
pinch ground mace   **wholemeal flour or oatmeal**

Melt butter and add cornflour to make a roux, stir in milk gradually to make a very thick sauce. Cook carefully for 5 minutes, blending in the Tastex. Add mace, eggs, onion and parsley. Season to taste. Shape into cutlets. Coat with flour, oven bake or 'fry' in greased non-stick pan. **(4)**

S EGGS IN A NEST

2 lb (900 gm) potatoes, sliced thickly   **3 tbsp chopped chives**
salty seasoning   **2 tbsp chopped parsley**
1 oz (25 gm) butter or vegetable   **1 tbsp chopped chervil**
   margarine   **1½ cups mung beansprouts**
¼ pt (150 ml) natural yoghurt   **4-8 eggs**

Boil potatoes with a little seasoning. Remove skins when cooked and mash flesh with butter, yoghurt and herbs. Check seasoning and reheat. Stir in 1 cup beansprouts. Fork mashed potato into a nest shape in a shallow casserole and keep hot. Soft-boil and shell the eggs. Nestle eggs in the centre of the nest, with remaining beansprouts around the edge. Serve immediately. (4)

AVOCADO EGGS

2 large ripe avocados
1 tsp lemon juice
4 small onions, chopped finely
1 tbsp butter OR vegetable oil
3 sprigs fresh tarragon, 2 chopped
  finely OR 1 tsp dried tarragon
2 sprigs fresh chervil, chopped
  finely OR 1 tsp dried chervil

2 tbsp wholemeal OR potato flour
½ pt (300 ml) vegetable stock,
  approx.
freshly ground black pepper
salty seasoning
4 free range eggs
hot potato mashed with own stock

Halve avocados and brush with lemon juice. Warm gently with the plates in oven at 150°F, 70°C, Gas ⅛. Sauté onions in hot butter with half the chopped or dry herbs. Make a sauce with the flour and stock, and simmer 5 minutes. Add seasoning, remaining chopped or dry herbs and onions. Reheat and cover. Poach eggs in water with tarragon sprig. Nestle warm avocado halves in supporting bed of hot mashed potato, with poached eggs in the hollows, and the herb sauce. (4)

RICE AND EGG CASSEROLE

S
GF

1 cup brown rice
4 cups water
1 large onion, halved
½ tsp herb salt
2 tsp tamari OR shoyu
6 oz (175 gm) French beans, in ½"
  slices
2 bunches spring onions, sliced
6 oz (175 gm) mushrooms, sliced

2 tbsp vegetable oil OR butter
3 tbsp chopped parsley
3 tbsp chopped chervil
3 tbsp chopped chives
4 hard-boiled eggs, shelled and
  sliced
salty seasoning
paprika
parsley sprigs

Cook rice in water with large onion, herb salt and tamari, till just tender (about 40 minutes). Drain and reserve stock, onion and 3 tbsp rice. Cook beans in rice stock. Sauté spring onions and mushrooms in hot oil. Mix in beans, rice and 2 tbsp of each herb. Transfer to greased casserole, arranging most of the sliced eggs in the centre of rice mixture. Make a sauce by liquidising onion, beanstock and sufficient of reserved rice to thicken. Mix in remaining chopped herbs. Season to taste. Pour over rice casserole and heat through. Garnish with reserved egg slices, dusting of paprika and parsley sprigs. (6)

CURRIED EGGS

1 oz (25 gm) butter
1 oz (25 gm) wholemeal flour OR ½ oz
  (15 gm) cornflour
1 tsp curry powder

½ pt (300 ml) vegetable stock
4 hard-boiled eggs, sliced
salty seasoning to taste
wholemeal toast OR hot brown rice

Melt butter, add flour and curry powder and cook, stirring. Add stock slowly, whisking to make a smooth sauce. Simmer for 5 minutes. Add sliced eggs and season. Heat through and serve on toast or brown rice. **(4)**

S STUFFED MARROW

3 oz (75 gm) sliced mushrooms
2 large onions, chopped
2 tbsp vegetable oil
4 oz (100 gm) fresh wholemeal
  breadcrumbs
4 fl oz (125 ml) stock OR water

4 oz (100 gm) hazelnuts, grated
1 egg beaten
½-1 tsp dried sage
salty seasoning
black pepper
1 small marrow

Sweat mushrooms and onion in hot oil. Add all ingredients except marrow and cook for a few minutes. Check seasoning. Cut marrow lengthwise and remove seeds. Fill with stuffing. Put in greased casserole with 2 tbsps of stock or water and cover with buttered greaseproof paper. Bake at 325-350°F, 160-180°C, Gas 3-4 for about 1 hour, until marrow is tender. **(4-6)**

MACARONI CHEESE

2 onions, chopped
2 sticks celery, chopped
3 tbsp vegetable oil
6 oz (175 gm) wholemeal OR
  buckwheat cut macaroni
2 pt (1,100 ml) stock OR water
2 tsp vegetable bouillon powder

¾ pt (450 ml) milk, approx.
4-6 tbsp 100% wholemeal flour
¼ tsp mustard powder
1 tsp Worcester sauce
8 oz (225 gm) Lancashire, Edam OR
  Cheddar cheese

Sweat onions and celery in oil till tender, then drain. Cook macaroni in boiling stock (or water with bouillon powder) till just tender – about 15 minutes. Strain and make up stock to 1 pt (600 ml) with milk. Mix 4 tbsp flour and mustard with ¼ pt (150 ml) cold milk to a smooth paste. To the residual oil add sufficient flour to be absorbed and cook gently. Stir in milky stock and bring to the boil. Thicken with flour paste and cook, stirring, for 5 minutes. Add Worcester sauce, onions, celery, cheese and the macaroni, and heat through, stirring. Check seasoning. Transfer to greased casserole and sprinkle remaining cheese over the top. Either place in oven or under grill until slightly brown on top. **(4)**

For a less rich dish, conservatively cook the vegetables instead of sautéing, or boil the onions with the macaroni. Other vegetables, e.g. peas, beans, mushrooms, carrots, parsnips, leeks may also be used.

SPEEDY CHEESY PIE   S

4 slices wholemeal bread, buttered
1 lb (450 gm) onions, sliced thinly
1 lb (450 gm) tomatoes, sliced OR
   tinned tomatoes, sliced

8-12 oz (225 gm) sliced or grated
   cheese
4-8 fl oz (125-250 ml) stock, water OR
   tomato juice

Line a deep casserole with bread slices. Add repeated layers of onions, tomatoes and cheese. Top with bread. Add liquid. Bake at 350°F, 180°C, Gas 4, ¾-1 hour, until nicely brown. Serve with greens or salad. My favourite pie. (4-5)

SIMPLICITY SUPPER   S

8-12 oz (225-350 gm) onions, halved
   or thickly sliced
pinch salty seasoning

3-4 oz (75-125 gm) Lancashire OR
   Edam cheese, grated
wholemeal bread and butter

Simmer onions in barely seasoned water till just done. Serve in soup bowls covered in grated cheese, the onion stock poured over to melt the cheese. Eat with fingers of bread, lightly buttered. Ideal for a quick snack meal – another of my favourites. (2)

FORESIGHT AU GRATIN SUPREME   S

1 lb (450 gm) waxy potatoes (reds)
1½ tsp vegetable bouillon powder
1 lb (450 gm) runner OR French beans
12 oz (350 gm) onions, chopped
2 tbsp vegetable oil
3 oz (75 gm) flaked almonds
8 oz (225 gm) Edam cheese, grated

1 pt (600 ml) milk, approx.
6 tbsp 85% wheatmeal flour OR 3 tbsp
   cornflour
2 tsp Worcester sauce
15 oz can sliced peaches in fruit
   juice

Peel potatoes, cut in ¼" slices and into ½" squares. Season with ½ tsp bouillon powder and boil gently till just tender (not mushy). Drain. Use this stock to cook sliced beans similarly. Sauté onions in hot oil till nearly transparent. Into deep greased casserole arrange repeated layers of potato, onions, almonds, beans and cheese, finishing with cheese. Measure vegetable stock and make up to 1½ pt (900 ml) with milk. Use a little milk to mix flour, 1 tsp bouillon powder and Worcester sauce to smooth paste. Thicken stock and cook sauce 5 minutes, stirring. Ladle over casserole. Arrange peach slices over top. Bake 350°F, 180°C, Gas 4 ¾-1 hour, till just bubbling. I like to serve this top favourite party dish with calabrese. (6-8)

s CAULIFLOWER AU GRATIN

cauliflower
½ pt (300 ml) stock from cauliflower
1 oz (25 gm) wholemeal flour
¼ pt (150 ml) milk
¼ tsp mustard powder

5 oz (150 gm) grated cheese
salty seasoning and paprika
1 tsp Worcester sauce
2 tbsp wholemeal breadcrumbs

Cut cauliflower into serving size florets. Steam until just tender (10-15 minutes), retaining stock. Keep hot. Make a sauce with the flour, milk, mustard and stock. Cook, stirring for 5 minutes. Add most of cheese and seasonings to taste. Pour over cauliflower in casserole dish. Scatter cheese and breadcrumbs over the top. Brown under grill. Leeks, celery, artichokes, marrow, courgettes or broad beans are all delicious made in the same way. (4)

CHEESE PIE

½ tsp Tastex or Vecon
1 pt (600 ml) milk, warm
⅓ pt (200 ml) soft wholemeal
  breadcrumbs or barley flakes or
  oat flakes

2 large eggs, beaten
salty seasoning
pinch cayenne pepper
6-8 oz (175 gm) grated cheese

Dissolve Tastex in the milk. Soak the breadcrumbs, or rolled oats in it for ½-1 hour. Mix in the eggs, seasoning and grated cheese, beating well. Put in greased pie dish. Bake at 275°F, 140°C, Gas 1 for about 1 hour until set and nicely browned. (4)

s CHEESE SOUFFLÉ

1½ oz (40 gm) margarine, butter or
  oil
1 oz (25 gm) cornflour
½ pt (300 ml) milk
2 eggs

6 oz (175 gm) tasty cheese, grated
1 small onion, finely chopped or 2
  tbsp chopped chives
¼ tsp dry mustard

Make a thick roux with the butter, cornflour and milk and cook, stirring, until thick. Remove from heat. Beat in egg yolks, singly, and other ingredients. Whisk egg whites until stiff and fold into mixture. Turn into greased deep soufflé dish. Bake at 350°F, 180°C, Gas 4 for about 30 minutes. Serve immediately it is ready. Flaked fish, chicken or meat (for non-vegetarians) or cooked mushrooms, asparagus or celery may be used in addition to the cheese. (4)

PULSES

There is a wide, colourful range of pulses available. Their high fibre content ensures good filling meals for those watching their weight – and their pocket! Keep a stock of the dried beans, peas and lentils you like best. They store well and are good emergency rations when the hordes descend and you do not have time to get out to the shops. Soya beans are high in good value protein. Other pulses when served with grains also produce a dish high in protein.

Adzukis, black eyed beans, brown and green lentils, cooked with wholegrains and vegetables, are recommended for enjoyable cheap complete protein meals (see Proteins, page 8). Beans added to a little meat (e.g. Cassoulet) can make a meaty dish which goes a long way! Do not serve pulses with fish – together they make an indigestible combination.

Soya beans tend to be the least tasty of the pulses but you can overcome this by mixing cooked soya beans with other recipe ingredients the day before, to allow time for flavours to be absorbed. Soya beans are also least digestible but cooking with sea vegetables will help offset this.

Tips for cooking dried beans, peas and lentils

- Plan ahead – most beans need to be soaked overnight in plenty of water, and need long cooking. Soya and lima beans are better soaked 24 hours. (Use 3-4 cups water to each cup of beans)
- When you need beans in a hurry, choose mung beans, brown, green and orange lentils, split peas and blackeyed beans. These can be cooked satisfactorily without the need to soak them.
- As a compromise when you cannot soak overnight, add 3 cups water to each cup of beans (not soya or butterbeans), bring to the boil, and boil rapidly for 2 minutes. Remove from heat and leave standing for an hour. Again bring to rapid boil (for 10 minutes) then simmer till cooked.
- Never add salt wait until the beans are almost cooked. Salt prevents the proper absorption of water during cooking. (Or use unseasoned stock).
- To prevent wind-promoting tendencies, rinse beans and change water 2 or 3 times during soaking. Use sufficient fresh water to cover the beans well when you start cooking, and do not allow them to dry out.
- To avoid the mealy taste of beans, add a very little vegetable oil or fat to the cooking water.
- Add to the flavour of your dish by using herbs and spices e.g. basil, oregano, bay leaves, onion, garlic, celery, etc. – and kombu.
- A 4"-6" strip of kombu sea vegetable added to beans during cooking adds trace minerals, helps soften the beans, brings out their flavour and makes them more digestible.
- Regardless of final cooking methods, always begin by boiling beans rapidly for 10 minutes, to inactivate potentially dangerous enzyme blockers.

- Five cooking methods, following the initial rapid boiling:
  Simmer in heavy saucepan with close-fitting lid.
  Use a pressure cooker, to speed up the cooking process.
  Long cooking in a slow oven, about 250°F, 130°C, Gas ½ if you have an Aga
  or Raeburn, for 6-8 hours.
  Use a slow cooking pot in the same way.
  Economize on fuel by transferring the beans and their boiling stock into a
  heated, wide-necked vacuum jar. Leave them in this for 6-8 hours or
  overnight, when they should be tender.

Guide for cooking times for pulses

After pre-soaking the chosen beans, boil rapidly for 10 minutes, then simmer for
approximate time given:

Chosen pulse, soaked	cooking time	pressure cooking time
Adzuki	1½-2 hours	(unsuitable method)
Chickpeas (garbanzos)	3 hours	1 hour
Brown and green lentils	½-1 hour	15-20 minutes
Black eyed beans	1½ hours	35 minutes
Butterbeans (lima beans)	1½-2 hours	35-40 minutes
Haricot beans (navy beans)	1½-2 hours	35-40 minutes
Red kidney beans	1½-2 hours	35-40 minutes
Split peas	1 hour	(unsuitable method)
Soya beans (soy beans)	3-4 hours	1 hour

TVP (Texturized Vegetable Protein) is soya processed to imitate the texture of
meat. The advantage of this convenience food is in saving time. Follow instructions given on the packet. (But I prefer unprocessed beans.)

s BROWN LENTIL SAVOURY

4 oz (100 gm) brown whole lentils	¼ tsp mixed herbs
1 large onion, finely chopped	pinch of mace
1 large carrot, finely chopped	¼ tsp garam masala OR curry
2 tbsp vegetable oil	powder
1 large clove garlic, crushed	¼ tsp salty seasoning
4 tbsp tomato purée	¼ tsp paprika

Cook lentils until soft. Sauté onion and carrot until softened. Roughly mash
lentils leaving a few whole. Combine and mix all ingredients. (4)
  Choose one of the following cooking methods. 2, 3 & 4 are suitable for
slimmers:
1. Roll into small rounds, dip each into beaten egg, then wholemeal breadcrumbs, and grill, oven bake or fry.
2. Heat all through in the saucepan and serve immediately.
3. Put into shallow greased casserole and heat through in a cool oven.
4. Roll into balls and leave to cool. Serve cold with salad.

CASSOULET – FRENCH CASSEROLE

8 oz (225 gm) haricot beans,
  soaked 24 hours
freshly ground black pepper
bouquet garni
3 onions, sliced
2-4 cloves garlic
3 tbsp vegetable oil

14 oz (400 gm) can tomatoes
1 tsp basil
salty seasoning
1 lb soya sausages (optional)
4 oz (100 gm) wholemeal
  breadcrumbs

Cover soaked beans with water, add pepper and bouquet garni, and boil till soft. Remove bouquet garni. Sauté onion and garlic in hot oil. Add to the beanpot with tomatoes, basil and season to taste. Grill the TVP sausages. Transfer beans and sausages to greased casserole and cover top with breadcrumbs. Bake ¾-1 hour in moderate oven. Also good without the soya sausages. OR meat-eaters could use meaty sausages for traditional flavour. (6-9)

BEANBURGERS   S

8 oz (225 gm) adzuki beans, soaked
  overnight
piece kombu (optional)
2 carrots, grated
3-4 sticks celery, finely chopped
1 large onion, finely chopped

½ tsp oregano
2 eggs, beaten
salty seasoning
½ tsp black pepper
approx 12 oz (350 gm) wholemeal
  flour OR flaked oats

Rinse and cover beans with cold water, add kombu and soak 10 minutes. Cook till soft. Drain. Mix in vegetables, herbs, eggs and season to taste. Add sufficient flour or oats to give firm consistency. Shape into 12 patties and roll in flour or oats. Bake on oiled tray about 1 hour at 350°F, 180°C, Gas 4. Serve hot with Tomato and Onion sauce, or cold with salad. Vary with other beans, herbs and grains. (6-8)

BOSTON BAKED BEANS

8 oz (225 gm) haricot beans
1 large onion, chopped

1 tbsp molasses

For Sauce:
1 onion, finely chopped
4 tbsp vegetable oil
½ tsp mustard
1 oz (25 gm) wholemeal flour
bean stock

1 tbsp cider vinegar
1 tbsp molasses
salty seasoning to taste
a little honey (optional)

Soak the beans overnight in plenty of water. Cook them slowly in fresh water with onion and molasses. Drain and reserve stock for the sauce. Sweat the finely chopped onion in the oil, stir in the mustard and flour and gradually stir in enough bean stock to make a smooth sauce. Add vinegar and molasses and simmer for five minutes, stirring. Add the beans and heat through. Taste and add salt as desired, and possibly a little honey. (4-6)

s HOTPOT OF MIXED BEANS

4 oz (100 gm) red kidney beans OR
adzuki beans
4 oz (100 gm) haricot beans OR black
eyed beans
4 oz (100 gm) split yellow peas
1-2 onions, chopped
1-2 sticks celery, chopped
soya OR sunflower oil
1-2 carrots, chopped
1-3 cloves garlic, pressed

2 tbsp tomato purée
1 tbsp black treacle OR molasses (not
bitter)
2 tbsp apple cider vinegar
1 tsp Worcester sauce
½ tsp freshly ground allspice OR ¼
tsp mixed spice
6 oz (175 gm) brown rice
salty seasoning

Garnish:
3 tbsp chopped parsley OR 1 cup
alfalfa sprouts

Soak beans and split peas for 24 hours. Cook for 1 hour in a large pan. Gently
sauté onion and celery in oil. Stir these and all ingredients except salty seasoning
into the beanpot. Continue cooking till tender, about ¾ hour. Season to taste.
Garnish with chopped parsley or alfalfa sprouts. This is a complete protein dish as
well as a tasty, satisfying one. (6-9)

DHAL – INDIAN CURRIED LENTILS

2 cups red lentils
4½ cups water
1 bay leaf
2 onions, sliced
2 tbsp vegetable oil
½ tsp each of cumin, chilli, ginger,
mustard seed

1 lb (450 gm) tomatoes
2 cloves garlic, crushed
1 tsp each of turmeric & coriander
1 tbsp fresh lemon juice
boiled brown rice
natural yoghurt

Soak the lentils overnight. Rinse and cook gently with the bay leaf till soft. Sweat
the onions in the oil with the mustard seeds. Add quartered tomatoes, garlic and
spices and cook gently for ten minutes. Add to the lentil mixture and simmer ten
minutes more. Stir in the lemon juice. Serve with lots of boiled brown rice,
natural yoghurt and vegetables. (4-6)

PEASE PUDDING AND SPREAD

1 lb (450 gm) split yellow peas
2 sage leaves
1 large onion, sliced
onion salt, to taste

freshly ground black pepper
2 tbsp vegetable oil
1 egg
1 tbsp wholemeal flour

Soak the peas for 12-24 hours. Rinse, add fresh water, sage and onion and cook
till soft. Remove sage leaves and strain, saving stock. (For low-fat Spread: season,
mash till smooth with a little of its stock, and use as it is.) For pudding: liquidize
while hot with the onion, oil, egg and flour to produce a smooth paste. Season to
taste. Spoon into greased pudding bowl, cover and steam for one hour.

Desserts and Puddings

APPLE AND ORANGE FOAM

1 lb (450 gm) cooking apples
¼ pt (150 ml) orange juice
3 cloves (optional)
2 tbsp honey

½ lemon, grated zest and juice
¼ pt (150 ml) evaporated milk,
   chilled
1 orange, peeled, sliced small

Core and slice apples into orange juice. Cook with cloves until pulpy. Remove cloves. Mash or liquidize with honey, lemon juice and zest. Whip evaporated milk in large basin until light and fluffy. Stir in apple mixture. Decorate with orange slices. (4)

BAKED APPLES

4 ripe cooking apples
dates and/or sultanas

1 tbsp brown sugar OR honey
2 tbsp water

Remove apple cores with potato peeler. Stuff the cavities with dates and sultanas. Sprinkle over sugar. Add water to oiled dish. Bake in moderate oven till soft – about one hour. (4)

HURRY CRUMBLE

2 lb (900 gm) cooking apples, finely
   sliced
2-4 tbsp water
¼ tsp cinnamon

6 oz (175 gm) raw brown sugar
4 oz (100 gm) butter OR vegetable oil
8 oz (225 gm) wholemeal
   breadcrumbs

Stew apples gently in covered saucepan with the water, cinnamon and 2 oz (50 gm) sugar. Warm butter or oil and stir in remaining sugar and breadcrumbs, heating right through. Put hot stewed apple in greased pie-dish and smooth the crumble over the top. Put under hot grill for a few minutes to crisp the top. Or oven bake until cooked. Rhubarb, plums, damsons, gooseberries, apple and blackcurrants, apple and blackberries all make good crumbles too. (8)

APPLE SPONGE PUDDING

1 lb (450 gm) cooking apples, sliced
3 tbsp orange juice OR water
raw brown sugar to taste
5 oz (150 gm) 100% SR wholemeal
  flour

¼ tsp cinnamon
4 oz (100 gm) butter OR vegetable
  margarine
3 oz (75 gm) raw brown sugar
2 eggs

Stew apples gently in orange juice. Add sugar to taste. Transfer to greased casserole. Sift flour and spice. Cream butter and sugar and beat in eggs with a little of the flour. Fold in remaining flour and spread over the apple. Bake in moderate oven (350°F, 175°C, Gas 4) until sponge is firm to the touch, about ½ hour. (6)

APPLE CRACKNEL

1 lb (450 gm) cooking apples, sliced
4 tbsp orange juice
honey to taste

4 oz (100 gm) butter OR vegetable
  margarine
8 oz (225 gm) cornmeal OR oatmeal

Gently cook apples in orange juice. Add honey. Pour into greased pie-dish. Melt the butter and mix in the cornmeal. Sprinkle over the apple. Bake in moderate oven till crisp and golden. (6)

COPENHAGEN APPLE PUDDING

1 lemon
2½ lb (1,225 gm) cooking apples,
  sliced
3 oz (75 gm) washed sultanas
3 cloves (optional)

3 oz (75 gm) raw brown sugar
1-2 tbsp water (approx)
3 oz (75 gm) butter
6 oz (175 gm) digestive biscuits,
  crushed

Using potato peeler, finely peel off the yellow lemon rind in one long piece and add to apples. Add squeezed juice, sultanas, cloves, sugar and just sufficient water to avoid burning. Simmer, stirring, to allow evaporation. When cool, remove and discard lemon peel (and cloves if prefered). Melt butter and mix in crumbs. About an hour before serving assemble pudding with alternating layers of apple and crumb mixture. Serve warm or chilled. (8)

GF SURPRISE APPLE TART

1½ lb (675 gm) steamed potatoes
2 oz (50 gm) butter OR vegetable
  margarine
½ tsp sea salt

brown rice flour as required
1½ lb (675 gm) cooking apples
3 tbsp thin honey

Mash potatoes with some butter and salt till smooth. Melt remaining butter and add to cooled potato on a work surface sprinkled with rice flour. Knead to produce a soft pliable pastry, not too dry. Roll out for two tarts. Cover with sliced apples, drizzled with honey. Bake at 350°F, 180°C, Gas 4. **(8)**

NUT AND APPLE PUDDING

1 lb (450 gm) cooking apples, sliced
2 tbsp orange juice
honey to taste
3 oz (75 gm) butter OR margarine
3 oz (75 gm) raw brown sugar

1 egg
4 oz (100 gm) walnuts OR cashew
 nuts, grated
2 oz (50 gm) rice bran OR oatflakes

Mix apples, orange juice and honey. Put in oiled casserole. Cream butter and sugar and beat in egg. Whisk in mixed nuts and oats until blended. Spread over the apples and bake in a moderate oven, about one hour. (Gluten free when rice polishings are used.) **(4-6)**

FLUFFIN

4 tbsp barley flour
2 cups milk

grated nutmeg
honey

Mix barley flour and milk to a smooth paste. Bring to boil, stirring, and simmer for five minutes. Add grated nutmeg and honey to taste. **(2-3)**

OLD ENGLISH FRUMENTY

½ cup kibbled wheat
1 cup water
2 tbsp currants OR sultanas

pinch mixed spice
Gran's Cream

Soak kibbled wheat in the water for 8-24 hours. Simmer in the soaking water with sultanas and spice, about 3 minutes. Serve with Gran's Cream. (See also Kruska recipes in Muesli chapter.) **(1-2)**

BROWN BREAD PUDDING

1-2 tsp honey OR marmalade
1 pt (600 ml) warm milk
5 oz (150 gm) mixed dried fruit,
 washed (see p. 141)
¼ tsp dried cinnamon OR nutmeg

4 slices wholemeal bread and Butter
 Plus
OR dry bread and 1 tsp vegetable oil
3 eggs, beaten

Dissolve honey in milk and pour over dried fruits, spice, bread and butter (or oil). Leave soaking 1-3 hours. Whisk in eggs. Pour into oiled pie-dish, placed in pan of hot water. Bake at 325°F, 160°C, Gas 3 till set, about ½-¾ hour. **(4-5)**

SWEET PANCAKES

1 egg, beaten
¼ pt (150 ml) natural yoghurt
¼ pt (150 ml) milk
2 oz (50 gm) honey

1 oz (25 gm) butter OR vegetable
   margarine
4 oz (100 gm) 100% wholewheat flour

Whisk egg, yoghurt and milk. Melt honey and butter and stir together over gentle heat. Cool a little. Make a well in the flour and pour in milk and melted butter mixtures. Whisk wet ingredients into flour to form a smooth batter. Cook spoonfuls of the batter in a hot oiled frying pan. Serve with lemon juice and a drizzle of honey, or with orange or strawberry sauce (p. 110). (2-4)

CORNMEAL AND CINNAMON PUDDING

1 cup yellow cornmeal (maize meal)
4 cups milk
3 tbsp molasses
1 tbsp butter OR vegetable oil

1 tsp cinnamon
¼ tsp nutmeg
½ cup raisins OR sultanas
1 egg, beaten

Mix cornmeal with sufficient cold milk to make a smooth paste, free from lumps. Heat remaining milk and beat into the cornmeal. Bring to the boil, stirring constantly, and boil for 7 minutes. Stir in molasses, butter, spices and raisins. Mix in beaten egg. Pour into a greased casserole and stand in a baking tin of hot water. Bake at 275°F, 140°C, Gas 1 for ¾-1 hour. (6-8)

SOFT FRUITS

Fresh raw raspberries, dessert and alpine strawberries, red and white currants, dessert gooseberries, plums, greengages and blackberries are often appreciated 'solo' by children – eaten in the fingers like grapes. When they are a little sour, try them also served with unsweetened orange, pineapple, apple or grape juice. Or serve with Cottage Cream, Gran's Cream, Orange Sauce, Non-Dairy Topping or Cashew Cream. Sharper raw fruit (e.g. blackcurrants, loganberries, damsons) may be delicious with the addition of wheatgerm or oatgerm to the naturally sweet fruit juice. There are many delicious healthier alternatives to the traditional cream and sugar!

RASPBERRY DUET

¾ pt (450 ml) natural fruit juice –
   pineapple, grape or apple
1½ lb (675 gm) ripe dessert pears

½ lb (225 gm) raspberries (fresh OR
   frozen raw)
clear honey if required

Pour fruit juice into serving dish. Peel, core and slice raw pears into the juice, and stir in the fresh or frozen raspberries. Add honey to taste. Serve unaccompanied after rich main course, or with cream substitute. This is my favourite Christmas dinner dessert. (6-8)

COOKED PEARS AND PEACHES

While ripe peaches and pears are delicious eaten raw – and more nutritious also – sometimes they become 'sleepy' and unappetizing. These fruits are improved by stewing gently in fruit juice or a little water sweetened with either honey or raw brown sugar.

BAKED BANANA

4 ripe bananas, peeled
1 tbsp lemon juice

1-3 tsp Runny Honey
2-3 tbsp desiccated coconut

Paint bananas with lemon juice and place in oiled casserole. Drizzle over Runny Honey and sprinkle with coconut. Bake in moderate oven about 20 minutes. OR Bake unpeeled bananas for 20-25 minutes, until skins are totally black. Skin and serve. (4)

BANANA FLUFF

2-3 sweet apples (Coxes), chopped
¼ pt (150 ml) unsweetened
   pineapple juice

¼ pt (150 ml) natural yoghurt
3-4 very ripe bananas
honey if necessary

Liquidize apple with pineapple juice and yoghurt. Add bananas and blend until smooth. Serve as soon as possible. This is one of my favourites! (4-6)

FRUIT JELLY

1 pt (600 ml) pineapple, grape,
   orange OR apple juice OR a mixture

1½ tbsp (1 packet) gelatine OR 2 tbsp
   in hot weather

Heat ½ cup of the juice. Sprinkle over the gelatine, stirring to dissolve. (Stand cup in pan of boiling water if necessary.) Mix with remaining juice and pour into jelly mould or serving dish. Refrigerate to set. Vary by adding sliced bananas, or any soft fruits, to total volume of 1 pint. Good for children's parties. (4)

BANANA ICE-CREAM

juice of 1 lemon
orange juice
2 cups very ripe bananas, mashed

1½ cups soft brown sugar OR honey
2 cups evaporated milk

To the lemon juice, add sufficient orange juice to make up to 1 cup. Add bananas, sugar and milk. Liquidize or whip thoroughly. Put to freeze. Re-whip before quite frozen to break up ice crystals. Freeze. (8-10)

ORANGE ICE-CREAM

1 packet gelatine   ¼ pt (150 ml) double cream
1 pint (600 ml) orange juice
4 oz (100 gm) honey OR soft brown
  sugar

Dissolve gelatine in 3 tbsp orange juice, heated over boiling water. Add honey or sugar and remaining orange juice and beat to dissolve sugar. Cool. Whip in the cream. Put to freeze. Re-whip before quite frozen to break up ice crystals. Freeze. (6-8)

ORANGE SAUCE

4 fl oz (100 ml) natural yoghurt   honey to taste
4 fl oz (100 ml) orange juice

Whisk together – or vary proportions, and add honey to taste. Use on pancakes or as an alternative to custard.

RUNNY HONEY

3 tbsp apple juice   3 oz (75 gm) honey

Heat juice until nearly boiling. Stir in honey till dissolved. Use for sweetening natural yoghurt, cereals, porridge or raw or stewed sour fruit.

STRAWBERRY SAUCE

4 oz (100 gm) strawberries, hulled   ½ pt (300 ml) natural yoghurt
1 ripe tomato   1 tbsp honey OR to taste
1 sweet eating apple, chopped

Choose a sweet flavoured tomato, scald for ½ minute in boiling water and remove skin. Liquidize tomato, apple, strawberries and yoghurt. Stir in honey. Serve with pancakes, with home-made ice-cream or sponge pudding, or add to sliced ripe bananas as a dessert on its own.

CUSTARD SAUCE

3 eggs   1 pt (600 ml) milk
1 tbsp arrowroot   honey to taste

Beat eggs with arrowroot. Add warmed milk and honey and cook gently in a double saucepan, stirring occasionally, until custard starts to thicken. Cover and keep hot in the double saucepan. Use for trifle, stewed fruit, crumble or sponge pudding.

COCONUT CUSTARD

1 pt (600 ml) milk
1 tbsp honey
3 eggs, beaten

4 oz (100 gm) fresh wholemeal
   breadcrumbs OR barley flakes
2 oz (50 gm) desiccated coconut

Warm milk and dissolve honey. Whisk eggs, milk and breadcrumbs together. Pour into casserole standing in a pan of hot water. Bake at 275°F, 140-150°C, Gas 1-2 till set. Sprinkle coconut over the top and serve hot or cold. (4)

CHRISTMAS CUSTARD

3 tbsp home-made mincemeat OR
1 tbsp chopped dates, 1 tbsp
   currants and 2 tsp honey

1 pt (600 ml) warm milk
3 eggs, beaten

Beat all ingredients together. Pour into casserole and stand in pan of hot water. Bake in cool oven (275°F, 140°C, Gas 1) until set, about 1 hour. (4)

COTTAGE CREAM

3 tbsp natural curd cheese
2 tbsp natural yoghurt
2 tsp honey OR to taste

1 tsp cold-pressed safflower oil OR
   All Blend Oil

Whisk all the ingredients well together and use instead of cream with fruits and desserts.

GRAN'S CREAM

honey
natural yoghurt

dried milk powder (optional)

Mix honey and yoghurt, adding milk powder to thicken if necessary. Use proportions suited to the acidity of the yoghurt and to your personal preference.

NON-DAIRY TOPPING

1 tsp agar-agar
1 tbsp boiling water

¼ pt (150 ml) soya milk
2-3 tsp apple juice concentrate

Sprinkle agar-agar on to boiling water, stirring to dissolve. Whisk in other ingredients. Chill. Whisk lightly before use.

CASHEW CREAM

5 oz (150 gm) broken cashew nuts   5 fl oz (150 ml) water

Liquidize together to produce a creamy fluid. Strain through a sieve to remove any remaining lumps. Almonds or walnuts may similarly be used to produce a nut cream.

MILK JELLY WITH GELOZONE

1 tsp gelozone
2 tbsp cold water
1 pt (600 ml) milk

1 tbsp honey
vanilla essence OR grated nutmeg
OR 2 tbsp carob powder

Sprinkle gelozone on to cold water, stirring to a smooth paste. It thickens as it mixes. Whisk in the cold milk to avoid lumps. Bring to the boil and simmer for 2 minutes, stirring continuously. Sweeten and flavour to taste. Leave to set. (3-4)

NOTE: Gelozone is made from caragheen moss and is a vegan alternative to gelatine. Used in greater concentration it is a valuable herbal remedy for digestive disturbances, e.g. diarrhoea.

PRUNE SWIZZ

½ lb (225 gm) prunes, soaked 24 hrs
   in ½ pt (300 ml) water
juice of 1 small lemon

1 tbsp raw brown sugar
1 tbsp gelatine
small tin evaporated milk, chilled

Simmer prunes gently until soft. Remove stones. Mash. Stir in juice and sugar. Cool. Dissolve gelatine in 2 tbsp hot prune juice. Cool. Whip evaporated milk until doubled in volume. Stir gelatine into prunes. Fold in milk foam. Pour into individual dishes. Refrigerate. (4-6)

GOOSEBERRY FOOL

1 lb (450 gm) dessert gooseberries
2 fl oz (50 ml) natural yoghurt

honey to taste

Choose ripe, sweet, gooseberries and liquidize with yoghurt, adding honey to taste. (4)

RHUBARB SNOW

1 lb (450 gm) rhubarb, sliced
sweet cicely sprigs (optional)
¼ pt (150 ml) pineapple juice

1 packet gelatine
8 tbsp powdered milk (optional)
honey to taste

Simmer rhubarb with herb sprigs and pineapple juice till tender. Remove leaves. Taste and add honey. Sprinkle gelatine on half cup of the hot rhubarb juice. Stir till dissolved. Mix with rhubarb. Cool until tepid. Liquidize with powdered milk. Pour into serving dish to set. (4)

CREAMY GRAPE GATEAU

1 lb (450 gm) sweet ripe grapes
sweet white grape juice to taste (1-6 tbsp)
1 lb (450 gm) Loseley Greek-Style yoghurt OR Lebnie OR quark

6 oz (175 gm) digestive biscuits, crushed

Halve grapes and remove pips. Stir grape juice into Greek-style yoghurt, Lebnie or quark. In a deep dessert bowl arrange repeated layers of digestive crumbs, grape-flavoured yoghurt and grapes, finishing with grapes decoratively arranged on the top. Refrigerate until ready to serve. While Loseley Lebnie is virtually fat-free, their Greek-style yoghurt is deliciously creamy and gives the party touch. Home-made quark is similar to the Lebnie, but may be more acid and need more sweetening. (6-8)

GOOSEBERRY PUDDING

1 lb (450 gm) green gooseberries
honey to taste
4 oz (100 gm) soft wholemeal breadcrumbs

2 eggs, well beaten

Gently stew the gooseberries in very little water. Mash. Add breadcrumbs and honey to taste. Cool. Whisk in eggs. Pour into greased pie-dish and bake 30-40 minutes at 300-325°F, 150-160°C, Gas 2-3. Also delicious without baking. Cooked with sweet cicely sprigs, less sweetening will be needed. (4-5)

FRUIT FLUFF

2 lb (900 gm) good flavoured apples (Coxes)
½ pt (300 ml) plain yoghurt
½ pt (300 ml) orange juice

1 lemon – grated zest and juice
2 oz (50 gm) apricots (soaked 24 hrs)
4 oz (100 gm) raisins (soaked 1-2 hrs)
chopped nuts for decoration

Slice apples, retaining skins. Liquidize with yoghurt, orange and lemon juice and zest. Add soaked dried fruit and sufficient soaking liquid to process into a purée. Sprinkle nuts across top. Eat soon, while full of vitamins. (8-10)

FORESIGHT FRUIT SALAD

1 lb (450 gm) good flavoured plums
(fresh OR frozen raw)
¾-1 pt (450-600 ml) pineapple juice
(unsweetened)
3 tbsp honey (OR to taste)
2 passion fruit (granadillos)
1 lb (450 gm) oranges, peeled and
sliced

2 lb (900 gm) ripe pears, raw, peeled
and diced OR ripe melon
½ lb (225 gm) grapes, halved and
de-pipped
2-3 ripe bananas, sliced
1 lb (450 gm) raspberries (fresh OR
frozen)

Simmer plums in pineapple juice with honey until tender. Cool. Remove stones, and slice. Stir in flesh and pips of the passion fruit, and all other fruits. Mix and add a little more honey or pineapple juice as necessary. Delectable. (**10-12**)

WINTER FRUIT SALAD

4 oz (100 gm) dried apricots
4 oz (100 gm) hard figs
2 oz (50 gm) dried peaches
4 oz (100 gm) dates, stoned
2 oz (50 gm) raisins

2 oz (50 gm) sultanas
1 pt (600 ml) orange juice
(unsweetened)
2 oz (50 gm) sunflower seeds

Wash dried fruit (see p. 141). Soak apricots, figs and peaches in boiling water and sunflower seeds in cold for 8-24 hours. Soak dates, raisins and sultanas for 1-2 hours, in orange juice. Slice larger fruits. Mix all together. Serve this very sweet dish with tofu, unsweetened baked custard or quark. (**8**)

FRESH FRUIT SALAD

2 ripe bananas, sliced
4 pears, sliced
juice and rind of 1 lemon
2 oranges, zest and flesh

6 oz (175 gm) grapes, halved and
de-pipped
2 oz (50 gm) cashews, almonds, OR
walnuts

Slice bananas and pears into lemon juice to prevent oxidation. Add grated peel from oranges and lemon. Add chopped orange flesh. Mix all ingredients. Served attractively with more nuts, yoghurt (or quark) and wheatgerm, this will make a meal in itself. Substitute fresh soft fruits for imported when available. (**4-6**)

EAGER FRUIT SALAD

12-16 dried prunes, soaked 24 hrs
2 oranges, peeled and chopped

2-3 really ripe bananas, sliced
natural yoghurt to taste

Stone prunes and cut into quarters. Gently mix all ingredients. (**4-6**)

RAINBOW FRUIT SALAD

2 tsp honey
2 tsp fresh lemon juice
2 tbsp water
Mixed nuts: cashews, almonds, sunflower seeds, as available
3-4 of the following fresh fruits, organically grown when possible:
ripe peaches, pears, grapes, strawberries, raspberries, bananas, pineapple
(choose fruits with a variety of colours)

2-3 soaked prunes, stoned
2-3 soaked dried apricots, sliced
1 tbsp raw wheatgerm

Mix honey, lemon juice and water. Add quartered prunes and apricots. Add larger fruits, slicing them into the mixture. Add grapes whole. Arrange decoratively and serve with wheatgerm, nuts and Cottage Cream. (4-8)

PARTY APRICOT DESSERT

12 oz (350 gm) dried apricots (see p. 141)
½ pt (300 ml) water
4 fl oz (100 ml) sweet white wine
1 tsp lemon juice

1-2 tbsp honey
1″ cinnamon stick
1 tbsp kirsch
flaked almonds for decoration

Soak apricots in water and wine for 24 hours, covered. Next day add lemon juice, honey, cinnamon and a little more wine if necessary. Simmer gently about 5 minutes. Remove cinnamon and add kirsch. Transfer to serving dish and decorate with flaked almonds. (6)

BANANA CHEESECAKE

2 tsp gelatine
3 tbsp hot water
3 very ripe bananas
1 lemon
8 oz (225 gm) curd cheese
1 tbsp honey

¼ pt (150 ml) double cream
9″-10″ cake tin with removable base
CRUST: 3 oz (75 gm) butter
2 tbsp honey
8 oz (225 gm) muesli base (cereals only)

Sprinkle gelatine on hot water and stir till dissolved. Cool. Mash two ripest bananas into juice from ½ lemon. Whisk in the curd cheese, honey and cool gelatine. Whip cream and fold in. Oil loose-bottomed cake tin and ladle in the almost setting mixture. Refrigerate to set.

To make the crust, melt butter, stir in honey then muesli base, till well mixed. Cool. When just hand hot, spread carefully over top of cheesecake, smoothing level and gently pressing down. Refrigerate to harden. When ready to serve, put large flat serving dish over the cake tin, invert and press out. Slice last banana, toss in lemon juice and use for decoration. (6-8)

PINEAPPLE CHEESECAKE

1 lb (450 gm) curd cheese OR quark	2 eggs, separated
1 lemon, grated zest and juice	¼ pt (150 ml) double cream
1 lb (450 gm) tin pineapple pieces in natural juice	9″-10″ cake tin with removable base
¾ cup pineapple juice (from above)	CRUST: 3 oz (75 gm) butter
1 oz (25 gm) gelatine (2 envelopes)	2 tbsp soft brown sugar OR honey
8 oz (225 gm) soft brown sugar OR honey	8 oz (225 gm) digestive biscuits, crushed

Put into liquidizer the cheese, lemon zest and juice, and most of the partly drained pineapple, reserving some for decoration. Sprinkle gelatine on cup of heated pineapple juice, standing in boiling water. Stir until dissolved. Add hot gelatine solution and sugar to blender and liquidize. Blend in egg yolks. Cool. Add cream and beat in quickly. Whisk egg whites until stiff. Fold into cheesecake mixture. Oil tin, blotting off excess. Ladle in the mixture and refrigerate to set.

To make the crust, gently melt butter with sugar. Mix in biscuit. When nearly cool, spread gently over the cheesecake, smoothing level and pressing down lightly. Refrigerate. Just before serving, invert on to flat serving plate. Decorate with pineapple pieces. (8-10)

PEAR TRIFLE

1 lb (450 gm) ripe pears	Custard sauce (p. 110)
apple juice	whipped cream for decoration (optional)
8-12 oz (225-350 gm) wholemeal sponge	toasted flaked almonds

Peel, core and slice pears into a little apple juice. Either use pears raw, or poach gently in the juice till tender. Arrange thin slices of cake in base of serving bowl. Cover with most of the fruit. Pour over sufficient pear/apple juice to soak into the sponge. Make custard sauce, sweetened appropriately, and pour over. When cold, decorate with reserved pear, piped cream and flaked almonds.

Other fruits may be substituted for pears – or use unsugared tinned fruit in its own juice. Similarly wholegrain fruitcake or soft biscuts may be used. (8)

Muesli and Grain Dishes

Muesli or wholemeal bread?

Both are made from whole grains, but one is raw and the other cooked. So which is better? Muesli! When made from raw ingredients, with the grains and seeds soaked overnight, muesli is a living food full of enzymes, amino-acids, vitamins and minerals, and should be eaten every day. The important factors with muesli are the pre-soaking, the higher proportion of fruit to cereals, and ample chewing – seldom practised by packet muesli eaters.

Muesli is the ideal quickly prepared meal, and should be considered for packed lunches, snack meals, home suppers as well as breakfasts, especially when salads are not eaten daily. When time is pressing, muesli can be made without adding the fruit – and fresh fruit eaten separately. Use good flavoured apples – tasteless apples spoil muesli.

Where a milk allergy exists, muesli can be made with a little soya milk or nut milk (see page 20), or made with fruit juice only.

Choose a muesli base composed of organically grown grains, free from sugar, milk powder and maize. Organically grown whole grains, sprouted (see page 49), are ideal inclusions and are preferable to crushed, cooked grains not organically produced.

Soak the crushed muesli grains overnight in just sufficient water to wet them. The growth enzymes will develop and multiply, increasing the amino-acids (pre-digested protein) and overcoming the phytic acid present in the bran (which otherwise binds the calcium, iron and zinc). So the effect of soaking for 8-24 hours in a cool place rewards us with many extra nutrients otherwise unavailable!

If you buy the flaked raw grains separately, you can **blend your mixture to help overcome specific mineral deficiencies**. You can even produce a nutritious gluten-free muesli, individually tailored. Whenever possible include oats (or oatmeal) which has a particularly health-promoting form of fibre, or linseed (e.g. Linusit Gold) if a more effective laxative food is needed. Here is a list to help you choose the ingredients you need:

Muesli ingredient:	*Rich in:*
Almonds	Magnesium, potassium, vitamin E, B complex
Apricots	Magnesium, iron, A
Alfalfa & other sprouts	Many vitamins (especially B and C), minerals, enzymes, amino-acids
Barley flakes†	Silica, manganese, molybdenum
Brazil nuts	Selenium
Brewer's yeast*	Many minerals, vitamins, B complex, chromium
Buckwheat	Manganese, B1, B5, B6, molybdenum
Caraway seeds	Silica

Cashew nuts	Magnesium, zinc, A, B5
Coconut	Manganese
Hard figs	Silica
Fresh fruits	Vitamins C and P
Hazel nuts	Magnesium, potassium, manganese, A, B2, E
Honey	Enzymes and trace minerals
Kelp powder*	Iodine and trace minerals
Lecithin granules*	B1, choline, inositol
Linseed, whole (soaked) or split	Potassium. Mucillaginous laxative – better than bran
Maize flakes	Zinc
Millet, whole (soaked) or flakes	Potassium, magnesium, iron, B1, B2
Oats (flakes or sprouted)†	Zinc, molybdenum, fibre
Peanuts (unsalted)	Potassium, manganese, E, magnesium
Pecans	Manganese
Pumpkin seeds (soaked)	Iron, folic acid
Raisins and sultanas	Potassium, magnesium, iron
Brown rice flakes	Manganese, zinc
Rice bran (polishings)	Manganese, B1, niacin, fibre
Brown rice (sprouted)	Selenium, zinc, manganese
Rye flakes (or whole sprouted)†	Potassium, folic acid, zinc
Sesame seeds (soaked)	Calcium, magnesium, niacin
Soya flour or flakes	Potassium, molybdenum, magnesium
Soya Bran	Potassium, fibre
Spirulina*	Iron, B12, F
Sunflower seeds (soaked)	Potassium, iron, B1, molybdenum
Walnuts	Vitamin F, manganese
Wheat bran†	Zinc, iron, potassium, fibre, manganese
Wheatgerm†	Selenium, zinc, iron, molybdenum
Wholewheat (sprouted)†	Selenium, zinc, iron, calcium, manganese
Natural yoghurt	Lactic acid

* Food supplements – to be used sparingly, if at all.
† Best avoided if on a gluten-free diet.
(Sources: 'Nutrition Almanac' – Nutrition Search. Inc.; 'Mental and Elemental Nutrients' by Carl C. Pfeiffer, Ph.D., M.D.)

ORIGINAL BIRCHER-BENNER MUESLI

2 tbsp raw rolled oats
2 tbsp raw wheatgerm
4 tbsp water
juice of ½ lemon
2 tbsp sweetened condensed milk
2 apples
2 tbsp chopped hazel nuts

Soak oatflakes and wheatgerm overnight in water. Next morning mix in lemon juice and condensed milk. Coarsely grate in the apples (unpeeled), stirring well. Add nuts and serve immediately. The author (now a granny) was brought up on this breakfast devised before the horrors of white sugar were realized! For my own children, I used 2 tsp honey and 4 tsp nut cream instead of the 2 tbsp condensed milk. Now we have many more enterprising recipes, using the Swiss doctor's principles of combining raw cereal grains and fresh fruit for a healthy start to the day. But for reluctant muesli eaters, the original recipe is a good introduction to better breakfasts.

BASIC MUESLI RECIPE

4 tbsp muesli base – raw crushed cereal grains, unsugared

1 tbsp sunflower seeds
1 tsp millet flakes

Soak these ingredients overnight in 5 tablespoons cold water. Next morning add:

½ cup orange juice
2-4 tbsp natural yoghurt

2 tsp honey (or to taste)

Stir together to mix in the honey then grate in:

1 cooking apple (Bramley)

1 large eating apple

and stir well. Use a coarse, stainless steel grater, or chop the apples, it should be necessary to chew the muesli.

To this basic muesli, add variations of choice; choose from:

1 tbsp desiccated coconut
1 tbsp raisins or sultanas
½-1 ripe banana, sliced

1 tbsp chopped nuts
1 tbsp chopped hard dates

Add any other fresh fruit available: e.g. blackberries, strawberries, raspberries, blackcurrants, redcurrants, cherries, grapes, sliced pears, apricots, peaches, plums or satsumas.

Similarly in winter a few home frozen fruits can be added occasionally. If really needed, powdered supplements such as kelp can be added judiciously – personally I prefer to keep them separate as muesli is too delicious a dish to be spoilt! **(1-4)**

DRY MUESLI MIX

8 oz (250 gm) jumbo oat flakes
8 oz (250 gm) barley flakes
4 oz (125 gm) sunflower seeds
4 oz (125 gm) dried figs, chopped
8 oz (250 gm) sultanas or raisins
4 oz (125 gm) dried bananas, chopped

8 oz (250 gm) wheat flakes
8 oz (250 gm) rye flakes
2 oz (50 gm) millet flakes
4 oz (125 gm) hard dates, chopped
4 oz (125 gm) dried apricots, chopped or minced

Mix all ingredients. Sufficient for each meal should be soaked overnight in just sufficient water to cover. This comprehensive muesli may then be used as in the basic recipe with fruit, or eaten alone with apple juice or milk, and the fresh fruit eaten separately. In order to add a crisp element, add some Grapenuts, almonds, peanuts or toasted coconut flakes when serving.

LAXATIVE MUESLI MIX

1 cup cereal muesli base
  (unsweetened)
½ cup oat bran OR Linusit Gold

½ cup chopped nuts
½ cup wheatgerm (raw)
½ cup mixed dried fruits

Mix. Soak serving portion overnight. Eat with milk or apple juice, or make into basic fruit muesli.

GF GLUTEN-FREE MUESLI

1 tsp sunflower seeds
1 tsp rice bran
dried fruit to taste
1 tbsp soyabean flakes

1 tbsp brown rice flakes
1 tsp ground almonds
1 tsp desiccated coconut

Soak sunflower seeds, rice bran and dried fruit overnight. Mix in all other ingredients. (1)

MUESLI RICH IN MANGANESE AND SELENIUM*

1 tbsp sprouted wheat
4 tbsp barley flakes OR wheat flakes

1 tbsp coconut
1 tbsp walnuts, chopped

Grow the wheatsprouts. Soak barley or wheat overnight. Add other ingredients and make as basic muesli recipe. (1-2)

MUESLI RICH IN IRON*

Soak choice of wholewheat flakes, wheatgerm, apricots, raisins, millet flakes and sunflower seeds overnight. Add orange or lemon juice and sprouted wheat before serving, with apples.

* Food samples vary, depending on the soil and production methods (see page 6).

MUESLI RICH IN MAGNESIUM* GF

Use soya flour or soya flakes, soya bran, peanuts, almonds, cashews, hazel nuts, millet flakes, raisins and apricots, soaking the last 3.

PURÉED SMOOTH MUESLI

2 tbsp sunflower seeds OR broken
  cashew nuts
2 sweet eating apples, sliced
2 tsp honey
½ cup natural yoghurt

½ cup orange juice
1 tsp cold-pressed safflower oil OR
  All Blend Oil
½ cup alfalfa sprouts
4 tbsp raw wheatgerm

Soak sunflower seeds overnight. Liquidize apples with honey, wet ingredients and alfalfa sprouts. Stir in wheatgerm. Serve with the soaked sunflower seeds or nuts to encourage chewing. (2-4)

HIGH PROTEIN MUESLI GF

1 tbsp millet flakes
3 tbsp sunflower seeds
½ cup natural yoghurt
½ cup orange juice
4 good flavoured apples

½ cup broken cashew nuts
2 cups beansprouts OR alfalfa
  sprouts
honey to taste
sultanas OR raisins to taste

Soak millet and sunflower seeds overnight. Add wet ingredients and grate in the apples, stirring. Stir in other ingredients. Variations: Use lemon juice instead of orange. Add ripe sliced banana, blackberries or any other available fresh or dried fruits. (2-4)

SLIMMER'S MUESLI

Any of these fresh fruit muesli recipes, with the proportions adjusted, are suitable for slimmers. The wholegrain cereal base, yoghurt and juice remain unchanged. Choose eating apples with a good sweet flavour so that less honey and dried fruit is needed. Add a squeeze of fresh lemon juice if liked. Add extra protein with soaked millet and sunflower seeds, sprouted wheat, alfalfa and beansprouts in preference to the calorie-laden nuts.

A large bowl of fresh fruit muesli makes a filling, satisfying start to the day and is a meal in itself at any time.

* Food samples vary, depending on the soil and production methods (see page 6).

COLD WEATHER RECIPES

If the weather is cold and a warming breakfast is needed, there are variations on traditional porridge made from soaked jumbo oats, oat flakes, oatmeal, barley flakes, millet flakes – or even potatoes!

GF GRAIN-FREE POTATO PORRIDGE

Boil about 2 cups water. Scrub a large potato thoroughly. Grate it into the boiling water. Stir and boil till the porridge thickens. This highly alkaline and cleansing dish is surprisingly good to eat with milk and perhaps a little molasses.

FIVE GRAIN KRUSKA

1 tbsp wholewheat
1 tbsp whole millet
1 tbsp whole oats
1 tbsp whole rye
1 tbsp whole barley

1 tbsp wheatgerm OR oatgerm
1 tbsp oat bran
2 tbsp raisins OR sultanas
1 cup water (approx)

Buy organically produced grains if possible – otherwise ensure that you have untreated grains, suitable for human consumption. Grind them in a grain mill, coffee grinder or Moulinex chopper. Soak overnight in the water. In the morning bring to boil, then transfer to a heated thermos jar for ½ hour for the completion of cooking at a lower temperature. The exact quantity of water will depend on the dryness of the grains – experiment to produce kruska with the consistency of thick porridge. It should not be mushy. Serve hot with milk and/or stewed apples or apricots.

This Scandinavian version of muesli is also full of vital nutrients. Eat it alone as a complete meal. (1)

GF RICE KRUSKA

3 tbsp brown rice
¼ pt (150 ml) water

1-2 dried figs (OR prunes)

Soak the organic brown rice with the dried fruit overnight. In the morning bring to boil and simmer 15 minutes. Transfer to heated vacuum jar or double saucepan for further 30 minutes cooking. Gluten-free. (1)

OAT KRUSKA

½ cup cracked oats   ¼ cup wheat, oat OR soya bran
½ cup raisins   2 cups water

Soak all together overnight. Bring to boil and transfer to double saucepan to continue cooking slowly for 30-40 minutes more. (2)

KASHA

1 cup raw buckwheat   1-2 dried figs OR prunes (optional)
3 cups water

Soak the buckwheat and dried fruit overnight. Bring to boil, simmer five minutes. Transfer to heated thermos for final 30 minutes cooking. Serve with little sunflower oil. (3)

Packet Cereal Eaters

Choose wholegrain, unsugared cereals, free of chemical additives, e.g. Shredded Wheat, Shreddies, Weetabix, GrapeNuts – and fruit and nut muesli! If serving cornflakes, add raw wheatgerm and Frugrains, dried fruit, honey or molasses to sweeten. Most commercial cereals are wheat based. In America unsweetened puffed whole brown rice, millet and corn (maize) cereals are available – we should press for these here!

Guide to Cooking Wholegrains

Sometimes a simple dish of one wholegrain may be better tolerated by those with allergies than compound preparations such as shop-bought wholemeal bread. For this may have some chemical additives (and yeast!) and may be made from high gluten flour, inorganically grown.

Buy organically produced wholegrains whenever possible, and wash in cold water. For cooking savoury dishes, stock is preferable to water. Measure by volume in the proportions given in the table.

BOILING: boil the measured water with ½ tsp salty seasoning to each 8 oz (approx 1½ cups) grain. Add the grain, bring back to boil, and stir once. Do not stir again or it will stick. Simmer, covered, till all fluid is absorbed, and the grain is tender but not mushy – remove lid near end of cooking time if needed to evaporate excess water. Heavy based saucepans are ideal, and gentle simmering. Serve with leafy vegetables, tomatoes, mushrooms, onions, etc., i.e. use in place of potatoes or bread.

SAUTÉING: this produces a nuttier flavour, and is traditionally used in cooking Spanish rice dishes, buckwheat and bulgar wheat. After washing and draining the grain, place in a dry saucepan and heat gently, stirring till dry. Add just sufficient oil to coat the grains and sauté them gently, stirring, until golden. Then add boiling stock or water and continue as for boiling, above.

VACUUM FLASK OR SLOW COOKER: this method is a fuel saving way of cooking the quicker grains, which preserves more of the vital nutrients and avoids the danger of boiling dry and burnt saucepans! Soak the grains in cold water overnight. Bring to the boil then quickly transfer to well heated vacuum jar for the completion of cooking at a lower temperature. Exact water quantity depends on dryness of grains – experiment to produce a cooked grain that has absorbed all the fluid but is not mushy. This method is recommended for Kruska and Kasha, but allow extra time for wholegrains.

Guide to quantities and cooking times:

Wholegrain	Water Needed	Simmer for	Proportion Grain:Water
8 oz (225 gm) wheat	3 pt (1.8 l)	2 hours	1:6
8 oz (225 gm) barley	3 pt (1.8 l)	2 hours	1:6
8 oz (225 gm) rye	3 pt (1.8 l)	2 hours	1:6
8 oz (225 gm) oats	3 pt (1.8 l)	2 hours	1:6
8 oz (225 gm) brown rice	1½ pt (900 ml)	40-50 mins	1:3
8 oz (225 gm) buckwheat	2½ pt (1.5 l)	20-30 mins	1:5
8 oz (225 gm) millet	2½ pt (1.5 l)	½ hour	1:5
8 oz (225 gm) bulgar wheat	2 pt (1.2 l)	½ hour	1:4

SAVOURY BROWN RICE

2 tomatoes, sliced
1 green pepper, sliced
2 onions, sliced
1½ tbsp vegetable oil

1 cup brown rice
2½ cups boiling water
1 tsp Tastex

Sauté the tomatoes, pepper and onions gently in hot oil to soften. Add rice and stir till glazed. Add boiling water and Tastex, bring back to the boil, stir once and cover tightly. Simmer gently till cooked (about ¾ hour) checking that it does not burn, but absorbs all the water. (3-4)

Bread and Pastry

BREAD

Breadmaking is a very satisfying activity. It is an art which may take a week or two to perfect. Persist, and you will be rewarded with the delectable aroma of nutty, delicious, satisfying bread.

Where 100% wholewheat bread, free from chemical additives, cannot be bought, it is logical to bake it at home, freezing extra loaves till required. Ideally, choose organically grown, stone-ground, 100% wholemeal flour. I like to go one step further and grind my own flour as I need it, from bio-dynamically produced grain. The flavour is magnificent!

Practical notes for breadmakers

Choose to make your bread when you have other jobs to do around the house and you don't have to watch the clock for a deadline.

Flour varies in its water content, so the exact proportion of water to flour must be flexible. Canadian 'hard' wheat, high in gluten, is not necessary for good home-made bread. Using the slow, cool overnight 'setting the sponge' or 'batter' method (as in many of these recipes) allows good gluten strand formation even with 'soft' English flours. With increasing incidence of gluten allergy this seems better sense to me. Use fresh, stone-ground, 100% wholemeal flour (as produced by Doves Farm, Allinsons, Prewetts and Loseley), organically grown if possible.

Different batches of bread will turn out differently. Active dried baker's yeast does not keep indefinitely – if it does not froth up well in 10 minutes, you could need a fresh supply. Do not use brewer's yeast. Fresh yeast can be kept in the refrigerator for 2 days or frozen for 4 weeks. It needs slow defrosting at room temperature and should be used immediately, in twice the quantity given for dried yeast.

ACTIVATING THE YEAST: Dissolve 1-3 tsp honey (or raw sugar) in a little hot water. Add more water to give ½ pt (300 ml) at 100-105°F, 38-40°C, in a deep basin, and sprinkle the dried yeast over (OR crumble over if fresh). OR cream fresh yeast with the honey (or sugar) and add water at this temperature. Leave in a warm place till the yeast froths up to produce about 1″ (2½ cm) of foam. Use remaining warm water to rinse out the yeast basin.

'SETTING THE SPONGE': Mix the frothed yeast with all the recipe water and whisk into half the flour to produce a smooth thick batter. Cover with oiled polythene sheet and rest in a warm place till spongy and covered with bubbles – 20-60 minutes (OR overnight in a very cool place).

126

PROVING, OR PUTTING TO RISE: Put kneaded dough into a well-oiled bowl (or greased tins) in a warm, draught-free place. Loosely cover with an oiled polythene sheet, allowing room for expansion. Leave until dough has fully risen if for final proving – i.e. doubled in size for all-wheat flour, by 50-75% for less glutinous or mixed flours, by 25-50% for sourdough loaves. Proving time varies also, depending on the yeast, the flour, the kneading and the humidity, as well as the temperature. Sourdough bread is much slower to rise (3-7 hours).

The dough-hook of an electric mixer, used at slow speed, is a useful energy saver – although I enjoy sharing the kneading with it. Food processors can make short work of the kneading. Don't keep working in extra flour to the elastic kneaded dough – it will make the bread dry.

Loaf tins need to be greased well, especially into the corners, preferably with salt-free butter. Fill the tins about ⅔ full to produce a nicely rounded loaf risen about an inch above the rim.

Preheat the oven before baking bread. Bread is cooked when it sounds hollow when tapped. Usually I remove loaves from their tins when they appear cooked on top, reversing them in the oven for their final 5-10 minutes, till sounding hollow when tapped on the bottom. Then I like to wrap them in a clean damp tea-towel, on a cake-rack, to prevent too hard a crust.

Choose a good bread knife which will slice your good home-made bread without tearing it into crumbs.

To refresh an uncut loaf which has become dry, or to produce quickly 'steaming fresh bread' from the freezer, wet the crust quickly all over and put in a cool oven 15-20 minutes for stale bread, 30-45 minutes for frozen bread.

Use left-over bread for making soft breadcrumbs (grate, or use dry liquidizer), bread and butter pudding, or for 'blotting' off fat from casseroles. Slices of dried-out bread are useful for making rusks for babies (and dogs) and for dry breadcrumbs (chop small and 'liquidize').

Basic method for breadmaking

Step I Start with the flour, bowl, etc. at room temperature (warm flour very gently in oven at 150°F, 70°C, Gas ⅛ in very cold weather. It must not exceed blood heat.) Sift flour to aerate, retaining bran. Put flour into large mixing bowl and make a well in the centre. Activate the yeast. Gradually stir the yeast water and other water (or milk) into the flour, producing first a smooth batter (for 'sponge', perhaps) which becomes a dough as more flour is combined. If necessary add a very little extra warm water to incorporate all the flour into the dough. Turn on to a floured work surface and knead – i.e. push, pull and punch with your hands – it's great fun and can be quite therapeutic! Continue kneading until the dough is firm, elastic and does not stick to your floured hands (3-8 minutes).

Step II Put the ball of dough into oiled container, covered, to prove until well risen, in a warm place to speed the process, but not over blood heat. Then turn on to floured surface again and 'knock back' the dough – i.e. knead it till firm, elastic and pliable again (3-5 minutes). This step may be repeated once or twice. If risen bread is left too long, and begins to go down again, or loaves to spill over the sides of the tin, a repeat is indicated.

Step III Cut the risen, knocked-back dough into loaf-sized portions – 1 lb for small (1 lb) loaf tins, 2 lbs for large (2 lb) tins, approximately. Knead each loaf separately for 2-3 minutes to produce a smooth, even, well-built loaf shape, just narrower than the tin. Place in greased tin OR roll out a long sausage of dough and cut into equal sized pieces (2-4 oz, 50-100 gm). Knead and roll each into a roll and place on floured tray, allowing room to spread as they prove. Loosely cover loaves and rolls with greased polythene sheets. Put in warm places to rise. Keep an eye on the expanding loaves to gauge when rising is complete and they are ready for baking in preheated oven.

Where exceptions occur, they are detailed in the recipes.

Remedies for specific problems
If the loaf has collapsed and slices reveal doughy sticky streaks, the last proving was probably too long, allowing the loaves to collapse when put into the oven. If the slices of bread reveal small, hard lumps, the original dough was not sufficiently well mixed. If the top crust separates away, the loaf was not sufficiently well kneaded into shape.

If your bread has large holes it indicates overlong kneading or overlong rising.

If a slice of bread is soggy with a sagging crust, the dough probably was too wet and needed more kneading.

SODA BREAD

Soda bread is not included, as alkaline bicarbonate of soda destroys B vitamins – it is better to make yeast breads or use baking powder in scone mixtures.

QUICK WHOLEMEAL BREAD OR PIZZA BASE

2 tsp raw brown sugar
2 tsp salty seasoning
½ pt (300 ml) very hot water
½ pt (300 ml) additional water
1 tbsp dried yeast

2 tbsp vegetable oil
2 lb (900 gm) plain 100% wholemeal
  flour
(see page 94 for toppings)

Dissolve sugar and salty seasoning in very hot water and add the ½ pt to give 1 pt (600 ml) at blood heat. Activate the yeast. Stir yeast water and oil into flour to make dough (as step 1). Knead till dough is firm and elastic (3-5 minutes).

Divide and knead into loaves (or 1 loaf and 4 pizza bases). Knead into shape. Put into greased tins and put to prove in a warm place until doubled in size (about 1 hour). Bake at 375°F, 190°C, Gas 5 for about 30 minutes for 1 lb loaf, 20 minutes for pizza bases.

s FORESIGHT FIVE GRAIN BREAD

1 tsp honey
1 pt (600 ml) warm water
2 tbsp dried yeast
3 oz (75 gm) rye flour
3 oz (75 gm) buckwheat flour
3 oz (75 gm) cornmeal

3 oz (75 gm) soya flour
1¼ lb (550 gm) 100% wholewheat
  flour
1 tbsp sunflower oil
2 tsp salty seasoning

In the evening: Dissolve honey in ½ pt (300 ml) warm water. Activate yeast. Sift the flours and divide into two, putting half into a large bowl. Whisk in all water, yeast and oil to form a smooth thick batter. Cover and leave in a cool place overnight to 'set the sponge'.

Next morning: Mix salty seasoning with remaining flour and gently stir into the 'sponge' to form a soft dough. Knead thoroughly till smooth and elastic. Knead into 3 loaves and put into 1 lb loaf tins. Leave to prove (till risen by 75%). Bake at 350°F, 180°C, Gas 4 for 30-40 minutes. A good-flavoured, dark bread.

s SLIMMER'S HIGH FIBRE BREAD

6 oz (160 gm) fine oat bran
3 lb (1,350 gm) plain 100% wholemeal
  flour
1 tsp honey
1½ pt (900 ml) warm water

2 tbsp dried yeast OR 2 oz (50 gm)
  fresh yeast
2 tsp salty seasoning
1 tsp kelp powder
2 tbsp vegetable oil

In the evening: Sift flour into large bowl and mix in bran. Dissolve honey in warm water and pour into hollow in flour. Sprinkle or crumble in the yeast. When the yeast is activated, gradually work yeasty water into the top flour, to make a thick batter (leaving dry flour underneath). Cover and leave in cool place.

Next Morning: Add oil and sprinkle over seasoning. Work all ingredients together. Knead for 3-5 minutes. Divide into 2 large and 1 small loaves (or 4 small) and put into greased tins. Allow to rise, covered till nearly double in size (½-1½ hours). Bake for about 35 minutes for large loaves, 23-30 minutes for small loaves, at 400°F, 200°C, Gas 6.

s RYE BREAD WITH SOURDOUGH

1 lb (450 gm) 100% wholewheat flour
1¼ pt (750 ml) tepid water

1½ cups sourdough starter (see
  next recipe)

In evening: Mix flour and water to a smooth thick batter in a large bowl (not metal). Stir in starter. Cover with cloth and leave in a warm place overnight.

Next morning: Remove 1½ cups of batter from the bowl and return to the sourdough starter crock.

2 tbsp molasses
2 tbsp sunflower oil
½ lb (225 gm) rye flour, sifted

1 tbsp salty seasoning
1 lb (450 gm) 100% wholewheat flour
2 lb loaf tin, warmed and oiled

To the remainder add molasses, oil, rye flour and salt. Fold in gently, adding sufficient wholewheat flour to produce a soft dough. Turn the mixture gently with long movements of the wooden spoon to avoid breaking up the gluten strands which have formed overnight.

Scatter the remaining flour thickly over the work surface, and turn the dough on to it. Knead gently for about 5 minutes until even, soft and moist, but not sticky – do not attempt to incorporate all the flour. Shape into loaf. Put the soft loaf in tin. Slash the top with a sharp knife to release any large bubbles which may form. Paint top with a little water. Cover and put to prove in a warm place for 4-5 hours, till risen by ⅓. Bake at 375°F, 190°C, Gas 5 for 30-35 minutes. This loaf keeps well in a cake tin for over a week. Delicious sliced thinly and spread with Butter Plus and Barmene or Tastex. Good for rusk making.

LIGHTER RYE BREAD   S

Quick sourdough starter – prepare 7 days before needed:

1 tsp dried baker's yeast	½ tsp honey
½ pt (300 ml) warm water (100-105°F, 38-40°C)	½ lb (225 gm) plain 100% wholewheat flour

Activate yeast in the honeyed water. Mix into a smooth thick batter. Put in a large glass screw-top jar (leaving plenty of headspace) and stand in a warm place for 48 hours (e.g. airing cupboard). Refrigerate for 5 days, when it will be ready for use. After use, add more plain flour and water to the remaining starter to make up to the original volume, leave in a warm place for 24 hours, then refrigerate till needed.

12 oz (350 gm) rye flour, sifted	¾ pt (400 ml) warm water
1 cup sourdough starter	(100-105°F, 38-40°C)

The evening before: Mix rye flour to a thick batter with water and whisk in the starter. Cover and leave overnight at room temperature.

1 tsp honey	1 tsp caraway seeds
¼ pt (150 ml) warm water (100-105°F, 38-40°C)	1¼ lb (575 gm) plain 100% wholewheat flour
1 tbsp dried yeast	3 tbsp vegetable oil
1 tbsp salty seasoning	2 × 2 lb loaf tins, greased
1 tsp poppy seeds	

Next morning: Dissolve honey in the warm water and activate yeast. Add salt, seeds, the wholewheat flour, 2 tbsp oil and frothing yeast to rye mixture. Work together to a soft dough. Knead for 10 minutes. Use remaining oil to grease large mixing bowl. Roll dough around bowl to coat with oil. Cover and leave in a warm place to prove (about 2 hours). Knead again, divide and knead into 2 loaves. Cover and leave to rise (about 1 hour in warm place).

Bake for 30-35 minutes at 350°F, 180°C, Gas 4. Good with smoked fish and for sandwiches. Keeps well.

The replenished starter will be ready for more breadmaking one or two weeks later.

QUICK WHOLEMEAL LOAF OR ROLLS

1 × 25 mg vitamin C tablet, crushed   ½ tsp kelp powder (optional)
2 oz (50 gm) fresh yeast   1½ tsp salty seasoning
¾ pt (450 ml) water (100°F)   2 tbsp sunflower oil
1½ lb (675 gm) wholewheat flour   1 beaten egg

Cream vitamin tablet with fresh yeast. Add tepid water and leave to foam. Sift flour, kelp and salt. Pour on yeast liquid and oil and mix into a soft dough ball. Knead for 3-5 minutes.

Divide into 2½-4 oz pieces and work into rolls. Place on baking tray and cover while rising. When proved, paint top lightly with beaten egg and bake for about 15-20 minutes. Or divide into two loaves, knead and put into greased tins. Cover and put to rise. Bake for 22-25 minutes at 400°F, 200°C, Gas 6.

LIGHT SPONGY WHOLEMEAL BREAD

½ lb (225 gm) potatoes   4 tsp salty seasoning
  (to give 1 cup mashed potato)   2½ lb (1,125 gm) 100% plain
½ pt (300 ml) water   wholemeal flour
  (to give 1 cup potato stock)   1 tbsp soft butter or extra oil
2 tbsp raw brown sugar   2 × 2 lb loaf tins, greased
1 cup warm water (100-110°F)   Glaze: (optional)
2 tbsp dried yeast   1 tbsp egg white (reserved from the
2 eggs   eggs)
¼ pt (150 ml) vegetable oil   1 tbsp cold water

Scrub potatoes and slice in three. Cook in water till tender. Drain, reserving the stock. Peel and mash thoroughly. Dissolve sugar in the warm water and activate the yeast. Beat the eggs (reserve 1 tbsp egg white for glaze). Whisk oil, beaten egg and cool stock into potatoes.

Sift salt into flour in a large mixing bowl. Stir in the yeast and potato mixtures, gradually working in the flour to make a firm dough. Knead for about 10 minutes. Generously grease a large bowl with the butter and roll dough in it to coat it with butter. Cover and place in refrigerator to rise slowly. When doubled in size, punch down. Rest the dough for about 5 minutes. Knead for about 5 minutes. Knead into two loaves. Cover and leave to rise until doubled in size (it may be slow rising, so keep an eye on it). Gently brush on the egg glaze (made by combining the egg white and water) and bake for 35-45 minutes at 375°F, 190°C, Gas 5.

Remove loaves from tins for the final 5-10 minutes of baking to colour the crust. Cool thoroughly before cutting. This bread keeps very well and is very good toasted. It is slow to make but appeals to those accustomed to the soft 'sponginess' of English white bread.

Doris Grant, nutritionist author of *Your Daily Bread* and *Food Combining for Health* has kindly sent the following recipe for her renowned 'no kneading' loaf – 'easier to make than a mud pie!'

THE GRANT LOAF

3 tsp dried yeast OR 1 oz (25 gm) fresh yeast

6 tsp Barbados sugar OR honey OR black molasses

2 pt (1,200 ml) water at blood heat

3 lb (1,350 ml) stone-ground 100% wholewheat flour

2 tsp salt (according to taste)

If using fresh yeast, mix it in a small bowl with 4 tsp sugar and add ¼ pt (150 ml) water at blood heat. Leave to activate before adding to the flour with the rest of the water. (To make 1 loaf, use a scant ½ oz fresh yeast mixed with 2 tsp sugar, etc., with about 8 tbsp water.) Sift the salt with flour (in very cold weather, warm flour slightly – enough to take off the chill). Place in a cup 3 tbsp of the water at blood heat; the temperature is important – it is best to check with a cooking thermometer which should register 35-38°C. Sprinkle the dried yeast on top. Leave for 2 minutes or so for the yeast to soak, then add the sugar, honey or black molasses. In about 10-15 minutes this should have produced a thick, creamy froth. Pour this into the flour and add the rest of the water. Mix well – by hand is best – for a minute or so, working from sides to middle, till the dough feels elastic and leaves the sides of the mixing bowl clean; this helps to make a well-built loaf. (To test if the dough is of the right consistency, hold a handful above the basin – it should drop slowly back into the basin. The tendency is to make the mixture too dry.)

Divide the dough into three 2-pint tins which have been warmed and greased. Put the tins in a warm place, cover with a cloth and leave for about 20 minutes or until the dough is within half an inch of the top of the tins. Bake at 400°F, 200°C, Gas 6 for approximately 35-40 minutes.

Quantities for 1 loaf

1 tsp dried yeast

2 tsp Barbados sugar, honey OR black molasses

13 fl oz (375 ml) water at blood heat

1 lb (450 gm) flour

1 tsp salt (to taste)

CHEWY WHEAT BREAD   S

1¾ pt (1 l) water (approx)

8 oz (225 gm) wholewheat or bulgar

2 tbsp honey

2 oz (50 gm) fresh yeast

1 tbsp salty seasoning

3 lb (1,350 gm) 100% wholewheat flour

1 oz (25 gm) sunflower margarine

3 oz (75 gm) oat bran

2 × 2 lb and 2 × 1 lb loaf tins

1 tbsp milk OR water

1 tbsp egg white

a little cracked wheat

Boil ½ pt (300 ml) water and pour over wholewheat. Leave till tepid, adding most of the honey. Whisk fresh yeast with one tsp honey and ½ pt (300 ml) warm water (100°F). Sift salt with flour and lightly rub in margarine. Strain water from wholewheat and make up to 1¼ pints (750 ml) liquid. Mix wheat and bran into flour before adding total liquid. Mix into dough ball and knead till dough is elastic. Put into greased bowl, cover and prove. Knock back the dough, divide and knead into loaves. Cover and prove again. Whisk egg with milk and brush over loaves. Sprinkle with cracked wheat. Bake at 425°F, 220°C, Gas 7 for 30-40 minutes.

SOYA BREAD

6 oz (175 gm) soya flour
1¾ lb (800 gm) 100% wholemeal flour
1¼ tsp salty seasoning
4 tsp honey

22 fl oz (650 ml) warm water
1 oz (25 gm) dried yeast
2 tbsp vegetable oil
3 × 1 lb (small) loaf tins, greased

Barely warm the flour. Add salt. Sift to aerate, retaining the bran. Dissolve honey in water and activate the yeast. Add oil. Stir into tepid flour to produce dough.

Knead for about 5 minutes. Prove in large oiled mixing bowl in a warm place for about 2 hours. Knead dough for further 5 minutes, make into 3 loaves, and press down well into prepared tins. Cover and put to rise till doubled in size. Bake for 30-35 minutes at 375-400°F, 190-200°C, Gas 5-6.

POPULAR 'ONE-BOWL' BREAD

4 tbsp raw brown sugar
1 oz (25 gm) butter OR vegetable
  margarine
¾ pt (450 ml) boiling water
¾ pt (450 ml) chilled milk
2 eggs, beaten

2 oz (50 gm) fresh yeast OR 2 tbsp
  dried yeast
4 tsp salty seasoning
3 lb (1,350 gm) wholemeal flour,
  sifted
a little cracked wheat

Dissolve sugar and butter in the water in a large mixing bowl. Add cold milk to give fluid at blood heat. Add yeast and leave to froth. Add eggs. Mix salt with some of the flour, and mix in gradually to produce a smooth batter. Leave 20 minutes to set sponge. Beat in sufficient extra flour to produce a soft dough which leaves the sides of the bowl clean. Tip on to floured surface and knead thoroughly (7-10 minutes). Put in greased bowl, covered, to prove. Knock back the dough and knead into rolls or loaves, rolling their surface in cracked wheat. Put into greased tins, cover, and leave to rise again. Bake at 400°F, 200°C, Gas 6 about 15-20 minutes for rolls, 25-35 minutes for loaves. A sweet-flavoured, softer wholemeal bread popular with all the family.

S HIGHER PROTEIN BREAD

1 tsp honey
1 pt (600 ml) warm water
1 tbsp dried yeast OR 2 tbsp fresh
  yeast
1¾ lb (800 gm) 100% wholewheat
  flour

3 oz (75 gm) dried milk powder
2 oz (50 gm) soya flour
3 oz (75 gm) wheatgerm
3 tsp salty seasoning
2 tbsp vegetable oil

In the evening: Dissolve honey in water and activate the yeast. Whisk into 1 lb (450 gm) of the wholewheat flour to make a smooth batter. Cover and leave overnight in a cool place to 'set the sponge'.

Next morning: Sift remaining dry ingredients. Add the oil to the 'sponge' and gradually work in flours to give a soft dough, adding more flour or water as necessary. Knead thoroughly. Put into greased bowl to prove. Knead and shape into 3 loaves, cover and leave to rise again. Bake at 350°F, 180°C, Gas 4 for 30 minutes then reduce the heat to 325°F, 160°C, Gas 3 until cooked (about 45-60 minutes altogether).

ENRICHED BREAD

S

1 tsp honey
½ pt (300 ml) warm water
2 tbsp dried yeast
1½ lb (675 gm) plain 100%
  wholewheat flour
1 pt (600 ml) tepid milk

4 oz (100 gm) wheatgerm
8 oz (225 gm) chick pea flour
12 oz (350 gm) wholewheat flour
4 tsp salty seasoning
2 tbsp sunflower oil

In the evening: Dissolve honey in the water. Activate the yeast. Sift the 1½ lb (675 gm) wholewheat flour. Mix with the tepid milk to produce a smooth thick batter. Cover and leave overnight to 'set the sponge'.

Next morning: Sift remaining flours and salt. Add oil to the 'sponge' and gradually work in the dry ingredients to give a pliable dough. Knead thoroughly. Put into greased bowl, covered, to prove. Knock back and knead into 3 loaves, two large and one small. Prove. Bake at 375°F, 190°C, Gas 5 for 20 minutes then reduce heat to 350°F, 180°C, Gas 4 till cooked, 45-55 minutes in total.

ANN'S GRAIN-FREE BREAD

A

5½ oz (160 gm) potato flour
5 oz (150 gm) gram (chick pea) flour
1 tbsp carob powder
½ tsp fine sea salt OR Biosalt
4 tsp special gluten-free baking
  powder

1½ tbsp ground whole almonds
3 tsp vegetable oil
9 fl oz (275 ml) cold water
1 × 1 lb loaf tin

Oil tin and dust with potato flour. Sift the mixed flours, carob, salt and baking powder. Stir in almonds. Whisk oil and water together and beat into flours, to give soft dropping consistency. Smooth into tin. Bake ¾-1 hour at 350°F, 180°C, Gas 4, till cooked (test as for cake). Cool on rack. Slice and spread carefully – liable to crumble.

Vary your bread batch by using some of the dough for these variations:

CHEESE AND HERB ROLLS

4 oz (100 gm) grated strong cheese
½ tsp dry mustard powder
2-4 cloves garlic, pressed

2-3 tbsp finely chopped parsley
1 lb (450 gm) prepared bread dough
  ready for final proving

Mix first 4 ingredients. Punch dough into thin circle and cover with mixture. Roll up the dough and continue to knead until evenly distributed. Divide and knead into 6-8 rolls. Place on greased baking sheet, cover and prove. Bake 15-20 minutes at 400°F, 200°C, Gas 6.

SWEET CINNAMON BREAD

4 oz (100 gm) dark muscovado sugar
1-1½ tsp powdered cinnamon
½ tsp powdered allspice

1 lb (450 gm) prepared bread dough
ready for final proving

Mix dry ingredients together. Punch dough into thin circle and cover with mixture. Roll up the dough and continue to knead until evenly distributed. Shape into small loaf. Cover, prove and bake with other loaves.

WHOLEMEAL SCONES

¼ tsp salty seasoning
2 oz (50 gm) dark Muscovado sugar
¼ pt (150 ml) milk OR water, warm
1½ oz (32gm) sultanas, washed

2 oz (50 gm) butter OR vegetable
margarine
8 oz (200 gm) SR 100% wholemeal
flour, sifted

Dissolve the salt and sugar in milk. Add sultanas and leave to swell. Rub fat into the flour. Add the liquid and sultanas and lightly work together, adding a little more milk if necessary to give a smooth soft dough. Knead on floured board till smooth and free from cracks. Roll to ½" thick, cut into shapes, and put on floured baking tray. Brush tops with milk. Bake at 375-400°F, 190-200°C, Gas 5-6 for about 20 minutes. Wrap in clean tea-towel on a wire rack while cooling.

SPICED WALNUT SCONES

½ tsp cinnamon or mixed spice
2 oz (50 gm) raw brown sugar
2 tbsp chopped walnuts
2 oz (50 gm) butter OR vegetable
margarine

8 oz (200 gm) SR 100% wholemeal
flour
milk to mix
1 egg, beaten
(see Wholemeal Scones recipe)

Mix the cinnamon, nuts and half the sugar together. Make scones with remaining sugar and roll out quickly. Sprinkle with the nut mixture, fold into three and roll quickly again. Cut or mark into scone shapes and bake at 375°F, 190°C, Gas 5 for about 15 minutes.

BARLEYMEAL SCONES

10 oz (275 gm) barley meal
⅛ tsp salty seasoning
1¼ tsp baking powder

2 oz (50 gm) butter
1 egg
¼ pt (150 ml) milk (approx)

Sieve dry ingredients together to mix and aerate. Rub butter into the barley flour. Beat the egg with half the milk. Make a well in the centre of the barley mixture and add egg to make a smooth soft dough, adding more of the remaining milk as necessary. Turn on to surface sprinkled with barley meal and knead gently with hands until free from cracks. Transfer to a greased baking sheet and roll out to ½" thick. Mark into squares by almost cutting through. Bake at 375-400°F, 190-200°C, Gas 5-6 for about 20-25 minutes, till lightly browned. Wrap in clean cloth while cooling. Good served warm with Butter Plus.

POTATO GIRDLE SCONES   **GF**

8 oz (225 gm) potato
½ oz (15 gm) butter
Paprika OR cayenne

salty seasoning to taste
potato flour OR brown rice flour

Scrub potatoes and slice in 2 or 3 pieces. Steam and remove skins. Mash potato with butter and season.
  Add sufficient flour to make a workable dough and use for rolling out very thinly. Cut into scone shapes, prick well with a fork and cook on a hot girdle – or a large shallow frying pan, lightly greased, turning carefully. Serve hot with Butter Plus or vegetable margarine.

RYE FRUIT LOAF

16 oz (450 gm) washed sultanas
  (p. 141)
4 oz (100 gm) raw brown sugar
½ pt (300 ml) hot strained herb tea
10 oz (275 gm) 100% rye flour

2 tsp baking powder
2 eggs, beaten
little water
2 × 1 lb loaf tins, greased & floured

Put sultanas and raw sugar into a large bowl and stir in the hot tea. Leave several hours for the fruit to swell. Sift rye flour and baking powder, retaining the bran. Stir eggs into the soaked fruit mixture. Add rye flour and mix thoroughly, adding a little water if necessary to give a soft loaf mixture. Bake for 50-60 minutes at 350-375°F, 180-190°C, Gas 4-5, covering top after 30 minutes to prevent over-browning. Cool on rack, wrapped in a tea-towel. Serve cold sliced with Butter Plus or margarine.

MOLASSES AND APPLE LOAF

6 oz (175 gm) apples, thinly sliced
4 fl oz (125 ml) water
4 oz (100 gm) molasses sugar
1 tsp cinnamon
¼ tsp powdered cloves
¼ tsp powdered nutmeg

3 oz (75 gm) butter OR vegetable
  margarine
12 oz (350 gm) SR 100% wholemeal
  flour, sifted
1 egg, beaten

Gently cook apples in water with sugar until soft. Cool and liquidize with spices. Rub butter into flour. Add gradually to the apple mixture with the egg, stirring to keep smooth. Pour into greased tin and bake at 350°F, 180°C, Gas 4 for about 30 minutes.

PASTRY

Wholemeal pastry-making is different from white pastry. Forget about keeping everything cool. Wholemeal pastry has not the elasticity of white and so cannot be stretched or rolled so very thinly. The wholegrain flour is heavier, of course, so there are fewer pastry variations. But, with a little practice, you will soon be making delicious short wholemeal pastry. Experiment to find the method which suits you best.

Practical tips for wholemeal pastrymaking

Choose finely ground flour. Using SR (self-raising) 100% wholemeal flour will help lighten the pastry more. Butter makes better pastry than margarine.

Sift the flour to aerate, reserving the residual coarser bran. Keep back enough bran for rolling out, and return the rest to the measured flour. For rubbing fat into the flour, use a large mixing bowl. Cut the fat into the flour with a knife, then gently rub it in with the fingertips in an upward finger-rolling movement. Shake the bowl occasionally to bring the larger lumps to the top. Continue rubbing in until the mixture resembles fine breadcrumbs.

Stir in sufficient water or egg to just bind, without being too wet and sticky, or dry and crumbly. Knead lightly into a ball. Place pastry on large sheet of greaseproof paper on working surface, well sprinkled with bran, for rolling out lightly. Keep the pastry from sticking by sprinkling more bran or flour. Lift the paper to slide off the pastry into flan tin or over pie. Stretching the pastry will encourage tears, but these can be patched with off-cuts, first damping the edges with a wet finger.

Wholemeal pastry scorches readily in a hot oven. Using dark Muscovado sugar darkens the pastry, so heightens this tendency. So bake your pastry at 350°F, 180°C, Gas 4. For flans and quiches, pre-bake the pastry case unfilled (blind) for 15-20 minutes, add the hot filling and complete baking for a further ¼-¾ hour as required by the filling.

Add hot filling to hot pastry; cold filling to cold pastry.

For fruit tarts, gently cook the fruit with very little fluid in a heavy saucepan or closed greased oven casserole before transferring to pastry case.

The best wholemeal pastrymaker I know always creams the fat before mixing it into the flour with sufficient boiling water to bind it into a workable pastry dough. The warm fat keeps the pastry flexible while working. She also advises rolling out and baking all the pastry as soon as it is made. I like to bake excess pastry in wedge-shaped pieces on a flat baking tray, to store in an air-tight tin for use later.

WHOLEMEAL SHORTCRUST PASTRY

8 oz (200 gm) wholemeal flour
4 oz (100 gm) butter OR vegetable
  margarine OR a mixture

1 egg, beaten (optional)
1-2 tbsp water

Make as described above in Tips for Wholemeal Pastrymaking. Bake at 350°F, 180°C, Gas 4.

WHOLEMEAL 'FLAKY' PASTRY

8 oz (200 gm) 100% wholemeal flour
¼ tsp salty seasoning
3 oz (75 gm) soft lard OR butter

1 tsp lemon juice
2 tbsp water, cool
3 oz (75 gm) soft butter OR margarine

Sift finely ground wholemeal with salt. Rub in the lard. Mix lemon juice with water and blend into a workable dough. Cream the butter till light and fluffy. Roll out the pastry into an oblong, then spread ⅓ of the butter over ⅔ of the pastry. Fold over the unspread third, and then the remaining third and pinch edges together to seal in air. Turn to the right and repeat the process till all the butter has been incorporated into the pastry, keeping the board well floured to prevent sticking. For final rolling use greaseproof sheet as the pastry is very brittle. Best for savoury dishes. Bake at 375°F, 190°C, Gas 5.

RICH SHORTCRUST PASTRY

12 oz (350 gm) SR 100% wholemeal
  flour

7½ oz (210 gm) butter
2 eggs, beaten

Tip flour on to a large surface and shape into circle with a hollow in the centre. Chop the butter into the flour. Tip eggs into the well and continue working with fingertips to incorporate all into a pastry dough, kneading lightly. Roll out lightly into an oblong shape and then fold into 3 and seal edges. Turn clockwise, and repeat the rolling and folding twice. Use as required. For two large flan tins, cut pastry into 2 pieces and roll out each to fit one tin. Bake blind, at 350°F, 180°C, Gas 4.

SWEET PASTRY

8 oz (225 gm) 100% wholewheat flour
2 oz (50 gm) raw brown sugar
1 whole egg & extra yolk beaten

5 oz (150 gm) butter OR soft vegetable
  margarine, sliced

Mix flour and sugar and tip on to work surface, make a well in the centre and put in egg and butter. Using fingers, gradually work fat and egg into the flour until all is incorporated. Knead. Roll out once. Bake at 350°F, 180°C, Gas 4.

RICH WHOLEMEAL PASTRY

6 oz (175 gm) butter or margarine

8 oz (225 gm) 100% wholemeal flour

Cream the butter till light and fluffy. Gradually blend in the flour to form a soft dough. Roll out thinly on well floured greaseproof paper. A good short pastry with a good flavour, suitable for sweet or savoury use. Bake at 350°F, 180°C, Gas 4.

QUICK & EASY SHORTCRUST

4 oz (100 gm) 100% wholemeal flour   **½-¾ tsp salty seasoning**
2 oz (50 gm) soya flour   **3 tbsp water**
2 oz (50 gm) barley flour   **6 tbsp vegetable oil**

Sift flours and salt together – or use all wholewheat flour. Whisk water and oil together in a cup. Add liquid all at once to flours and stir lightly together to form a soft dough. Roll out between greaseproof paper sheets. Bake blind at 350°F, 180°C, Gas 4.

WHOLEMEAL QUICHES

Line sandwich tin with wholemeal pastry. Trim top and crimp edge. Pre-bake blind, 15-20 minutes (OR cook completely 20-30 minutes for use cold with a filling requiring no further cooking.)
For base filling, choose from the following:

A. SAVOURY CUSTARD BASE. Use in proportion of 3 eggs to 1 pt (600 ml) milk. (I use 1 egg and 6 fl oz (180 ml) milk for 7″ sandwich tin, twice this for 8″ tin). Warm milk, add choice of herbs, spices, and salty seasonings (see p. 20) and whisk in beaten eggs. Fill hot pre-baked pastry shell with chosen filling, pour over warmed savoury custard to within about ¼″ of pastry rim (allowing for expansion). Bake immediately at 350°F, 180°C, Gas 4, till set and golden (40-55 minutes).

B. THICK SAVOURY SAUCE. A versatile base which can include sliced onions if liked. Use 2 tbsp vegetable oil or butter, 4 tbsp 85% wheatmeal flour and 12 fl oz (350 ml) stock, water or milk (or a mixture). Sauté 8 oz (225 gm) onion in hot oil. Drain and remove. Stir flour into oil till smooth, cooking gently without browning, 1-2 minutes. Remove from heat and stir in fluid and seasoning. Bring to boil, stirring, and simmer 4-5 minutes. (If lumpy, liquidize briefly to rectify.) Stir in onions. Add other quiche filling ingredients, adjust seasoning. Use hot to fill hot pastry case. Bake 30-45 minutes till cooked through.

C. INDIVIDUALITY BASE. Quark, cottage or curd cheese, blended with a little natural yoghurt or savoury sauce, with herbs and salty seasoning to taste can make a good, low-fat, high-protein base for a variety of vegetables. Can be baked or used cold as it is in its fully baked shell.

QUICHE FILLINGS
  • Salmon and tomato in base A or B.
  • Cheddar, Lancashire or Edam cheese, grated, with tomato, oregano or
    chives, in base A or B seasoned with a little mustard, paprika or cayenne.
  • Portuguese – sardine and tomato, with tarragon, in base A or B.
  • Asparagus and cheese in base A, B or C.
  • Maryland – cooked chicken pieces with sweetcorn in base B.

- Cooked chicken, mushroom and onion in base A or B.
- Grilled soya or beef chipolatas and onions in base A or B.
- Cowboy – baked beans and ham pieces (or sliced soya sausages); stir in a beaten egg. Or just baked beans with the beaten egg stirred in.
- Mushrooms and chopped spring onions in base C.
- Vegetable – cooked sweetcorn, peas, carrot rings and green pepper strips in base C.
- Sicilian – green pepper pieces with mushrooms, ham, onions and tomato in base A or B with oregano.
- Prawns and cooked peas in base A or B.

REFRIGERATOR MINCEMEAT

1 lb (450 gm) currants
1 lb (450 gm) seedless raisins
½ lb (225 gm) sultanas

2 oz (50 gm) dried peel
1 lb (450 gm) cooking apples, peeled
  and cored

Use special washing procedure for dried fruits (see page 141). Mince these ingredients together coarsely.

½ lb (225 gm) grapes, halved and
  de-pipped OR seedless grapes
1 lb (450 gm) soft light brown sugar
4 tbsp sherry OR rum

2 oz (50 gm) finely chopped almonds
2 lemons, zest and juice
2 tsp mixed spice

Add these to minced fruits and mix well. Pack into sterilized jars, seal and refrigerate. Can be used uncooked. Will keep up to 6 months in refrigerator.

MINCE PIES

pastry e.g. Rich Wholemeal Pastry
  (p. 137)
6-12 oz (175-350 gm) cooking apples,
  peeled

12 oz (350 gm) prepared mincemeat
  (see recipe above)
1 egg white, beaten
1-2 tbsp demerara sugar

Make pastry. Coarsely grate sufficient apple into mincemeat to adjust sweetness to taste. Roll out pastry thinly and cut into circles for patty pans. Put 1 tsp mixture in each, cover and seal with pastry. Glaze with egg white and sprinkle over the sugar. Bake for 25-35 minutes at 350°F, 180°C, Gas 4.

APPLE FLAN WITH PÂTE SUCRÉE

8 oz (200 gm) 100% wholemeal flour
2 oz (50 gm) soft brown sugar
4 oz (100 gm) firm butter, sliced

2 eggs
apples, finely sliced
honey, sparingly to taste

Pile flour and sugar on to working surface and make a well in the centre. Put butter in centre, with one whole egg and the second egg yolk (reserving the second white for glazing). Using a palette knife chop the butter and eggs into the flour, adding a little cold water to produce a stiff dough. Knead lightly. Roll out and transfer to pie dish. Trim. Bake blind. Cook apple and arrange over pastry base. Drizzle honey over (some apples, e.g. Coxes, need none). Bake at 350°F, 180°C, Gas 4 for about 30 minutes.

A ANN'S JAM OR FRUIT TARTS

2 oz (50 gm) gram (chickpea) flour
2 oz (50 gm) potato flour
½ oz (15 gm) soya flour

1 tsp gluten-free baking powder
2 tbsp vegetable oil
2½ tbsp cold water

Sieve flours and baking powder. Whisk oil and cold water and mix in. Knead into ball and roll out pastry. Cut into rounds and line tart tins. Bake blind near top of oven for 15 minutes at 425°F, 220°C, Gas 7. Allow to cool slightly before removing from tins. Fill with sugar-free jam, puréed or stewed apples or apricots. Eat same day as baked.

A ANN'S DATE TART

2 oz (50 gm) vegetable oil
2 oz (50 gm) potato flour

2 oz (50 gm) gram (chick pea) flour
3 oz (75 gm) grated apple

Mix ingredients, press into tin and cook at 375°F, 190°C, Gas 5 until just golden.
    Meanwhile cook together:

4 oz (100 gm) chopped dates
zest of ½ lemon

¼ pt (150 ml) water

until soft and smooth. Cool slightly and spread over pastry base. Return to oven and cook a further 10-15 minutes.

As a variation, top pastry with stewed apple flavoured with cinnamon and sweetened with sultanas. OR use a mixture of date and apple.

Alternatives to Pastry

However good wholemeal pastry may be, it is still a rich, fat-laden food, best avoided by some. For lower-fat, quick alternatives try wheatgerm, oatgerm, wholegrain breadcrumbs, soya grits, oat or barley flakes, sprinkled over the casserole or fruit. Slices of wholegrain bread, potato mashed with stock or semi-skimmed milk and Savoury Crumble are other possibilities.

SAVOURY CRUMBLE

8 oz (225 gm) barleyflakes, oatflakes
    OR cereal-only muesli base
½ tsp salty seasoning

6 tbsp stock OR water
3 tbsp vegetable oil

Mix dry ingredients. Whisk stock and oil together to blend and stir quickly into flaked cereal. Scatter over top of dish and grill or bake in oven (40 minutes at 350°F, 180°C, Gas 4 will cook the crumble, but be guided by the dish).

Biscuits and Cakes

We all love to reward ourselves with biscuits or cake sometimes, and with good wholefood ingredients it is less of a threat to our total health. At least they contain useful fibre and more trace minerals. As your palate adjusts, gradually decrease the sugar content. Using 100% wholemeal flour and dark Muscovado sugar also adds to the flavour and moisture-retaining qualities of cakes.

For lighter sponges, buy finely ground 100% wholemeal SR (self-raising) flour. Sift to aerate, replacing the bran in the measured flour. Remove all lumps from the moist sugar. The other secret is in the creaming. Use butter or soft vegetable margarine at warm room temperature (not melted). Beat together till really light and fluffy – in texture and colour (creamy). A cake mixer is indispensible for this. Beat in the eggs singly, with a little of the flour with the last 1 or 2, to prevent curdling. Fold in the flour alternately with enough fluid to give a soft dropping consistency (except when oil is substituted for butter, when it will be slacker). Prepare cake tins by lining with greaseproof or silicone paper; lightly oil and flour sandwich tins. Smooth cake mixture into the tins gently. Test cakes before removing them from the oven by inserting a fine skewer or knitting needle. The cake is cooked when no mixture sticks to the skewer. Cakes contract very slightly away from the edge of the tin when done, and when prodded gently with a finger, a cooked sponge will leave no lasting indentation. Let sponge-type cakes rest for 5-10 minutes before turning out of tin on to a wire rack to cool. Fruit cakes can cool in the tin; leave rich ones to go cold in the oven (to discourage sinking centres).

Remember that good cakes made from natural whole ingredients are living foods which will spoil if kept too long. Preserve rich fruit cakes with brandy or sherry: invert cake and prick all over the base with fine knitting needle or hatpin. Pour over the alcohol to moisten all the base. Wrap in greaseproof and then foil. Store in a tin in a cool place while maturing. Every 2 weeks re-moisten base with alcohol and rewrap, until coated with almond icing – or eaten!

Search for dried fruit free from added sugar, mineral oil coating and chemical preservatives – and don't be put off by the appearance of the real thing! (Taste before you judge the black-looking apricots – they are delicious.) As currants tend to be indigestible, I use sultanas and raisins instead. Avoid sticky or sugar-coated dates. Replace dyed glacé cherries with pieces of dried apricot.

Today we usually need to compromise with a special washing technique for dried fruits. Rinse them in 1-2 changes of very hot water to wash off most of the oil coating. Then wash in acidulated water – 1 tbsp cider vinegar to 1 pt (600 ml) water – to remove surface chemical sprays. Drain. Pour over boiling water, return to the boil and skim off any scum. Drain or leave to swell, as appropriate.

With biscuits, coarser flour is good. The secret is always to remove them from the baking tray a few minutes after taking out of the oven. Carefully transfer the still flexible biscuits to wire racks to cool, when they will become crisp. Ensure they are completely cold before storing in air-tight containers, or they will go soft.

BUTTER SPONGE FOR GATEAUX

6 oz (175 gm) SR 100% wholemeal
   flour
6 oz (175 gm) butter
6 oz (175 gm) Muscovado sugar

3 eggs, whipped to a froth
approx 3 tbsp milk to mix
2 × 8" or 3 × 7" sandwich tins, oiled
   and floured

Sift flour, retaining bran. Cream butter and sugar. Gradually beat in eggs with a little flour at the end. Fold in flour alternately with milk to give a soft dropping consistency. Smooth into tins. Bake 350-375°F, 180-190°C, Gas 4-5 for 20-25 minutes. Cool on rack. Sandwich together with cream and honey or home-made jam, fresh strawberries or raspberries and cream or a butter cream.

ORANGE CAKE

This recipe is based on the weight of 3 of the 4 eggs in butter, sugar and wholemeal flour – say 7 oz (200 gm).

7 oz (200 gm) butter or vegetable
   margarine
7 oz (200 gm) Muscovado sugar
grated zest of 1 orange
4 eggs

7 oz (200 gm) SR 100% wholemeal
   flour
orange juice to mix
2 × 8" or 3 × 7" sandwich tins, oiled
   and floured

Cream butter and sugar and beat in zest. Beat in eggs singly, adding a little flour with the last two. Fold in flour alternately with enough orange juice to mix to a soft dropping consistency. Smooth into prepared tins. Bake at 350-375°F, 180-190°C, Gas 4-5 about 25-30 minutes. When cold, sandwich together with home-made marmalade or lemon cheese, or make into a gateau with orange buttercream filling and decorate with flaked almonds.

ORANGE BUTTERCREAM FILLING

4 oz (100 gm) butter
3-4 tbsp honey, to taste
grated zest of 1 orange

2-4 oz (50-100 gm) fine oatmeal or
   wheatgerm or powdered milk
a little orange juice to mix

Cream butter and honey. Beat in zest, oatmeal or wheatgerm until smooth, with a little orange juice, to produce a light buttercream of desired sweetness and spreading consistency.

HEALTHY 'CHOCOLATE' CAKE

5 oz (150 gm) SR 100% wholemeal
  flour
1 oz (25 gm) carob powder
2 oz (50 gm) ground almonds
6 oz (175 gm) butter OR margarine

6 oz (175 gm) Muscovado sugar
3 large eggs
3-5 tbsp milk, to mix
2 × 8″ OR 3 × 7″ sandwich tins oiled
  and floured

Sieve flour and carob, retaining bran. Add almond. Cream butter and sugar. Gradually whip in eggs. Fold dry ingredients into creamed mixture, with sufficient milk to mix. Smooth into prepared tins and bake for 22-25 minutes at 350-375°F, 180-190°C, Gas 4-5. Cool on wire racks. When cold, ice with Mocha Cream Topping (see p. 151).

SPICED COFFEE CAKE

8 oz (225 gm) SR 100% wholemeal
  flour
1 tsp mixed spice
2 tbsp Barleycup or Pioneer
6 oz (175 gm) butter OR margarine

8 oz (225 gm) Muscovado sugar
3 large eggs
milk OR water to mix
3 × 7″ sandwich tins, oiled and
  floured

Sieve flour, spice and Barleycup, retaining bran. Cream butter and sugar. Gradually beat in eggs. Fold in flour alternately with milk to mix. Smooth into tins. Bake at 350-375°F, 180-190°C, Gas 4-5 about 25 minutes. When cool sandwich together with almond icing, mocha cream or quick demerara icing.

ALMOND ICING OR PASTE

8 oz (225 gm) dark Muscovado sugar
8 oz (225 gm) ground almonds/soya
  flour OR a mixture of both

1 egg, beaten
few drops vanilla/almond essence
1-3 tsp lemon juice, as required

Mix sugar and almonds. Mix in egg, flavouring and enough juice to bind into soft dough. Knead until smooth.

QUICK DEMERARA ICING

2 tbsp demerara sugar
carob OR Pioneer OR other flavouring

3 tbsp hot water
dried milk powder

Dissolve the demerara and carob (or other flavouring) in hot water. Add sufficient powdered milk to give a good spreading consistency.

SPICED SULTANA CAKE

6 oz (175 gm) SR 100% wholemeal
   flour
¼ tsp ground ginger
¼ tsp ground cinnamon
¼ tsp mixed spice
6 oz (175 gm) butter OR vegetable
   margarine
6 oz (175 gm) Muscovado sugar

grated zest of 1 lemon
3 eggs
1 tsp honey
3 tbsp warm milk
6 oz (175 gm) washed sultanas
1 oz (25 gm) demerara sugar
7" cake tin, paper lined

Sieve flour and spices, retaining bran. Cream butter and sugar. Add zest. Gradually beat in eggs. Dissolve honey in warm milk. Cool. Fold in the flour alternately with sweet milk and sultanas. Smooth into tin and sprinkle with demerara sugar. Bake at 350-375°F, 180-190°C, Gas 4-5 for 45-50 minutes.

TROPICANA CAKE

8 oz (225 gm) SR 100% wholemeal
   flour
4 oz (100 gm) ground almonds
8 oz (225 gm) butter OR margarine
8 oz (225 gm) Muscovado sugar
grated zest of lemon
4 eggs

a little milk to mix
4 oz (100 gm) dried papaya pieces
2 oz (50 gm) blanched almonds,
   chopped
1 oz (25 gm) whole OR split almonds
8" cake tin, paper lined

Mix flour and ground almonds. Cream butter and sugar. Gradually beat in zest and eggs. Fold in flour with sufficient milk. Mix in fruit and chopped nuts. Smooth into tin, arrange whole nuts across the top. Bake at 300-325°F, 150-160°C, Gas 2-3 about 1½ hours. Keeps well. May be iced with coconut topping, decorated with papaya pieces.

COCONUT TOPPING

6 tbsp butter
4 tbsp honey

desiccated coconut

Cream butter and honey together till light and fluffy. Mix in sufficient coconut to produce desired consistency.

UPSIDE-DOWN CAKE

For cake:
4 oz (100 gm) butter OR vegetable
   margarine
4 oz (100 gm) raw brown sugar
1 tsp thin honey
2 large eggs
4 oz (100 gm) SR 100% wholemeal
   flour
a little milk OR orange juice to mix

For Topping:
2 tbsp extra butter
demerara sugar
blanched almonds, walnuts
large raisins, dates, fig slices OR
   pineapple pieces as available

Line the sides only of 7″ cake tin with greaseproof paper. Topping: Generously spread base of tin with 'topping' butter, to approximate depth of $\frac{1}{16}$″ (1 mm). Sprinkle over even layer of demerara sugar. Arrange nuts and fruit, pushing them down into the butter. Cake: Cream butter and sugar. Beat in honey and eggs. Fold in flour with liquid to mix. Carefully smooth over the arranged base. Bake at 350-375°F, 180-190°C, Gas 4-5 about 30-40 minutes. Turn upside-down while hot. Ready to eat when cool.

FORESIGHT CHRISTMAS CAKE

4 oz (100 gm) dried apricots, minced
8 oz (225 gm) sultanas
6 oz (175 gm) raisins
4 oz (100 gm) cut mixed peel
1 can (15 oz) pineapple in natural juice
7 oz (200 gm) butter OR margarine
5 oz (150 mg) dark Muscovado sugar
3 large eggs
10 oz (275 gm) SR 100% wholemeal flour
9″ cake tin, prepared specially (see p. 141)
4 oz (100 gm) split almonds
2-4 tbsp sherry OR brandy (needed to preserve cake if not being eaten within 2 weeks)

Wash dried fruit (see p. 141). Drain, then soak 1 hour in the juice from the pineapple. Add chopped pineapple. Prepare tin with several layers of lining greaseproof paper. Cream butter and sugar. Beat in eggs with a little of the flour. Fold in flour and then drained fruit to give a soft dropping consistency. Spoon into tin. Bake for ½ hour at 325°F, 160°C, Gas 3 then arrange split almonds in a pattern on the top. After a further ¾ hour reduce heat to 300°F, 150°C, Gas 2 and cover top with layers of greaseproof paper if necessary to prevent over-browning. Bake until done (1¾-2¼ hours in all). Cool. Preserve cake with sherry while maturing (see p. 141). Decorate cake with wide red ribbon or a Christmas cake frill, and/or flowers.

RICH CHRISTMAS OR WEDDING CAKE

4 oz (100 gm) currants
1 lb (450 gm) raisins
2 lb (900 gm) sultanas
8 oz (225 gm) cut peel
8 oz (225 gm) dried apricots
10 oz (275 gm) tinned pineapple in own juice
6 oz (175 gm) chopped walnuts
1½ lb (675 gm) 100% wholemeal flour
1 tsp salt
1½ tsp baking powder
1½ tsp mixed spice
½ tsp cinnamon
6 oz (175 gm) ground almonds
1¼ lb (550 gm) butter
1¼ lb (550 gm) dark Muscovado sugar
3 dessertspoons black treacle
1 large lemon, grated zest & juice
9 large eggs
a little brandy

Line a 10-12″ tin with 3 layers of greaseproof paper and with a band of folded newspaper tied around the edge. Wash fruit (see p. 141) and drain. Chop apricots and pineapple into small pieces and mix with prepared fruit. Pour over pineapple juice from the tin. Leave soaking overnight. Add walnuts.

Sift flour, salt, baking powder and spice, retaining bran. Mix in almonds. Cream butter, add sugar and cream again till light and fluffy. Beat in zest and black treacle. Beat in eggs singly, adding a little of the flour with the last two. Drain fruit from any surplus juice. Coat in a third of the flour mixture. Fold dry ingredients into the creamed mixture, using lemon juice and drained soaking water as necessary to maintain a soft dropping consistency. Stir in the fruit to distribute it evenly. Spoon into prepared tin and smooth out to leave a slight hollow in the centre. Set on baking tray covered with several layers of newspaper.

Bake for 1 hour at 325°F, 160°C, Gas 3. Cover top of cake with several layers of brown paper and bake for the next hour at 300°F, 150°C, Gas 2. Complete baking at 275°F, 140°C, Gas 1, testing with fine skewer. Large deep cake will take about 5-6 hours. When cold use brandy as preservative (see p. 141).

EGGLESS FRUIT CAKE

12 oz (350 gm) SR 100% wholemeal
 flour
¼ tsp cinnamon
¼ tsp allspice
¼ tsp ground ginger
8 fl oz (250 ml) sour cream OR milk OR
 yoghurt OR buttermilk
1 tbsp black treacle

8 oz (225 gm) butter OR vegetable
 margarine
8 oz (225 gm) dark Muscovado sugar
½ tsp soda bicarbonate
1 lb (450 gm) mixed dried fruit,
 washed
8½" cake tin, paper lined

Sieve flour and spices, retaining bran. Slightly warm the sour cream or alternative and dissolve black treacle in it. Cool. Cream butter and sugar till light and fluffy. Fold in a little flour. Mix soda bicarbonate with sour milk till it froths. Fold into the mixture alternately with remaining flour and the fruit. Bake at 350-375°F, 180-190°C, Gas 4-5 for 1-1¼ hours.

MOLASSES TOFFEE TOPPING

1 tbsp butter
2½ tbsp molasses sugar

1 tbsp orange juice

Gently heat all together and simmer, stirring, for five minutes. Pour over cake while hot.

DATE AND WALNUT CAKE

½ pt (300 ml) boiling water
8 oz (225 gm) dates, chopped
1 tsp bicarbonate of soda
10 oz (275 gm) SR 100% wholemeal
 flour
3 oz (75 gm) butter OR 6 tbsp
 vegetable oil

8 oz (225 gm) raw brown sugar
2 eggs, beaten
½ tsp vanilla
3 oz (75 gm) chopped walnuts
8½" cake tin, paper lined

Pour boiling water over dates, and mash together with soda bicarbonate. Cool. Sieve flour, retaining bran. Either rub butter into flour, add sugar and mix in eggs and other ingredients OR use oil and mix all ingredients in one bowl, beating well. Smooth into tin and bake at 350-375°F, 180-190°C, Gas 4-5 about 40 minutes. Make Fudge or Molasses Toffee Topping, pour over, and decorate with walnuts.

FUDGE TOPPING

2 tbsp butter
5 tbsp raw Muscovado sugar

2 tbsp cream
walnuts for decoration

Heat butter, sugar and cream gently together and boil for one minute, stirring. Pour over cake while hot. Decorate with walnuts.

MARMALADE CAKE

4 oz (100 gm) marmalade
4 oz (100 gm) black treacle
3 oz (75 gm) butter OR vegetable
  margarine
8 oz (225 gm) raw Muscovado sugar
12 oz (350 gm) plain 100% wholemeal
  flour

¼ tsp ground ginger
¼ tsp ground cinnamon
2 eggs, beaten
2 tsp bicarbonate of soda
½ pt (300 ml) milk at blood heat
7" cake tin, paper lined

Weigh a large saucepan empty and then re-weigh as you add the marmalade, treacle, butter and sugar. Heat together gently, stirring, till dissolved. Cool. Sift flour and spices, retaining bran. Stir eggs into mixture in saucepan. Dissolve soda bicarbonate in warm milk. Mix in milk mixture alternately with flour. Smooth into tins. Bake at 300-325°F, 150-160°C, Gas 2-3 for 50-60 minutes. When cold, top with a spread made from marmalade, curd cheese and honey, creamed together.

HONEY AND COCONUT ROLL

3 oz (75 gm) fine SR 100% wholemeal
  flour
3 eggs
2½ oz (62 gm) clear honey

Swiss roll tin, lined with
  greaseproof paper and oiled
2-3 tbsp desiccated coconut
filling of choice

Sift flour 3 times, retaining bran. Whisk eggs and honey over hot water until light and thick enough to retain impression of whisk. Fold in flour gently. Transfer to prepared tin, tilting it to spread mixture. Bake 10-12 minutes at 425°F, 220°C, Gas 7, till golden. Sprinkle coconut over a second piece of greaseproof laid over a hot damp cloth. Without delay invert hot cake on to the coconut. Peel off oiled paper and roll up carefully with the coconut paper still in place. Cool on wire rack. Unroll, remove paper, and spread with warmed sugar-free jam OR ripe banana mashed with honey, coconut and curd cheese or tofu. Re-roll. Variation: for a 'chocolate' Swiss roll use 2 tbsp carob powder dissolved in 1 tbsp hot water. Add to sponge mixture when folding in flour. When cool fill with half quantity Curd Cheese Icing and re-roll. For low-fat cake, omit coconut.

BABY'S BIRTHDAY CAKE

4 oz (100 gm) fine SR wholemeal
 flour
4 oz (100 gm) dates, chopped
4-5 fl oz (100-125 ml) apple OR
 pineapple juice

½ tsp bicarbonate of soda
4 oz (100 gm) soft vegetable
 margarine, butter OR oil
2 eggs, beaten
7″ cake tin, paper lined

Sift flour, retaining bran. Heat dates in 4 fl oz fruit juice and mash till pulpy. Cool. Stir in bicarbonate. EITHER cream margarine and beat in other ingredients, adding extra fruit juice if needed. OR make in food processor, using oil instead of margarine, when consistency should be slacker. Smooth into oiled tin and bake ¾-1 hour at 350°F, 180°C, Gas 4. Cool on rack.

For novelty cakes choose appropriately shaped baking containers: e.g. Pyrex pudding basin for teddy, cat, snowman, etc., loaf tin for train, house, etc., empty can for locomotive boiler. (Allow longer baking time for denser containers.) Shape, join and fill cold cake pieces with date pulp (dates mashed in boiling water, cooled) or with Curd Cheese Icing (p. 161). Decorate with sultanas, raisins, apricots, halved grapes and satsuma segments to the limit of your imagination!

Jackie Applebee of the Wholefood Cookery School in Leicester, has kindly contributed her recipe for this easily digestible fruit cake:

VEGAN CAKE

20 oz (525 gm) mixed dried fruits
2 oz (50 gm) mixed dried peel
1½ pts (900 ml) boiling water
8 oz (225 gm) 100% wholemeal flour
1 tbsp carob powder
1 tbsp Barleycup
¼ tsp ginger or cinnamon

¼ tsp nutmeg or allspice
6 tbsp soya flour*
2 oz (50 gm) ground almonds
2 fl oz (50 ml) corn oil
¾ pt (450 ml) Guinness* (measured
 below froth)
1-2 tbsp brandy (approx)

Wash dried fruits as on p. 141. Leave fruit to swell in the boiling water. Cool. Sift dry ingredients, retaining bran. Stir in ground almonds and work in the oil. Mix in the Guinness, drained fruit, and sufficient of the fruit water to produce a creamy pouring consistency. Pour into lined tin and leave standing overnight (about 12 hours) in a warm place, for fermentation to take place. Bake at 300°F, 150°C, Gas 2 for 6-7 hours. When cold, prick base with needle and pour over brandy as a preservative. Store wrapped in greaseproof paper, in a cake tin.

* Denotes raising agents.

FRUITY GINGERBREAD

1 lb (450 gm) 100% wholemeal flour
¼ tsp salty seasoning
2 tsp ground ginger
1 tsp ground cinnamon
2 tsp baking powder
8 oz (225 gm) vegetable margarine
8 oz (225 gm) raw Muscovado sugar
  OR molasses sugar
4 oz (100 gm) currants
14 oz (400 gm) sultanas

4 oz (100 gm) chopped glacé ginger
2 oz (50 gm) chopped dried orange
  peel
8 oz (225 gm) black treacle OR
  molasses
¼ pt (150 ml) warm milk
1 tsp soda bicarbonate
3 eggs, beaten
10″ square tin OR roasting tin, paper
  lined

Sift flour, salt, spices and baking powder, retaining bran. Rub in the fat. Stir in sugar and washed fruits (see p. 141). Dissolve treacle in milk, and stir in the soda. Pour the milk mixture and eggs into the dry ingredients and mix to a soft dough. Smooth into large square lined tin and bake at 350°F, 180°C, Gas 4 about 1¼-1½ hours. Mature 3-4 days before cutting.

ARROWROOT SPONGE

GF
LF

2½ oz (65 gm) arrowroot
2 tsp gram (chickpea) flour
1 tsp gluten-free baking powder

pinch sea salt
3 eggs, beaten
4 oz (100 gm) light Muscovado sugar

Oil and dust 2 × 7″ sandwich tins with gram flour. Sift twice the arrowroot, baking powder, flour and salt. Whip eggs alone till thick and gradually beat in sugar. Fold in dry ingredients and smooth into tins immediately. Bake at 350-375°F, 180-190°C, Gas 4-5 for 8-10 minutes. Cool. Fill with ripe banana mashed with tofu and honey.

ANN'S GRAIN-FREE FRUIT CAKE

A

3 oz (75 gm) minced dried apricots
8 oz (225 gm) sultanas
5 oz (150 gm) raisins
12 fl oz (350 ml) pineapple juice
3 tbsp sunflower oil
3 oz (75 gm) grated carrot
6 oz (175 gm) grated sweet apple
2 oz (50 gm) soya flour

4 oz (100 gm) potato flour
3 oz (75 gm) chickpea flour
2 tbsp gluten-free baking powder
2 tsp mixed spice
2 tsp cinnamon
4 oz (100 gm) ground almonds (or
  nuts)

Oil and flour 8″ tin using potato flour. Wash dried fruit (see p. 141). Soak in pineapple juice. Add oil, grated carrot and apple, quickly stirring to prevent oxidation. Sift dry ingredients and mix well. Cook at 400°F, 200°C, Gas 6 about 1 hour till just done.

NOTE TO THOSE SENSITIVE TO WHEAT
Most of the recipes can be made with wholemeal rye and barley flour in place of wholewheat flour. Barley flour is better in pastry than in bread. Oatmeal is good in biscuits; yellow maizemeal in breads. Experiment! Chickpea flour (gram or garbanzo flour) tastes good in many recipes too. Potato flour is more refined and less recommended for extensive use.

MELROSE BISCUITS

8 oz (225 gm) butter OR margarine
6 oz (175 gm) Muscovado sugar
1 egg yolk
grated rind of 1 orange
10 oz (275 gm) 100% wholemeal flour

2 oz (50 gm) cornflakes
1 egg white, lightly whisked
pieces of dates OR dried apricots for
   decoration

Cream butter and sugar. Beat in the egg yolk and orange rind. Stir in flour and cornflakes. Space out teaspoonsfuls of the mixture on to 3 greased baking sheets and flatten slightly. Brush egg white over the biscuits. Top with a piece of date or apricot. Bake at 350-375°F, 180-190°C, Gas 4-5 for about 20 minutes, until golden. Remove carefully to rack to cool, when they will become crisp.

SULTANATES

4 oz (100 gm) butter OR margarine
6 oz (175 gm) raw brown sugar
2 eggs
8 oz (225 gm) SR 100% wholemeal
   flour

½ tsp powdered cinnamon
¼ tsp ground nutmeg
¼ tsp powdered cloves
10 oz (275 gm) sultanas, washed
3 oz (75 gm) chopped nuts

Cream butter and sugar, and beat in eggs. Sieve dry ingredients retaining the bran, and fold in. Stir in fruit and nuts. Drop teaspoonsfuls on to greased baking sheet or patty tins. Bake at 350-375°F, 180-190°C, Gas 4-5 for 10-20 minutes according to size.

MELTING MOMENTS

4 oz (100 gm) wholemeal flour
2 oz (50 gm) fine oatmeal
2 oz (50 gm) riceflour

7 oz (200 gm) butter (*not* margarine)
3 oz (75 gm) soft light brown sugar
½ tsp vanilla essence

Sift the 3 flours. Cream butter and sugar. Add vanilla. Fold in the flours. Put teaspoonsfuls on to greased baking trays. Bake at 350-375°F, 180-190°C, Gas 4-5 for 12-15 minutes. Cool on rack.

AFGHAN BISCUITS

9 oz (250 gm) butter OR margarine
4½ oz (135 gm) raw Muscovado
   sugar
½ tsp vanilla essence

8 oz (225 gm) SR 100% wholemeal
   flour
5 tbsp carob powder
3 oz (75 gm) cornflakes

Cream butter and sugar. Add vanilla. Sift flour and carob, retaining bran. Fold in, with the cornflakes. Space teaspoonfuls on greased baking sheets. Bake at 350°F, 180°C, Gas 4 for about 10 minutes. Cool on rack.

AUSTRIAN CHOCOLATE BISCUITS

1 oz (25 gm) carob powder
4 oz (100 gm) SR 100% wholemeal
   flour

4 oz (100 gm) butter or margarine
2 oz (50 gm) Muscovado sugar
¼ tsp vanilla essence

Sift carob and flour, retaining bran. Cream butter and sugar. Add vanilla. Fold in dry ingredients. Roll teaspoonfuls of the mixture into balls and space out on greased baking sheets. Flatten with wet fork. Bake at 350°F, 180°C, Gas 4 for about 12 minutes. Cool on rack. When cold, sandwich together in pairs with mocha butter filling.

MOCHA BUTTER FILLING (OR TOPPING)

1 tbsp Barleycup or Bambu
2½ tbsp carob powder
4 tbsp boiling water
2 oz (50 gm) butter

4 oz (100 gm) Muscovado sugar
vanilla or rum to taste (optional)
4-8 tbsp powdered milk (optional)
a little milk (optional)

Mix Barleycup and carob to a smooth paste with boiling water. Cream butter and sugar. For Mocha Butter Filling, beat in mocha paste, adding a few drops of preferred flavouring. To produce Mocha Cream Topping (less sweet and rich) beat in powdered milk with sufficient milk to give desired taste and consistency.

FORESIGHT SHORTBREAD

4 oz (100 gm) brown rice flour
4 oz (100 gm) 100% wholemeal flour

4 oz (100 gm) pale Muscovado sugar
6 oz (175gm) firm butter

Mix flours with sugar and tip on to work surface. Put lump of butter in the centre and cover with flour. Using the hands, gradually knead butter into the flour, till all is evenly incorporated. Divide into 3 flan tins, pushing and patting to obtain even depth (or roll out). Prick all over with a fork. Bake at 300-325°F, 150-160°C, Gas 2-3 till just done but not coloured. Cut into pieces while warm.

CRISP GINGER BISCUITS

4 oz (100 gm) plain wholewheat flour
1 tsp ground ginger
¼ tsp Garam Masala
2 oz (50 gm) butter or vegetable
   margarine

3 oz (75 gm) raw brown sugar
2 tsp honey
½ tsp bicarbonate of soda
1 tbsp milk, approx.

Sift flour and spices together. Cream butter, sugar and honey. Dissolve bicarbonate of soda in the milk. Mix flour into creamed mixture, adding the milk to make into a soft pastry dough. Add a little more milk if necessary. Roll out thinly (⅛"-¹⁄₁₀" thick) and cut into small round biscuits. Place on 2 greased baking trays and bake 10-12 minutes at 300°F, 150°C, Gas 2, until golden. Cool on rack.

FORESIGHT FOUR-GRAIN BISCUITS

7 oz (200 gm) butter
7 oz (200 gm) raw Barbados sugar
7 oz (200 gm) plain wholemeal flour
½ tsp bicarbonate of soda

5 oz (150 gm) sugar-free muesli base
   (Browns or Prewetts)
2 oz (50 gm) desiccated coconut

Cream butter and sugar. Sift flour and bicarbonate and mix with cereal muesli and coconut. Stir dry ingredients into creamed mixture. Roll into small balls and place on 2-3 greased oven trays. Bake 20-25 minutes at 325-350°F, 160-180°C, Gas 3-4. Cool on rack.

DATE CRACKERS

10 oz (275 gm) stoned dates,
   chopped
¼ pt (150 ml) boiling water
finely grated rind of 1 lemon
juice of ½ lemon
7 oz (200 gm) butter

7 oz (200 gm) dark or soft brown
   sugar
8 oz (225 gm) 100% wholemeal flour
½ tsp bicarbonate of soda
5 oz (150 gm) rolled oats (not
   pre-cooked)

Mash the dates with boiling water, heating if necessary. Stir in lemon rind and juice. Cool. Cream butter and sugar. Sift flour and soda bicarbonate, and mix in the oats. Mix with the creamed mixture. Spread half the crumb mixture over base of tin and press down firmly (about ¼" thick). Spread over the date pulp and then the remaining crumb mixture. Press down lightly. Bake 35-45 minutes at 325°F, 160°C, Gas 3. Cut into squares while warm.

OATMEAL DIGESTIVE BISCUITS

8 oz (225 gm) fine oatmeal
¼ tsp bicarbonate of soda
¼ tsp salty seasoning

2 oz (50 gm) raw Muscovado sugar
3 oz (75 gm) butter OR margarine
little beaten egg

Mix dry ingredients and rub in the butter. Add just sufficient egg to produce a pastry dough. Roll out thinly and cut into circular biscuits. Bake at 350°F, 180°C, Gas 4 about 8-10 minutes. Cool on rack.

OATCAKES

10 oz (275 gm) fine oatmeal
½ tsp sea salt

2 tbsp oil
7 tbsp water, approx.

Mix dry ingredients and make a well in the centre. Whisk oil and water together in a cup and pour on to oatmeal, combining to give a soft dough (add a little more water if needed). Sprinkle board with oatmeal and roll out very thinly. Cut circles for biscuits and place on greased oven trays. Bake at 375-400°F, 190-200°C, Gas 5-6 about 20 minutes without browning. Cool on rack. Serve with Butter Plus and Tastex or cheese.

BISCUITS FOR JOY

4 oz (100 gm) brown rice flour
½ tsp bicarbonate of soda
2 oz (50 gm) desiccated coconut

6 oz (175 gm) rolled oats
7 oz (200 gm) sunflower margarine
6 oz (175 gm) raw brown sugar

Sift rice flour with soda bicarbonate. Mix in coconut and rolled oats. Cream margarine and sugar. Mix dry ingredients into creamed mixture. Roll into small balls and place on 2 greased baking sheets. Bake 15-20 minutes in a slow oven 300°F, 150°C, Gas 2. Cool on rack. (Joy is allergic to wheat, rye, corn and milk.)

'REGULATORS'

8 oz (225 gm) SR 100% wholemeal
   flour
½ tsp mixed spice
¼ tsp salty seasoning
4 oz (100 gm) fine bran (oat, wheat OR
   soya)
4 oz (100 gm) raisins OR sultanas
1 oz (25 gm) chopped walnuts

4 oz (100 gm) honey
4 oz (100 gm) butter OR margarine
2 oz (50 gm) raw Muscovado sugar
½ tsp bicarbonate of soda
¼ pt (150 ml) natural yoghurt OR
   milk
2 eggs, well beaten

Sift flour, spice and salt, and mix in the bran. Wash the dried fruit and add to nuts. Weigh a saucepan empty, then add honey to right weight. Add butter and sugar and melt together gently till well mixed. Cool. Dissolve bicarbonate of soda in the yoghurt or milk. Whisk the egg into the honey mixture. Stir in flour and yoghurt alternately, then fruit and nuts, and mix well. Drop teaspoonfuls of the mixture on to a greased baking sheet. Bake 375°F, 190°C, Gas 5 for about 10 minutes. These spiced bran biscuits are useful for boarders and campers away from good wholefood cooking!

SULTANA BRAN MUFFINS

4 oz (100 gm) plain 100% wholemeal
   flour
1 oz (25 gm) dried milk powder
⅛ tsp salty seasoning
2½ tsp baking powder
4 oz (100 gm) fine bran, oat OR soya

8 fl oz (250 ml) milk
4 tbsp honey
1 egg
3 tbsp sunflower OR safflower oil
6 oz (175 gm) sultanas

Sift the mixed flour, milk powder, salt and baking powder into a large bowl. Lightly mix in the bran. Warm a little of the milk and dissolve the honey. Beat the egg with all the milk and the oil. Make a well in the centre of the dry ingredients, pour in the wet ingredients, add sultanas and stir to give a slack mixture. Grease and flour 24 patty tins or lay out paper cases on 2 baking sheets. Put spoonfuls of muffin mixture into each. Bake at 375-400°F, 190-200°C, Gas 5-6 for about 20 minutes.

154

A ANN'S TEA BISCUITS

3 oz (75 gm) chickpea (gram) flour
1 oz (25 gm) potato flour
3 tsp gluten-free baking powder

2 tbsp sunflower OR soya oil
3 tbsp water

Sieve dry ingredients. Whisk together the oil and water and add, kneading to mix. Divide into 6, roll into balls and flatten slightly on greased baking tray. Bake at 425°F, 220°C, Gas 7 for about 15-20 minutes, until golden. Serve fresh, with spreading of choice.

Note to those sensitive to wheat – see page 149.

Sweet Snacks

Why cut down on chocolates?

What is wrong with chocolate? Most of us will admit that, while we realize chocolates are not really good for us, we still enjoy indulging in them! We prefer to forget its association with acne, migraine, obesity, tooth decay, diabetes and coronary disease.

Cocoa and chocolate both contain caffeine and theobromine; drug-like chemicals which upset your digestion, make your heart beat faster and make you 'nervy'. Breast-feeding mothers are well advised to avoid cocoa and chocolates totally, as the caffeine and theobromine reaching baby through the breast milk may produce diarrhoea, constipation, eczema and/or irritability.

Chocolate is one of the most common sources of allergy. It can be a causative factor in headaches, migraine, depression, confused mental states, hyperactivity and anxiety neuroses. While it is commonly believed that milk chocolate drinks are a good source of calcium, the oxalic acid present in cocoa makes the calcium unabsorbable by the body.

Carob as a superior alternative

Carob (the 'locust bean' or 'St John's Bread' are the alternative names for the pods of the carob tree) has much to commend it, both in flavour and in nutritional value. Carob powder is prepared from grinding the roasted pulp of the carob bean pod. It is high in protein and in vitamins A, B1, B2 and niacin and D; and in minerals, calcium, magnesium, potassium, iron, manganese, chromium, copper and nickel. It also has a high pectin content, giving it herbal properties for regulating digestion and protecting against diarrhoea. So it has logical claims to its other name, 'the tree of life'.

Carob contains no caffeine or theobromine, no oxalic acid nor other harmful substances. It has none of the allergenic properties of cocoa and chocolate. It contains more natural fibre and more natural sugars, so it requires less added sweetening. Yet because it contains less fat, it is considerably lower in calories than cocoa. Add to all these advantages the pleasant chocolate-like flavour of carob powder and you will realize the great advantage of using it instead of cocoa.

MOSAIC SQUARES

10 oz (250 gm) broken digestive
  biscuits
2 oz (50 gm) walnuts, rough chopped
4 oz (100 gm) butter

4 oz (100 gm) honey OR Muscovado
  sugar
2 oz (50 gm) carob powder
2 eggs, beaten

Break biscuits into small pieces. Add walnuts. Melt butter, add honey and carob powder, stirring until boiling. Remove from heat. Stir in eggs, biscuits and nuts. Press firmly into a greased 7" square tin and refrigerate. Cut into squares.

CAROB BALLS

1½ oz (35 gm) butter
4 oz (100 gm) carob bar
1 tbsp honey

few drops oil of peppermint
7 oz (200 gm) stale wholemeal cake
   crumbs

Melt butter and carob bar on low heat with honey. Stir till blended. Remove from heat. Stir in peppermint oil and cake crumbs. Roll into balls and store in refrigerator.

FRUIT BALLS

2 oz (50 gm) dried figs OR dates
2 oz (50 gm) dried apricots
2 oz (50 gm) raisins OR sultanas

3 tbsp sunflower margarine
a little carob powder

Wash and dry the fruit (see p. 141). Chop finely or mince and mix well. Cream margarine and stir in. Add sufficient carob powder to enable rolling into balls. Rolling in carob powder will correct any stickiness.

FRUIT AND NUT FUDGE

1 lb (450 gm) raw brown sugar
3 tbsp butter
4 tbsp evaporated milk

4 oz (100 gm) sultanas
2 oz (50 gm) chopped nuts

Boil sugar, butter and milk together until thickened. Remove from heat and beat thoroughly till paler in colour. Add fruit and nuts. Press into greased tray while still hot and mark into squares.

BUBBLES

4 oz (100 gm) butter
2 tsp honey
6 oz (175 gm) raw Muscovado sugar

pinch salty seasoning
4 cups rice crispies, oat flakes OR
   barley flakes

Gently melt butter with honey, sugar and salt, stirring. Boil gently for 5 minutes, then stir in rice crispies and mix well. Press into a greased tin. Cut in squares when cool.

TREACLE CANDY

1 cup black treacle
½ cup cold water

2 tsp butter OR vegetable oil
a little potato flour OR alternative

Put treacle and water in thick based saucepan over low heat to dissolve slowly. Bring to brisk boil. Boil until a little dropped in cold water forms a soft ball. Generously butter a tin and pour in the candy, leaving to cool considerably. When cool enough to handle, flour the hands and work the candy into a ball. Stretch, tease and knead the candy until it becomes paler in colour. Twist into long pieces.

SWEET MILLET BALLS

4 oz (100 gm) butter OR margarine
4 oz (100 gm) raw brown sugar
2 oz (50 gm) coconut

3 oz (75 gm) rolled oats
1 oz (25 gm) flaked millet
flaked millet for coating

Cream butter and sugar till light and creamy. Mix dry ingredients and stir into creamed mixture. Roll teaspoonful into balls and coat with millet. Refrigerate.

FRIDGE SWEETS

4 oz (100 gm) butter OR vegetable
  margarine
4 oz (100 gm) clear honey

2 oz (50 gm) desiccated coconut
2 oz (50 gm) rolled oats
2 oz (50 gm) wheatgerm

Cream butter and honey till light and creamy. Mix dry ingredients and stir in. Press into shallow dish and refrigerate. Cut into squares. Store in fridge.

STRAWBERRY 'LOLLIES'

½ lb (225 gm) strawberries
½ pt (300 ml) natural yoghurt

1 tbsp lecithin (granular)
honey to taste

Liquidize strawberries with yoghurt and lecithin, adding honey to taste. Freeze in lolly moulds. Other fruit may be substituted as available.

Other healthy snacks
Dried fruits: raisins, sultanas, apricots, peaches, nectarines, prunes and bananas.
Nuts (unsalted): cashews, walnuts, cobnuts, peanuts, brazilnuts, tigernuts, almonds, dried broadbeans and sweet chestnuts.
Fresh fruits: especially washed grapes, apples, plums, clementines, etc.
Raw vegetables: carrots, celery, peas, red and green peppers, cauliflower florets, white cabbage stems; chick pea sprouts, etc.
Frozen bananas: just skin and roll them in carob powder before freezing.

Milk and Yoghurt Recipes

Cow's milk was intended by Nature to be the complete food of the young calf. Pasturization enables us to obtain 'safe, fresh milk' but the nutritional value is lessened. (Skimmed milk is not a whole food, but can contribute to lessening total fat in adult diets, and is suitable for yoghurt-making.) Bulgarian yoghurt made from raw goat's milk is the most easily digested and nutritious milk product, after breast milk.

For this you need the real Bulgarian culture but no special equipment. The culture resembles cooked white rice or cauliflower florets, and is a living bacterial 'plant'. The bacterial strain is much stronger than with other yoghurts, so there is no need to scald milk before use. Raw goat's or cow's milk (if obtainable – make sure it is TB tested) can be used to produce a yoghurt of the finest nutritional value.

Pour tepid milk on to the culture in a non-metal container, stirring once (using a wooden or plastic spoon), and leave in a warm room to set. This yoghurt is quite thin – like the whisked sub-cultured yoghurt or very thin cream. At this stage the yoghurt is separated from the culture by straining it through a nylon sieve without pressing the culture. The culture should then be rinsed in cold to tepid water and replaced in more milk to grow and carry on the process, whilst the made yoghurt can be refrigerated until needed. The taste is much stronger and more sour than bought yoghurts – an acquired taste.

These live yoghurts are especially valuable in re-establishing the natural lactobacilli acidophilus bulgaricus flora in the colon when these have been destroyed by antibiotics. Living yoghurt is the best form of pre-digested milk, i.e. can be a useful food in cases where milk is not well tolerated.

Home-made yoghurt from sub-culturing

There are many gadgets on the market for making yoghurt, but a simple way is to use a wide-necked thermos jar. Buy a small pot of natural living yoghurt (e.g. Loseley) and eat all but one tablespoon of it. Heat 1 pt or 1 litre of milk to boiling point, with a 'milk saver' in the large pan, and simmer for 5 minutes to destroy all the bacteria naturally present. Cool to 105°F (blood heat), add the tablespoon of yoghurt and whisk well. Pour into warmed thermos jar, close the lid and leave it in a warm place until set, when the yoghurt is ready. This natural yoghurt is not stabilized and will separate into curds and whey as you use it. So whisk it all well to produce evenly distributed curds in the yoghurt – quite a thin creamy consistency. If desired, the yoghurt may be thickened by stirring in 2 tablespoons skimmed milk powder to 1 pt yoghurt.

Enton Hall way to serve yoghurt

Try your home-made yoghurt stirred with thin raw honey and raw wheatgerm for an easily digested, most nutritious dessert. At Enton Hall it is served this way in the re-education of the digestive tract after fasting.

Fruit yoghurt
Sweeten the natural yoghurt with a little thin honey and/or pineapple juice and add chopped raw fruit as available: sliced ripe banana, red or black currants, chopped sweet apples, chopped ripe pears, dried apricots (which have been soaked for 24 hours, then chopped), strawberries, raspberries, dessert gooseberries chopped, or chopped plums or greengages. Or use stewed fruit.

Quark and soft curd cheese
Quark is made from yoghurt, curd cheese from sour milk. Make your home-made yoghurt with skimmed milk (or skim the cream off the bottle) and hang it in a cloth – or speed the process by covering a plastic colander with a clean tea towel, (standing it in a large bowl) and tipping in the yoghurt or soured milk. Keep a plastic spatula by the colander and give it a stir several times a day, to facilitate faster draining of the whey.

As pasteurized milk does not naturally sour, add a tbsp of fresh natural cottage cheese (e.g. Loseley) to milk at blood heat and incubate in a warmed large-necked thermos jar until set like junket. Then proceed as before to produce soft curd cheese. The whey can be used as a substitute for buttermilk in some recipes, or in scones in place of some of the milk. Any surplus milk available can be converted into quark or curd cheese and frozen ready for making cheesecake, cheese dips or cake frostings.

QUARK WITH FRESH HERBS

1 small clove garlic
4 oz (100 gm) quark OR curd cheese
    (made from 1 pt yoghurt OR milk)
2 tsp chopped parsley
2 tsp chopped tarragon
2 tsp chopped dill
salty seasoning
paprika

Mash pressed garlic into the cheese. Mix in fresh chopped herbs. Season to taste. Refrigerate. Make several hours before needed for the herb flavours to extend through the quark. Eat with salads, biscuits, bread or baked potatoes.

CURD CHEESE OR QUARK WITH DRIED HERBS

4 oz (100 gm) curd cheese made
    from 1 pt soured milk
1 tsp dried chervil
1 tsp dried thyme
herb salt
pinch cayenne pepper
freshly ground black pepper

Mix ingredients, seasoning to taste.
Variation: Coat cheese with crushed sesame seeds and thyme, mixed.

CRUNCH DIP

8 oz (225 gm) curd cheese OR quark
1 tbsp lemon juice
1 tbsp mayonnaise
3 tbsp crunchy peanut butter
4 tbsp natural yoghurt
1 tsp Worcester sauce OR tamari
1 tbsp onions and gherkins, finely
    chopped, lacto-fermented (Eden
    brand)

Mix ingredients. Serve with crudités of small pieces of raw carrot, cauliflower, celery, cucumber, radishes and spring onions.

CUCUMBER DIP

½ cucumber, chopped
1 tsp lemon juice
2 tbsp chopped chives

4 oz (100 gm) curd cheese OR quark
½ tsp garam masala

Liquidize together. Dunk crudités into the mixture: cucumber sticks, raw cauliflower florets, carrot sticks, baby courgette slices, celery sticks; young French beans (steamed for 2-3 minutes then cooled); cubes of sharp dessert or cooking apples dipped in lemon juice and put on toothpicks.

CURRY DIP

½ cup natural yoghurt
½ cup of home-made mayonnaise
¼ tsp paprika

½ tsp powdered ginger
½ tsp curry powder
few drops Tabasco sauce

Mix all ingredients, preferably 2 hours before serving, for flavours to blend.

CRABMEAT PARTY DIP

8 oz (225 gm) curd cheese OR quark
4 tbsp plain yoghurt
1 tbsp home-made mayonnaise

1½ tbsp lemon juice
flaked crabmeat

Mix together. Serve with crudités.

AVOCADO AND YOGHURT DIP

1 large ripe avocado
1 tbsp lemon juice
4 oz (100 gm) curd cheese OR quark

¼ pt (150 ml) natural yoghurt
salty seasoning to taste
freshly ground black pepper

Mash avocado flesh with lemon juice. Blend with cheese and yoghurt. Season. Serve with crudités or with wholemeal toast.

SAVOURY YOGHURT

Traditionally in Eastern Europe, yoghurt is served as a savoury dish. My favourite quick yoghurt snack meal is made from Bulgarian yoghurt mixed with:
    Chopped spring onions, chives, parsley or mint
    Grated raw carrot
    Any beansprouts (mung, alfalfa, etc.)

SPICED YOGHURT SAUCE

1 small onion, sliced
2 tbsp vegetable oil
1 cup chopped apple
1 cup grated carrot
½-1 cup sliced green pepper
1 tbsp wheatmeal flour

1-3 tbsp garam masala (to taste)
3 fl oz (75 ml) hot water
1 pt (600 ml) natural yoghurt
salty seasoning
freshly ground black pepper

Sweat onion in hot oil. Add apple, carrot and pepper and cook till soft. Stir in flour and spices, cooking for a few minutes. Stir in water and simmer till thickened, stirring. Cool slightly. Liquidize with yoghurt. Correct seasoning. Reheat without boiling. Serve with rice and grain dishes.

CURD CHEESE ICING

2-4 tbsp honey, or to taste
8 oz (225 gm) curd cheese

ground almonds, fine oatmeal,
desiccated coconut OR powdered
milk, as required

Cream honey and cheese, adding chosen dry ingredients to give required flavour and consistency. Or use home-made or Whole Earth marmalade or jam in place of the honey. Can be used on wholemeal sponge cakes and biscuits.

See other mock cream recipes in Puddings chapter.

Health Drinks

What should we drink?

The human body needs pure water and oxygen as well as nutrients for the health of every cell. While the answer to our question could easily be 'pure water', it is not the answer which would appeal to most people, accustomed to drinking lots of tea and coffee! We need to know the facts before leading our young children into unhelpful habits.

What is wrong with tea, coffee and cola drinks?

A cup of tea contains caffeine and tannin, as well as many other substances. A cup of coffee has twice as much caffeine as the tea, and soft cold drinks are also likely to be high in caffeine. These chemicals, caffeine and tannin, are comparable to drugs. Caffeine affects the brain by stimulating the central nervous system, producing an emergency 'alert' as stored blood-sugar is released into the bloodstream. This gives us the 'lift' we enjoy from our favourite 'cuppa'. But this false stimulation of the adrenal glands brings the compensating reaction of the pancreas, producing more insulin to rebalance the swinging blood-sugar levels. The same sequence is produced by eating refined sugar – and many people take sugar in, or eat sweet biscuits with their coffee and tea, so worsening the reaction.

Repeated cups of coffee and tea 'to buck you up' put a continued strain on the adrenals and the pancreas and could lead to nervous troubles, possibly to caffeine addiction and frequent headaches.

Caffeine stimulates the stomach to churn faster and encourages the body to excrete extra water as urine (acting as a diuretic). The acceleration of the digestion relieves an over-burdened stomach after an excessively large meal – hence the popularity of the after-dinner cup of coffee. The diuretic effect tends to flush away many needed water-soluble vitamins, to the body's loss.

The acidity of tea and coffee may also upset the digestion.

But you still want to drink tea, so . . . drink weak tea with lemon or milk and you will be binding the tannin in it, and getting less caffeine by choosing to drink it weak. Some teas have more tannin and caffeine in them than others (e.g. Matté tea). Try a variety of China teas – they vary in flavour. Rooibosch Eleven O'Clock Tea tastes similar to Indian tea and has the advantage of being tannin free, and almost caffeine free. Make in the usual way.

Heath and Heather's English Style Herb Tea is a herbal tea similar to traditional tea and can be served with milk or lemon juice.

Japanese twig tea is also tannin free and almost caffeine free, with a mild, pleasant flavour, not requiring milk, lemon or sweetening. The twigs should be simmered for 10-20 minutes, and may be re-used many times until the flavour disappears. This alkaline drink aids digestion and is high in calcium.

Camomile, Rose Hip, Mint and Frutee are other herbal teas to try. There are also many blends of herbs available for refreshing drinks, to which you might like to add a little apple, orange, lime, grape or pineapple juice. Herb teas take longer to infuse than the usual 'quick brew' Indian tea, and deserve to be made in a china teapot free from tannin stains. Use a cosy to keep the pot hot while the herbal tea infuses (5-10 minutes).

For coffee substitutes, see Alternatives, page 20.

Thirst quenchers

GREEN VITALITY

1 cup fresh orange juice	6-8 chives
handful green leaves e.g.	1 sweet ripe apple
2-3 small spinach leaves	4-5 small dandelion leaves
2 sprigs parsley	2 sprigs mint

(This selection of green leaves is available in my garden, compost grown, so I can pick them immediately before use. Otherwise use mustard and cress, parsley, watercress, spring onion tops, etc., as available.)

Wash leaves and apple. Finely slice apple into orange juice in the liquidizer. Remove woody stems and roughly chop the longer leaves. Liquidize till beautifully green. Strain through nylon sieve and drink immediately. (1)

HOME-MADE LEMONADE

6 lemons (or 4 lemons and 2 limes)	6-8 oz (175-225 gm) raw Muscovado
2 pt (1,200 ml) water	sugar

Scrub and dry the lemons. Finely grate the rind of three into half pint (300 ml) of the water. Squeeze the juice from all the lemons and add to the water with rind. Boil the remaining 1½ pt (900 ml) water and pour over the remaining six lemon skin halves and the sugar. Simmer for five minutes then leave to cool. Combine the two when cold: Remove lemon skins and store in clean bottles in refrigerator. Serve diluted 50:50 with water.

BARLEY WATER

½ cup pot barley	2 lemons
2 pt (1,200 ml) water	honey to taste
2 oranges	

Bring barley to boil in the water and simmer, almost covered, for two hours. Scrub fruit skins, squeeze juice. Strain off hot barley water on to fruit skins. Leave to cool. Remove skins. Add juice and honey.

TAMARI DRINK★

1 cup boiling water
1 tsp tamari soy sauce

½ tsp apple cider vinegar†

Pour the boiling water on to other ingredients – vary proportions to taste.

SHOYU REVIVER

1 tsp shoyu OR tamari

1 cup hot Japanese twig tea

Add the shoyu or tamari to the freshly made twig tea. Excellent when suffering from a tension headache.

BEDTIME DRINK

2 tsp apple cider vinegar†
1 glass hot or cold water

2 tsp honey

Mix all ingredients together. This acid drink can aid relaxation and help balance the alkaline salad and vegetable meals.

SLIMMER'S DRINK★

2 tsp apple cider vinegar†
OR juice of ½ lemon

1 glass water

CHILLED ORANGE REFRESHER

2 tsp China tea
1 pt boiling water
juice of 1 lemon
juice of 2 oranges

honey to taste
1 orange sliced thinly
fresh borage OR apple mint
ice cubes

Make the China tea and leave to infuse. Strain and cool. Add other ingredients and serve.

PINEAPPLE VELVET

¼ glass natural yoghurt
½ glass pure pineapple juice

¼ glass pure orange juice

Whisk together, or vary proportions to suit your taste.

★ Not to be taken more than twice a day.
† NB Apple cider vinegar contains malic acid, the acid nearest to that produced by the body. It helps regulate the intestines, dissolve mineral wastes (i.e. in cases of rheumatism and arthritis) and aids digestion and sleep. Small amounts only.

MIXED FRUIT CUP

2 cups orange juice
1 cup pineapple juice
½ cup lemon juice

2 cups water OR rejuvelac (see below)
fresh mint springs

Mix and preferably leave standing for an hour before serving.

REJUVELAC

2 oz (50 gm) organic soft wheat   filtered or bottled spring water

Soak wheat for 10-15 hours. Sprout it for 2 days (see p. 50). Rinse in filtered water. Cover wheatsprouts with 3 cups filtered water in large, ventilated bottle. Keep at room temperature for 24 hours. Strain off the rejuvelac and refrigerate excess till needed. These used wheatsprouts may be used twice more before discarding. The enzyme-rich rejuvelac tastes primarily of water, but is a worthwhile substitute when milk cannot be tolerated.

DO-ME-GOOD DRINK

4 oz (100 gm) carrots
1 bunch parsley including stems
few comfrey leaves (optional)
Tastex, tamari OR shoyu
4 oz (100 gm) celery, including leaves

4 oz (100 gm) spinach (leaves and stems)
green lettuce leaves as available

Wash, but do not peel, then chop vegetables finely and cover with cold water. Simmer gently for 30-40 minutes in covered saucepan. Strain the stock and flavour with Tastex or shoyu to taste. Drink hot or cold as a revitalizing health drink which helps to clear the skin, harden the nails, add life to tired hair and tired people. Taken before retiring it helps to promote sound sleep. A good tonic to take regularly as a health and beauty drink, high in potassium and silicon. It will keep, refrigerated, for 2-3 days.

See also Recovery Broth, p. 64.

Meals in a glass
Not advised for prolonged meal replacement, but for occasional use. All should be sipped very slowly, 'chewing' to mix with saliva, to start the digestion of the liquid meal.

STRAWBERRY SHAKE

½ cup fresh strawberries
1 egg yolk
1 tsp honey

1 cup natural orange juice
3 tbsp natural yoghurt

Blend in liquidizer. Sip slowly. (1-2)

SLIMLINE LUNCH

1 cup tomato juice
2 tsp chopped chives
½ tsp cold-pressed safflower,
   sunflower OR All Blend Oil
2 oz (50 gm) cottage OR curd cheese

2 tsp fine bran (oat, soya OR wheat
   bran)
a little shoyu, tamari OR Worcester
   sauce

Blend in liquidizer. Sip slowly. (1)

FRUIT SALAD SHAKE

1 ripe pear, unpeeled, sliced
1 small sharp ripe apple, sliced
1 cup orange juice

1 small ripe banana, chopped
1 tbsp ground sweet almonds
1 tbsp washed raisins

Liquidize pear and apple with orange juice. Add banana, ground almonds and
raisins. Liquidize till blended. Sip slowly. (1-2)

MANNA FOR MAMA

½ cup natural yoghurt
½ cup orange juice
1 tsp cold-pressed safflower,
   sunflower OR All Blend Oil
½ tsp lecithin granules
½ cup alfalfa sprouts (OR other
   sprouted seeds, beans OR grains)

2 tsp honey
2 sweet eating apples, sliced
1-3 tsp brewer's yeast powder
4 tbsp raw wheat OR oat germ
a little extra orange juice
2 tbsp sunflower seeds OR broken
   nuts

Liquidize yoghurt, orange juice, oil, lecithin, alfalfa sprouts and honey. Add
apple, brewer's yeast and wheatgerm and blend again. Pour into 2 bowls, using
extra juice to rinse out all the Manna. Sprinkle over nuts or sunflower seeds. Eat
immediately, chewing well. This pick-me-up complete meal is high in protein,
vitamins E, F, C and B complex, trace minerals and enzymes. It is palatable and
quickly prepared – good for enhancing the quality of breast milk of a lactating
mother. (2)

FRUIT FOAM

juice of 2 lemons
½ cup natural yoghurt
1 sweet apple, sliced

1½ cups natural orange juice
3 ripe bananas, chopped

Liquidize. Sip slowly. (2)

CAROB PROTEIN DRINK

1 cup milk
1 raw egg yolk
½ tsp cold-pressed All Blend Oil

1½ tsp carob powder
1 tsp honey
1 tbsp raw wheatgerm

Mix well or liquidize. Drink slowly. (1)

MOCK CHOCOLATE MILK SHAKE

1 tbsp carob powder
¾ pt (425 ml) cold milk
¼ tsp cold-pressed safflower OR All
  Blend Oil

honey to taste
a little block carob, grated

Liquidize powdered carob with milk and oil, adding honey to taste. Serve immediately, decorated with a little grated carob. (2)

HOT MOCK CHOCOLATE DRINK

¾ pt (425 ml) warm milk
2 tsp honey OR raw brown sugar

1 tbsp carob powder

Blend milk, carob and honey. Heat till almost boiling and serve. (2)

BANANA SPECIAL

1½ cups water OR rejuvelac
½ cup ground OR broken almonds

1 tsp clear honey
1 very ripe banana

Liquidize. Sip slowly. (2)

MILK-FREE PROTEIN DRINK

2 tbsp sunflower seeds
1 cup water
2 tsp honey

2 tsp wheatgerm
½-2 tsp spirulina powder

Soak sunflower seeds in the cold water for 8-12 hours to start sprouting. Liquidize with other ingredients. Sip slowly. (1)

VITAMIN COCKTAIL

½ cup natural pineapple juice
1 tsp lemon juice
½ tsp cold-pressed safflower OR All
  Blend Oil

1 small carrot, grated OR 2 tbsp
  Biotta carrot juice
½ tsp brewer's yeast powder
1 tsp wheatgerm

Liquidize. Drink immediately, sipping slowly. (1)

SALAD COCKTAIL

1 cup tomato juice
1 tsp chopped parsley
2 tbsp grated carrot
1 tsp lemon juice

1 tbsp chopped watercress (p. 62)
2 tbsp chopped celery
½ tsp brewer's yeast powder
¼ tsp kelp powder

Blend. Sip slowly. (1)

INSTANT NOURISHMENT

1 free range egg yolk
2 tbsp protein powder
1 tbsp lecithin granules
2 tsp cold-pressed safflower,
  sunflower OR All Blend Oil

½ pt (300 ml) milk, rejuvelac OR
  yoghurt
1 large ripe banana, sliced
¼ pt (150 ml) orange juice

Blend briefly the egg yolk, protein powder, lecithin and oil. Add milk, banana and orange juice and liquidize. Savour slowly. This instant meal is suitable for nursing mothers. (2)

Drinks for babies (First see chapter on infant feeding.)

FRESH GRAPE JUICE: Choose large ripe grapes, black or white. Skin, halve and de-pip them. Put into a strong clean finely woven cloth (old handkerchief is ideal) and twist and squeeze to extract the juice. Dilute.

FRESH MELON JUICE: Choose a really ripe melon. Press the melon flesh through a fine nylon sieve. Do not mix with any other fruit as melon digests better when separated from other fruits. Dilute.

FRESH STRAWBERRY JUICE: Cut washed, organically grown strawberries into several pieces and squeeze through a finely woven cloth. Dilute.

FRESH CARROT JUICE: Scrub the carrots, grate them finely, then squeeze through a fine cloth. Dilute.

CASHEW MILK: Soak 4 tbsp broken cashew nuts in 8 tbsp water for one to two hours. Add ½ tsp honey* and blend till smooth.

ALMOND MILK: Liquidize together:
  4 tbsp freshly ground or finely chopped almonds
  8 tbsp cold water
  ½ tsp honey*
OR pound the almonds in a pestle and mortar before liquidizing with the honey and water. Strain through fine cloth before serving. A most nutritious liquid food.

SESAME MILK: Soak 4 tbsp washed sesame seeds in ¼ pt (150 ml) of water for eight to twelve hours in a cool place. Liquidize till well broken up. Strain through fine cloth before serving.

SUNFLOWER SEED MILK: Make as for sesame seed milk.

* Note: Omit honey for babies under 6 months old, or use raw Muscovado sugar instead.

Packed Lunch and Picnics

A packed meal should be balanced, ideally containing wholegrain starch, protein and raw salad stuff and/or a raw fruit. Check that there is at least one ingredient high in vitamin C. Make it varied and appetizing, giving plenty so that the eater is well satisfied. (Dried fruits or home-made biscuits will please those who have a sweet tooth.) Here are some basic suggestions for packed meals:

Muesli† in a jar
Soup† in a vacuum flask or jar
Slice of wholemeal quiche†
Slice of wholemeal pizza†
Wholemeal sandwiches*
Wholemeal scones†
Filled wholemeal rolls†
Special meal in a drink†, chilled in a vacuum flask
Salads† in a closed pot
Unsalted nuts and raisins
Cheese, apples and celery
Wholemeal patties
Ripe bananas and nuts
Stuffed baked potatoes†
Home-made beefburger, celery and watercress
Beanburger†, celery and tomato
Nut rissoles†, cos lettuce and tomato
Pot of ratatouille†, cheese and watercress
Avocado with cottage cheese and walnuts
Home-made fish cakes† with cucumber and carrot sticks
Jar of natural yoghurt†, honey and wheatgerm
Natural yoghurt†, sunflower seeds, chopped red pepper and mung beansprouts†.
Natural yoghurt†, banana and pear
Dip† with crudités (raw vegetables e.g. asparagus, radish, spring onions, cauli-
flower florets, strips of cucumber, celery, red and green pepper).
Vary sandwiches and rolls with special bread recipes†, Ryvita, Nairn's oatcakes,
Healthy Life biscuits, gluten-free Rice Cakes and other additive-free savoury
wholegrain biscuits. Spread sparingly with Butter Plus*, Herb butters†,
clarified butter*, vegetable margarine (see p. 20), Mayonnaise†, Avocado
Dip*, Houmous*, Pease spread†, Tahini Dip*, Sesame Paste*, Crunch Dip†,
Cucumber Dip†, Curry Dip†, Curd Cheese†, Quark† or cottage cheese. Or
drizzle vegetable oil over thick rolls or hunks of wholemeal bread, as some
Spaniards do.

* Recipes follow.
† See index for recipes or instructions.

Suggestions for fillings for your 100% wholemeal bread sandwiches or rolls:

- Tastex and mung beansprouts† (chop the beansprouts into ¼-½ inch lengths to make the sandwich easier to manage!
- White Cheddar cheese, home-made mayonnaise†, alfalfa sprouts†.
- Mashed sardine and chopped watercress.
- Tastex and chopped walnuts with few alfalfa sprouts† or lettuce.
- Grated carrot with coconut and sultanas.
- Watercress, orange slices, chicory and chopped walnuts.
- Cold scrambled egg with a little horseradish sauce.
- Softly boiled egg mashed with lots of fresh chopped chives or parsley.
- Cottage cheese, lentilsprouts† (cut shorter) and natural peanut butter.
- Tastex, sliced tomato and parsley.
- Avocado pear and grapefruit slices with alfalfa sprouts†.
- Sliced cheese with grated carrot and pinch summer savory.
- Cottage cheese with Tastex and either chopped watercress, sliced tomato, cut beansprouts†, finely sliced celery, mustard and cress, sliced cucumber, alfalfa sprouts† or any combination.
- Tartex paste with chopped celery, lettuce or alfalfa sprouts†.
- Cottage cheese mixed with cooked chicken, Tastex or Worcester sauce and cut beansprouts†.
- Cold lamb, sliced dressed salad beetroot† and finely chopped mint.
- Cold chicken with home-made mayonnaise†, shredded lettuce, chopped beansprouts†, mustard and cress, or cucumber and tomato
- Quark† with chopped nuts (and drizzle of honey if desired).
- Quark† with sultanas and chopped nuts.
- Hard boiled egg slices with home-made mayonnaise† and sliced olives.
- Hard boiled egg slices with home-made mayonnaise† and salad ingredients.
- Cottage cheese or quark† mixed with a little blue cheese, with chopped watercress, sliced cucumber, or cut beansprouts†.
- Sliced cold beef with grated carrot and chopped parsley.
- Sliced cold pork with little mayonnaise† and thin slices of apple.
- Sliced cold pork with mashed banana and alfalfa sprouts†.
- Sliced cold pork with cooked stoned prunes and crisp lettuce.
- Home-made mayonnaise† with cut beansprouts†, chopped raw pear and finely sliced red pepper.
- Finely chopped raw cabbage with walnuts and raisins in home-made mayonnaise†.
- Houmous† with sprouted alfalfa†, chopped celery or cut beansprouts†.
- Home-made liver pâté* with cucumber slices or alfalfa sprouts.
- Peanut butter and sultanas.
- Peanut butter, home-made mayonnaise†, sliced tomato and alfalfa sprouts†.
- Tuna fish mixed with home-made mayonnaise†, cut beansprouts† or celery.
- Home-made mayonnaise† with chopped walnuts, celery, apple and grated carrots.

* Recipes follow.
† See index for recipes or instructions.

- Chopped hard dates, softened with a little boiling water, with a squeeze of lemon juice and chopped fresh mint.
- Mashed banana with a trickle of honey and chopped nuts.
- Chopped hard dates, softened with a little orange or pineapple juice, with chopped nuts.
- Soya bean sandwich spread★ with sliced tomato.
- Potted rabbit† with chopped beansprouts or tomato slices.
- Home-made 'jam'★ with sliced apple or banana.
- Cold meat slices with home-made chutney★.
- Cheese slices with home-made chutney★, and alfalfa sprouts†.
- Cashew nut pâté★.
- Sesame paste★ with lettuce, sprouted seeds or roasted buckwheat.
- Grated carrot with home-made mayonnaise†, chopped raisins and nuts.
- Mashed tuna fish with finely sliced onion and tomato.
- Cottage cheese or quark† creamed with home-made mayonnaise†, with finely chopped tart apples, celery and parsley.
- Cottage cheese or quark† mixed with home-made mayonnaise†, slivers of cold chicken and shredded lettuce.
- Tofu mixed with flaked millet and a little Tastex and chopped parsley.
- Tofu mixed with Pear 'n' Apple spread and desiccated coconut.

BUTTER PLUS

4 oz (100 gm) fresh butter (without chemical colouring or preservative)

4 tbsp fresh safflower, sunflower OR All Blend Oil (preferably cold pressed)

Cream butter and gradually beat in the oil. Use for spreading on bread, biscuits, etc., or for butter cream fillings for cakes. Do not heat it or the value of the cold-pressed oil will be lost. This has the flavour of butter plus the advantage of natural (unhydrogenated) polyunsaturates, a good compromise.

AVOCADO DIP

3 tbsp ripe avocado
2 tsp lemon juice

¼ tsp vegetable bouillon powder

Mash avocado into lemon juice and mix in bouillon powder. Use quickly.

CLARIFIED BUTTER

Butter as required

Slowly heat butter and bring to a gentle boil without colouring. Simmer 2-3 minutes. Remove from heat and leave till bubbling ceases. Skim off any surface froth. Decant the liquid clarified butter carefully into serving dish, leaving residual sediment in the pan.

★ Recipes follow.
† See index for recipes or instructions.

CASHEW NUT PÂTÉ

4 oz (100 gm) potato
2 tsp vegetable margarine
1 tsp Tastex
1 egg, beaten
1 tbsp tomato paste

4 oz (100 gm) grated cashew nuts
1 tiny onion, crushed in garlic press
1 tsp chopped fresh mint
1 tbsp chopped fresh parsley

Steam potatoes unpeeled. Skin and mash them with margarine and Tastex. Cool. Beat all ingredients together. Press into small bowl or terrine. Needs no cooking.

HOUMOUS – CHICKPEA PÂTÉ

8 oz (225 gm) chickpeas
1 clove garlic, crushed

1 pt (600 ml) water
Tahini Dip (see below)

Soak the chick peas overnight. Rinse and add water and garlic. Simmer till soft, adding more water if necessary. Drain, mash and measure the mashed peas, adding 5 parts of the peas to 2 parts of Tahini Dip, made as follows:

TAHINI DIP

¼ pt (150 ml) Tahini (sesame seed cream)
7 tbsp finely chopped parsley
5 tbsp lemon juice (approx)
1-3 cloves garlic, crushed

chick pea stock (from above recipe)
    OR water
salty seasoning to taste
½ tsp ground cumin (approx)

Mix first 4 ingredients adding a little chick pea stock if needed to give consistency of smooth cream. Adjust quantities of salt, cumin and lemon juice to taste. This dip is tasty to use as it is. Combine it with the puréed chick peas to produce Houmous in the proportions given above. Houmous makes a nutritious dip for crudités for party, lunchbox, or filling for sandwiches and baked potatoes.

CHICKEN LIVER PÂTÉ

6 oz (150 gm) onion, sliced
1½ lb (675 gm) chicken livers
2 tbsp vegetable oil

1 slice wholemeal bread
2 tbsp parsley, finely chopped
salty seasoning and paprika

Sauté the onion and then the chicken liver in the oil, until tender. Mince with the bread. Blend in chopped parsley and season to taste. Press into bowl or terrine. Needs no further cooking. Eat within 2 days, with salad.

SUGAR-FREE CHUTNEY

½ lb (225 gm) prunes
1½ pt (900 ml) cider vinegar
juice of 1 lemon
1 lb (450 gm) sultanas
2 cloves garlic, crushed
1 lb (450 gm) onions, finely chopped

1 tbsp ground allspice
1 tsp cinnamon
1 tbsp whole cloves
1 tsp mustard seed
4 lb (1.8 kg) prepared cooking apples

The day before soak prunes in vinegar. Remove stones and chop prunes. Into a large preserving pan (not aluminium) put vinegar, prunes, lemon juice, sultanas, garlic, onion and spices. Windfall apples may be used for this recipe, using only the perfect parts of the apples, cut small. Add immediately to the vinegar. Bring to the boil and simmer, uncovered, until sufficiently thick, stirring more frequently as the water evaporates. Pot into hot sterilized jars and seal immediately.

LOW-SUGAR RASPBERRY JAM

4 lb (1.8 kg) raspberries   **2 lb (900 gm) Guyanan demerara**
1 tsp fine sea salt   **sugar**

Gently heat raspberries in preserving pan and bring to the boil. Boil until soft and pulpy. Stir in salt and sugar. Boil for further 10 minutes and test for a set. Pour into heated jars and seal immediately. Redcurrants can be used in place of raspberries. With other fruits longer boiling will be necessary.

FREEZER 'JAM'

While this is not strictly a jam, it is my favourite, as no sugar is needed and the lovely fresh flavour of the raw fruit is retained.

1½ tbsp brown rice flour OR ground   **2 lb (1 kg) raspberries**
    rice   **honey to taste**
7 fl oz (200 ml) water

Mix rice flour to smooth cream with a little of the water, add to the rest of the water and bring to the boil, stirring. Simmer gently for about 4 minutes, until thickened and cooked. Cool. Mash fruit with honey to taste and beat in the rice when it is just warm. Pot into small clean containers, allowing head-space. Freeze. Once thawed, the freezer jam should be stored in the refrigerator, and consumed within three days, hence the need to choose small containers.

APRICOT 'MARMALADE'

4 oz (100 gm) dried apricots   **½ pt (300 ml) orange OR apple juice**
2 oz (50 gm) sultanas   **honey to taste**

Wash the fruit (p. 141). Soak overnight in fruit juice. Bring to boil and simmer till soft. Liquidize with just sufficient juice to produce a thick purée. Mix in honey. Pot and store in refrigerator.

SOYA BEAN SANDWICH SPREAD

3 tbsp cooked soya beans   **3 tbsp crunchy peanut butter**
1 tbsp chopped fresh chives OR   **1 tbsp chopped parsley**
    chopped spring onions   **little Tastex**

Mix everything together. This is a high protein filling.

SESAME PASTE

2 tsp tahini   **1 tsp tamari**
2 tsp lemon juice

Whisk together to produce a tasty protein spread.

Appendices

1. Infant Feeding from Birth to 18 Months

By Mrs Belinda Barnes, Chairman of Foresight Charity, the Association for the Promotion of Pre-conceptual Care.

Mothers who have been on the Foresight programme should be able to approach childbirth in rude health and enjoy a natural birth. From the start the Foresight mum will be able to provide drug-free colostrum (the first breast milk) to an enthusiastically sucking baby. If neither partner is sedated, the baby will become hungry every few hours or even more often and start searching around for the breast. Hopefully he will be kept close beside his mum, so that he can feed on demand, making for contentment for both.

Colostrum is an important first food which contains exactly what the baby needs to cleanse the digestive tract and start the digestive system working smoothly. No other species is denied this vital start – and no other species has 'feeding difficulties' and constant screaming from their young! When the colostrum is laced with anaesthetic, however, the value is more dubious – another reason for making every possible effort to achieve a natural birth.

Gradually, after three or four days of frequent suckling, the colostrum changes to whole breast milk. During the first few months, there should be no arbitrary feeding times – just let the baby feed on demand.

If he is still feeding at 2-3 hourly intervals by three months, it may be that the breast milk is slightly lacking in quantity or in quality. The best way to ensure a steady supply of top quality breast milk is for mothers to take 2 Foresight Vitamins and 2 Foresight Minerals each morning, 2 Foresight Iron Formula each evening and include raw polyunsaturated fats in a wholesome diet. That is, use sunflower seed oil or safflower oil in salad dressings and include such foods as fresh raw nuts, nut butter, milk shakes, seeds, avocados and cooked oily fish in her wholefood diet.

A nursing mother should try to live as 'hassle-free' a life as possible. A contented mum makes for a contented baby.

Let your mother or the neighbours do everything they offer to do – do not underestimate how much they love doing it! In many primitive cultures, mothers with new babies are looked after by female helpers for up to 40 days and nights. It is a deep-seated primitive driving-force to want to help new mothers, so you will be pleasing them by accepting their help, instead of claiming that you are 'all right' while you become more and more tired!

At first, the baby will need a night feed. His tiny tummy will not hold enough to last till morning. Leaving him to cry will not teach him that it is night and he should sleep longer! Far from having this effect, the terror of feeling abandoned and left to starve alone in the dark may stay with him all his life, leaving him with a fear of the dark and nightmares. If he is fed whenever he cries – as every other species (rabbits, horses, pigs, kittens, etc.) can take for granted – as his tummy grows bigger and he takes more milk at each feed, gradually he will be able to do longer and longer stints. After about two months the night gap gets to about eight hours and things begin to look up! By now breast-feeding should be well established and he will probably be gaining 6-10 oz per week.

Despite pressures not to weigh babies for fear of worrying the mother, I think recording successful weight gains each week is a great morale booster. The usefulness of the warning sign of no weight gain is also worth consideration. If the weight gain is poor then a mother will know she needs to look more closely to her diet and increase her intake of fresh natural foods, the B vitamins and polyunsaturated fats. Maybe he should be wakened for more frequent feeding. See the chapter on Health Drinks and the 'meal in a glass' recipes.

Some babies are upset by cow's milk in the mother's diet, in which case all bovine products – milk, cream, butter, cheese and yoghurt – should be avoided while breast-feeding.

Starting mixed feeding

Start from a position of strength, i.e. with the fully breast-fed baby thriving and sleeping well. If the baby is grizzling on a cow's milk, sugar and water formula, or an inadequate supply of breast milk, both mother and baby may be tempted to rush the transition to solids resulting in an upset stomach and the possible start of allergies. There is no need to add fruit juice drinks and cod-liver oil (for vitamins C, A and D) as supplements to the very young baby totally breast fed by a mother who is eating an ideal diet. This consists of natural wholefoods with plenty of fresh fruits, salads, some cold-pressed sunflower oil or safflower oil as salad dressings every day and taking 2 Foresight Vitamins, 2 Foresight Minerals and Foresight Iron Formula to ensure no trace mineral deficiencies. Her breast milk will contain all the nutrients the baby needs in the most easily digested, natural form. It is important that breast-feeding is correctly managed and going well, before introducing any other factors. Ideally start somewhere between 16 and 24 weeks (probably around 16 lbs in weight), with little tiny tastes of fresh fruit juice or strained fruit diluted with a little cooled, boiled water. Pear, grapes, ripe bananas, tomato and stewed unsulphured prunes, raisins and apples are good 'first tastes'. Put half a teaspoon of the puréed fruit into an egg cup and mix with a teaspoon of boiled water, given in tiny sips from a teaspoon. Sit him up on your lap and feed him carefully so that he does not feel in danger of drowning!

First tastes (of one new food only in one day) are best given around 10 am so that should it disagree with him, the complaints will be over by bedtime! When the fruit tastes are happily introduced, half a teaspoon of sieved vegetable can be given after the lunchtime feed and later bone broth. At this stage, always give the full breast feed first and give his tiny tastes afterwards.

Gradually increase the morning helpings of pulped fruit and after 20-24 weeks you can add the first carbohydrate feed – a little baby rice or other gluten-free baby cereal mixed with boiled water at first and later with a few teaspoons of cow's milk. Cow's milk is more likely to produce an allergic reaction when a) either parent has allergies, or b) cow's milk has been introduced in hospital during the first few days of baby's life. Allergy may cause nappy rash, other skin rash (e.g. eczema), runny nose, catarrh or asthma. Crying may indicate it has produced colic or headpains – never ignore crying. There are suitable soya milk alternatives if he proves allergic to cow's milk or he may be able to tolerate goat's milk (see Alternatives).

Remember to start with the smallest amount and increase very gradually. A baby's stomach has to learn how to digest each new food, so never give more than one new food each day. Then if baby grizzles, gets a nappy or other rash, has a runny nose or diarrhoea, you know which food to suspect and can remove it from his diet. Right at the start if a food upsets him, leave it out. Six months later he may be able to take it – but notice again if it upsets him and cut it out. This is the way to avoid developing allergies.

If many dietary restrictions have to be continued after the cessation of breast-feeding, seek professional advice from a Foresight Clinician, or a qualified dietician or nutritionist who fully understands allergy problems. Refer to Allergy chapter to see how other pre-disposing factors (e.g. chlorinated tap water, North Sea gas and cigarette smoke) can pre-dispose to food sensitivities.

From 22 weeks half a teaspoon of soft boiled egg yolk can be added to the cereal, twice and then three times a week. This can be gradually increased until he is taking the whole yolk. His lunch can be extended to include bone broth with strained vegetables gradually increased and thickened up with cereal, potato, or pulses put through a fine sieve or liquidized. After a few weeks, brains, herring roes, sieved soft fish and meat (e.g. plaice, liver and chicken) can be introduced, in tiny amounts at first, keeping the consistency smooth so that he encounters no 'chokey' lumps which frighten him and so make him react by spitting them out.

Postpone starting solids later in the day until about 30 weeks. Two meals incorporating solids require quite a lot of digesting. Also if he goes down at 6.30 pm on a very full stomach he may not need his 10 pm guzzle, whereas the mother's breasts need this late evening feed-time in order to go through the next eight hours in comfort! So it is a good idea to try to keep to the five feeds in 24 hours as long as possible.

Around 30 weeks, when he is awake more in the afternoons, he can be introduced to rusks while sitting on your lap. Never leave him alone with a rusk in case he chokes. The ideal rusk can be grasped in his hand and the business end sucked and chewed on, so that it gradually dissolves, but does not break off. Rusks can be made by soaking fingers of wholemeal bread in meat stock and drying out in a very cool oven. Rye bread is excellent for protecting new teeth. Little helpings of fruit – pulped pear, mashed ripe bananas or stewed apple, etc., can be given at this time with egg custard, or milk and cereal, if this suits him. Later little sandwiches can be introduced, with honey. Harmony natural peanut butter or mashed bananas. After one year try thinly scraped Tastex or Marmite (the salt in these yeast extracts is a stress on the kidneys of too young a baby).

If he is not milk-allergic, a little finely grated cheese can be added to the baby's diet at about one year of age; and once he has cut his molars cress, tomato, cucumber, grated apple and carrot can all take a turn. Chopped salad sandwiches make a good tea, and when he is old enough to chew, 'cheese parcels' – tiny cubes of white cheese wrapped in a small piece of lettuce.

If the baby is still breast fed at bedtime (approx 6.30 pm) he can have a drink of diluted fresh fruit juice at teatime (at about 4-4.30 pm).

At around 30 weeks, wheat, rye, barley and oat cereals (containing gluten) can be cautiously introduced – again a very little at a time – at breakfast. Gradually these can be extended to a little Weetabix, baby muesli, wheatgerm, etc. (i.e. natural, unsugared, wholegrain cereals). By 9-10 months he will probably have a commanding position from the high chair, and be demanding little tastes of whatever everyone else is eating – so the value of setting a good example cannot be too highly stressed! Pinhead oatmeal, brown rice, and millet porridge make excellent breakfasts too.

Foods for your baby to enjoy from about 12 months include natural wholegrain cereals (muesli should be soaked overnight), porridge (with cow's milk, goat's milk or nut milk), egg, mild white low fat cheeses, pounded fish, meat, all offal (liver, kidney, brain, heart, tongue, sweetbreads) and poultry, mixed whole grain breads and toast, Ryvita, unsugared rusks, oatcakes, vegetable soups, and all fresh vegetables and fruits. Sieve, pulp or grate the food until his teeth are through for chewing.

It is as well to avoid giving puddings too soon. Refined sugar is not a good item to add to any diet and avoiding the development of a 'sweet tooth' will greatly benefit his health and his teeth for the rest of his life. Later any of the following can be given as a second course: egg custards, boiled or baked and sweetened with a little honey and perhaps a little molasses, wholegrain semolina, brown rice pudding, sago, tapioca, cornmeal (polenta), barley flakes and honey, Gelozone milk jelly, stewed prunes or apricots, or baked eating apples stuffed with dates or sultanas, or stewed fruit sweetened with a little honey or raw Muscovado sugar. Sponges and crumbles can be made with wholegrain flours, etc.

Keep a small supply of Milupa, Gerber, Heinz or Johanus ready prepared savoury baby foods on hand for the odd emergency and use them occasionally without being consumed with guilt!

Protect your baby from pollution

If you live in a soft water area, it would be as well to use a water filter to remove toxic metals such as lead, cadmium and copper, which may leach off from the plumbing, or use bottled spring water.

When taken shopping, babies in low push-chairs and toddlers on foot tend to be at exhaust pipe level, and so are likely to inhale more lead from exhaust fumes. A carrying sling and an old-fashioned high pram keep the baby a little further from the source of the fumes.

Use stainless steel or enamel saucepans to avoid aluminium toxicity (see page 19).

If you live in a city and the baby has a consistently poor appetite, it is a good idea to get him out for a day in the country or at the seaside as often as possible. Never try to force him to eat, but ask yourself 'Why has he a poor appetite?' In city children, the answer is very often the high level of lead in the air, and it may be well to get in touch with our organisation, Foresight, for specific advice and possibly hair analysis. Leaking gas, or stuffy smoke-filled rooms can also inhibit appetite – open the windows, even in a town. Just follow your baby's lead, notice what he is ready for, what he enjoys, and what seems to suit him and do not bother too much about what the books say! You know him, we do not!

Remember, though, that with your first baby you will perhaps feel a great need to prove you are an adequate mother, and this can be quite hard on both the baby and mum! Everything about his feeding and progress may develop into a matter of great concern to you both. But with the second baby you will be more relaxed; and with number three you will forget to weigh him, fail to write down his milestones, not pay a lot of concern to what he says, does or eats at each meal – and he will still be cheerful and bouncing at the end of the day!

2. The Problem of Overweight

Extremes of both overweight and underweight are signs of wrong nutrition. With obesity they are directly related to ill-health, loss of vitality and premature ageing.

If your Doctor has told you that you need to lose weight, choose a method which will help you to reduce your weight and improve your general health at the same time. Crash diets are not the long term answer. Weight quickly lost is usually soon regained. As our 'normal' Western diets tend to be short of the nutrients our bodies need, a reducing diet may increase our deficiencies. This can bring greater risk to the new baby conceived by a parent who has previously been slimming. Hence the need for constructive suggestions for overweight future parents.

Stress, food, ecology and genetic traits all contribute to make you the shape you are. Here we will concentrate on the dietary factor.

Calorie-cutting is not the whole answer

Most slimming diets explain how you must cut down your calories. A glance at the section on Fats and Carbohydrates (page 10) soon reveals how inadvisable it is to include high fat foods (full fat cheeses and other dairy products, fatty meat, sausages, oily food, fried foods, etc.), alcohol, refined sugar and white flour products in *any* diet. Furthermore, all of these foods are calorie laden and have no place in a healthy weight-reducing diet.

The basis of *our* successful weight-reducing diet is whole foods – wholegrain cereals, plenty of raw and cooked vegetables, fresh and dried fruits and a balanced amount of proteins, in three meals a day. Wholefoods are high in natural dietary fibre; they are satisfying, nutritious, keep the digestive tract working more efficiently and do not linger in the intestines.

With the replacement of refined starches and sugar by wholegrains, pulses, vegetables and fruits, there will be no rebound hunger (that is the craving for more food soon after a full meal). Take the time to chew your food thoroughly. Mastication mixes saliva with the food and helps you feel satisfied as it aids the digestion.

Whole fruits which require chewing are advised in preference to drinking them as juices. You are unlikely to eat seven oranges at one time, but might easily drink half a litre of orange juice when really thirsty! The best low calorie thirst quencher is pure water.

Aim to lose weight slowly but steadily, and you will gain good health at the same time. You will simply be avoiding food that your body is better without anyway. Cutting down on salt intake is another important factor – salt encourages waterlogging of the tissues (fluid retention).

By eating moderate amounts of protein (see pages 8 and 92), the metabolism

180

is not so stressed and the diet is not expensive. Daily exercise is strongly recommended – not that it will 'burn up' the calories faster, but fresh air and exercise enhance all health-building regimes.

Some people will lose weight much faster than others. We are all different. Perseverance is what matters. Too rigid a regime that leaves you feeling hungry will tempt you to 'go off the rails'. If you genuinely keep to this reducing diet and do not lose any weight, it may be that you have a sensitivity to wheat and should seek professional help (see allergy chapter).

Suggested reducing breakfasts (for 1)

- Fresh fruit muesli.
- Porridge made with 1 oz oats, water and a pinch of Biosalt or sea salt (eaten with molasses if preferred sweet) and little milk. Apples.
- One large slice of wholemeal bread (Foresight 5-grain Bread, Slimmer's High Fibre or Rye Bread, or toast, cooled), little Butter Plus or alternative spread (p. 170). Half a grapefruit or orange.
- 2 oz dried apricots or prunes, soaked and stewed without sugar with 5 oz natural yoghurt.
- Slimmer's muesli with skimmed milk or unsweetened apple juice.
- Special nourishment in a glass – see chapter on drinks – to drink slowly.

Lunch or supper daily

Fresh salad made from several of the following raw ingredients: watercress*, celery, parsley*, cucumber, beansprouts*, tomato*, lettuce, carrot, cauliflower*, shredded cabbage*, spring onions*, French beans, artichokes, beetroot, apples.

With your salad eat either two slices of wholemeal bread or a wholemeal roll, or 2 tbsp cooked brown rice, millet, etc, or baked jacket potato and either 3 oz cottage cheese or hard boiled egg or 2-3 oz lean meat or lentil paté. Choose a salad dressing based on natural yoghurt or a slimmer's dressing if required. 1 tsp of cold pressed safflower or sunflower oil which provides the essential polyunsaturated oils can be included either in the dressing or on the bread or potato, etc.

Instead of the salad, try a good thick vegetable soup made with many vegetables and either some fish, meat or a combination of pulses and grains to provide balanced protein (see page 9).

Another alternative would be a nourishing 'meal in a glass' – see drinks chapter – sipped very slowly, 'chewing' each mouthful to mix it well with saliva. This mastication aids digestion and appetite satisfaction. 'Fluid meals' should only be an occasional or temporary substitute for 'solid' whole foods.

Cooked meals

Many of our cooked dishes are marked for their immediate suitability for slimmers (see page 22), as well as being good for all the family. Most others are readily adaptable, bearing the above points in mind.

* Be sure to include a good serving of the vegetables marked as these are good sources of vitamin C.

If you like to have a starter, choose a salad made of fresh green salad-stuffs, or clear or all vegetable soup, or raw unsweetened fruits such as grapefruit or melon, or unsweetened fruit juice or tomato juice.

For the main course, your choice of protein dish, with several conservatively cooked vegetables – at least one green vegetable and one steamed root vegetable. For the protein dish, choose non-oily fish dishes, oven baked, lean cuts of meat casseroled with vegetables (and any excess fat blotted off with kitchen paper before serving), lean slices from roast and braised joints, chicken with the skin removed, mixed grain and pulses (all with only a little added oil, if used at all). Avoid rich sauces and gravies. Avoid adding sugar, spirits or too much salt.

Choose fresh fruit for dessert – or a piece of fresh celery, or small bowl of seasonal salad.

Suggestions for packed lunches for slimmers

- For slimmer's sandwiches – make the special slimmer's wholemeal breads with added bran, or rye and mixed grain breads and use these for sandwiches – they are very filling!
- Choose one of the special nourishing drinks and take it chilled in a vacuum flask.
- Take a vacuum flask of hot home-made puréed soup or broth containing vegetables. Several fresh fruits and a few walnuts, almonds, sunflower seeds or hazelnuts.
- A mixed salad in a sealed container – eaten with a fork or spoon, whichever is easier, with protein of choice, or sprouted or cooked wholegrains.
- Fresh fruit muesli (in the right-sized container, so that no air is left to cause oxidation) with sunflower seeds.

Nibbles

Cut out the old pattern of snacks between meals: biscuits, salted nuts and crisps are very high in calories and can upset an otherwise well-balanced diet. Instead nibble celery, cucumber, raw carrots, peas, cauliflower, apples and pears. If you are consistently hungry between meals, eat a little more at mealtimes, chewing it longer. The natural high fibre content of wholefoods will help satisfy the appetite and aid the slimming efforts.

To begin with, a little hunger is a good sign indicating that you are eating less than usual! But if you feel dizzy or depressed, seek professional help – there might be a tendency to hypoglycaemia.

The less sugar and sugary foods you eat, the more sensitive will your taste become to the natural sweetness found in fresh and dried fruits and many vegetables.

Be miserly when buttering your bread – even with Butter Plus. Use a low-fat alternative sometimes (see p. 170).

Change over gradually to this new dietary plan high in salads and wholegrain cereals, to allow your digestion to adjust to the greater bulk of health-building wholefoods.

Monitor your weight

Since we are all different in metabolism, build and energy needs, it is not possible to specify quantities for individual diets. Weigh yourself once a week and eat to maintain a gradual, steady weight loss.

Two kitchen aids for lessening fat intake:

- A 'Romertopf' or 'clay baker' casserole for producing tasty roasts of meat without any added fat. The juices extracted during cooking can be strained and then put into
- A 'saucière' or 'gravy-separator', enabling the meat stock to be poured off from the bottom without the fat.

3. Allergies, Hyperactivity and Metal Toxicity

It is common practice for seed wheat to be dipped in mercury to ensure that no mould spoils the seed or rodents eat it before it is sown. These poisoned seeds are then usually grown in soil that is unbalanced by years of chemical fertilization. The plants are fed with the principal chemical nutrients to stimulate fast growth, with the result that the other essential trace minerals (zinc, chromium, manganese, etc.) are not taken up from the soil. The wheat is then chemically sprayed to inhibit further growth of the stem – heavy ears of grain too readily blow over and spoil when supported by long stems. After harvesting, the wheat is usually heavily processed to produce white bread, with many nutrients removed (see page 12) and chemical anti-staling agents added.

Is it surprising that more and more people are showing sensitivities to wheat? You can understand why we keep stressing the value of growing food organically – without poisons, unbalanced fertilizers, chemical pesticides and herbicides!

Human beings have evolved over hundreds of thousands of years, during which time all foods were entirely natural and wholesome. Our bodies and metabolism have developed to flourish on these natural whole foods. The situation has dramatically altered in such a short space of time – about three generations – 'the blinking of an eye' in comparison with the aeons before. Now food is chemically grown, heavily processed and fractionalized (divided up, with parts removed) and then stabilized. Our bodies have not had time to develop the means to assimilate these modern flavour-enhanced foods with their long shelf life. Nature gives us living, balanced foods. Even today's salads, fruits and brassicas may be sprayed with poisonous insecticides (see page 7).

From the 1950s to the 1970s the chemical barrage has steadily increased. Recently enlightened farmers are becoming more aware of the nutrient losses and health hazards thus caused: we must encourage them.

Edison said: 'The doctor of the future will give no medicine but will interest his patients in the care of the human frame, in diet, and in the causes and prevention of disease'.

When enough housewives keep asking for pesticide-free, organically grown produce, the demand will become so great that the supply will increase, and farming policies will be changed. Women have achieved much through such bodies as the Women's Institute – let us speak out for the health of our children and our nation, now!

Cooking for people with suspected allergies
When you encounter a friend with symptoms of allergy (skin problems, breathing problems, headaches, digestive disorders, etc.) show sympathy and under-

standing. He could easily be made very ill by being given even a very little of any food to which he is sensitized.

Everyone is a unique individual. Sensitivities vary in different people, even those exhibiting similar symptoms. 'Gluten-sensitive' people cannot tolerate any food containing gluten i.e. wheat, barley, oats, rye or buckwheat. Others may be very allergic to wheat, barley and rye, and yet able to tolerate oats or buckwheat. Remember grains are constituents of many drinks as well as cereals, flours, breads, cakes, biscuits, gravy, and sauces.

To give you an idea of the complexity of the problem of avoiding 5 foods commonly found to trigger allergic type reactions, here are 5 lists:

Foods which may contain wheat:
Bread (even if sold as cornbread or ryebread), biscuits, buns, batter, cereals, wheatgerm, bran, muesli, cornflour, ryeflour, white flour, wholemeal flour, gluten flour, kibbled wheat, cakes, pastries, puddings, pancakes, dumplings, gravy, sauces, spaghetti and macaroni, etc., ice-cream cones, chocolate, sausages, stuffings, mustard, stews, meat or fish coated in flour or breadcrumbs before cooking, stock cubes, some salad dressings, beer, whisky, malted milk, (Vitaquel margarine contains wheatgerm oil).

Foods which may contain milk:
Biscuits, cakes, bread, prepared food mixes, pancakes, puddings, custards, ice-cream, sauces, soups, boiled salad dressings, scrambled eggs, cream, butter, cheese, buttermilk, whey (in most margarines – check the label), yoghurt, soufflés, au-gratin dishes (with a cheese sauce), quiches, mashed potato, chocolates, toffees, chocolate drinks, foods cooked in batter. 'Added protein' can mean added powdered milk (e.g. in sausages).

Substances which may contain corn (maize):
Adhesives on envelopes, stamps, etc., toothpaste, cough syrup, medicinal tablets (e.g. aspirin), baking mixes, baking powder, bleached flours, corn-on-the-cob, cornflour, gelatin, desserts, popcorn, cornflakes, starch, corn oil, frying oil, sweets, frosted icing, glucose products, instant coffee, instant tea, creamed vegetables, creamed soups, some sausage meat, salad dressings, gravy, margarine, jams, jellies, cakes, biscuits, puddings, ice-cream, sauces, custards, soya bean milk, chewing gum.

Foods, etc., which may contain refined sugar:
Sweets, chocolates, candyfloss, icings, jam, jellies, ice-cream, puddings, tinned fruit, stewed fruit, glacé fruit, some fruit juices, cakes, biscuits, pastries, most breads, buns, fruit squash, soft drinks, cola, beers, wines, fruit punches, some drugs and medications, cough syrup, toothpaste, pickles, chutneys, salad dressing, mayonnaise, tomato ketchup, sweet and sour sauce, barbecue sauce, tinned carrots, tinned peas, cooked beetroot, corned beef, fruit yoghurt, many breakfast cereals including some mueslis and some made with bran, hot chocolate powder, Ovaltine, malted milk, milk shakes, cordials.

Foods which may contain yeast organisms:
Breads, fungi, mushrooms, canned fruit juice (as rotting fruit may have been used), vinegar, and all salad dressings, etc., made with vinegar; and vitamin-enriched foods containing brewer's yeast.

Check the small print on everything you buy. Watch out for chemical additives too. Maurice Hanssen's *E for Additives* explains their nature and function. Many books on allergy e.g. *Chemical Victims* (p. 191), show how these permitted additives are affecting some of us.

Other pre-disposing factors
The contraceptive pill, the IUD, coil, North Sea gas, cavity wall insulation, tobacco smoke, traffic exhaust, moth-proofed carpets, chemicals used to destroy woodworm, etc., damp mould, aerosol sprays as well as fresh paint, glue and varnish can all pre-dispose the body to allergy.

Dr. Jean Munro has found many children allergic to tap water – fluoride, chlorine, lead or copper may be the cause. Bottled water or good water filters are the answer here. It is wise to keep a few bottles of spring water in reserve to use when tap water looks brown and smells strongly of chlorine.

Simple home detection work
Food and chemical sensitivities can affect physical, mental and emotional health, being one possible cause of hyperactivity, antisocial behaviour, depression, catarrh, wheeziness, headaches, fatigue, 'jumpy legs', colic, eczema, asthma, migraine, etc. Where severe allergies or asthma exist, professional help from a clinical ecologist should be sought. For lesser allergies, home detection work, though slow, can be most rewarding. Seek professional help too.

When symptoms suggest a hidden allergy, Dr. Keith Mumby suggests making 1) a careful inventory of all foods eaten twice a week or more frequently, 2) list of foods known to disagree and 3) favourite foods and drinks which you consume most frequently. Catalogue all your symptoms, large and small, as an objective guide for checking your progress. A diet eliminating all the foods and drinks in 2) and 3) and the most frequent items in 1) should then be followed meticulously for 10-14 days. If you now feel fitter, happier and more alive, you may have removed the worst troublemakers from your diet. (He finds the most common offenders to be wheat, corn, egg, milk, colourings and chemicals, tea, coffee, sugar, yeast and cheese.) Then comes the painstaking task of unmasking the culprit foods from those omitted. He clearly explains how in his most helpful book *The Food Allergy Plan*.

Dr. William G. Crook's *Tracking Down Hidden Food Allergy* is a very helpful, amusingly illustrated book for explaining the procedure to a child. Dr. Doris Rapp's *Allergies and Your Family* gives, in question and answer format, a wealth of information including the psychological causes and effects of allergies, how to 'allergy-proof' your home, and how the 'bioessay titration' method can help. *Allergies, Your Hidden Enemy* by pioneer clinical ecologist Dr. Theron Randolph, and *Psycho-Dietetics* by Drs. Cheraskin and Ringsdorf show how much mental, emotional and physical illness is related to our polluted environment, and to our food and nutrition, and what we can do to help overcome these problems with sympathetic professional guidance.

Stone-age or cave-man diet
One way to ensure balanced eating while removing all most likely allergens is to return to the diet of our stone-age ancestors. The cave-man diet includes fresh free-range meats, offal, poultry, fish, organic local vegetables, fruits and nuts, with pure spring water or suitable herb tea to drink – all in the unadulterated form of pre-civilization days. All sugars, flours, sweets, grains, milk, butter, margarine, eggs, cheese, citrus and dried fruits are eliminated. Removed also are tea, coffee, alcohol and all processed or refined foods, drinks – and cigarettes.

Ideally, when needed to help a child, the cave-man diet is followed for two weeks by all the family together, thus saving many complications. All can benefit from it and make it a detection game as each 'new' food is subsequently introduced, one at a time. The reactions, if any, should be recorded for each individual on a Food/Reaction Diary Chart.

Foresight's booklet *Guidelines for Future Parents* gives directions for a 'rotation diet' for the detection of allergy and suggestions for starting a milk-free, gluten-free and egg-free diet. There are some suitable recipes given here under the appropriate sections, and many other recipes can be adapted to exclude unwanted ingredients. We recommend the specialized recipe books by Rita Greer, Louise Templeton and Hilda Cherry Hills (see page 190), to help you further with these problems.

Improved stone-age diet
Ongoing research shows that a diet based on the total removal of beef, pork, wheat and dairy products often proves beneficial in overcoming food sensitivities. This diet should include other wholegrains, pulses, local fruits, vegetables, sea vegetables, nuts and seeds – as well as fresh fish, free-range poultry and lamb.

Professional assistance should always be sought to ensure balanced nutrition when preparing for pregnancy.

The cleansing diet
During thirty years' association with Enton Hall Health Hydro, the authors have seen thousands of patients find renewed good health and vitality from undertaking fasting and cleansing diets based on fresh organically grown fruit and vegetables, under professional supervision. These are age-old methods of 'spring-cleaning' the body of waste products accumulated over the years, but are not recommended for self-administration.

To understand the 'how and why' of this natural cleansing process, read *Health Secrets from Europe* by Dr. Paavo Airola, *My Healing Secrets* by Boris R. Chaitow, *Natural Remedies for Common Ailments* by Constance Mellor or *The Grape Cure* by Basil Shackleton.

Foresight does not, however, advocate using these cleansing diets less than six months prior to embarking on pregnancy, nor without the consent and supervision of your Foresight Clinician.

For those planning a pregnancy, see Foresight's *Guidelines for Future Parents* and Margaret Brady's *Having A Baby Easily*.

Recommended food combinations for specially sensitive digestions – the Hay diet
Where wholefoods produce 'allergic' digestive disturbances, it may possibly be found that it is the wrong combining of foods which is the true culprit. Compatible food combinations are achieved by:

- Removing raw and dried fruits from any meal containing raw salads and vegetables.
- Combining starchy foods (potatoes and wholegrains) with fats, green vegetables, root vegetables, sweet fruits and honey in one meal.
- Combining predominantly protein foods (meat, fish, cheese, eggs and nuts) with green vegetables and salads. Acid fruits, (citrus, rhubarb, sour plums, etc.), may be included at this meal.

Incompatible food combinations:
Starches and proteins; and starches and acid fruits. It is possible that those can set up internal fermentation, which may produce ill-health in some 'sensitive' or 'allergic' people. *Food Combining for Health* by Doris Grant and Jean Joyce explains it all.

Pollution from heavy metal poisoning
Hyperactivity and allergic reactions can be caused by metal toxicities, as heavy metals such as lead inhibit the production of digestive enzymes. The rejuvenation programmes outlined here break the habit pattern of constantly repeated devitalized foods and drinks, and may help lessen the sensitivity to previously allergenic foods. These should be reintroduced in small quantities gradually, and increased cautiously if less sensitivity is demonstrated. In some cases a food may be tolerated once every 4-5 days, but not more frequently. In many cases it may be better to eliminate the allergen from the diet permanently.

Small amounts of heavy metals may actually be eliminated by use of the cleansing diet or with the Improved Stone-Age Diet (on your Foresight Clinician's advice) or by a diet including the following detoxifying factors.

Nutritional detoxification of toxic metals
Exposure to toxic metals in heavily industrialized and heavy traffic areas, and in some occupations, is unavoidable. The foods listed below give some degree of natural protection and can be used to help loosen these toxins which otherwise tend to accumulate in the body.

- Sea vegetables are useful as they can gently loosen toxic minerals and encourage their elimination from the body by normal excretion. (See page 62.)
- Pulses are valuable cleansing foods.
- Garlic, long famed as a prime blood and lymph purifier and natural antiseptic, has deep cleansing properties. To combat infection I like to eat it raw with apples – a tiny garlic slice with each bite of apple. Its infamous smell helps disinfect lungs and sinuses too!

- The pectin from apples is especially effective for heavy metal removal – cook the apples gently with the pips (as the pips contain more pectin) and then sieve to remove pips. Eating raw apples helps too.
- Vitamin C is a well known detoxifier.
- The fibre contained in wholegrains and vegetables is a protective agent.
- Vitamin E helps prevent heavy metal toxicity, but needs to be supplemented cautiously.

The Feingold diet to combat hyperactivity

Sometimes hyperactivity is caused not by toxic metal poisoning, nor by allergy to the foods themselves, but by intolerance to the chemical additives in foods and drinks.

Refined sugar can also increase hyperactivity.

The most troublesome chemicals come under the heading of artificial colourings, flavouring and anti-oxidants. So read the listed ingredients and avoid products with these additives. See *recommended books on hyperactivity* (page 191) to learn more about this vast problem.

Orange squash, jellies, and brightly coloured sweets are all suspect 'baddies' likely to contain chemical colourings, flavourings *and* refined sugar. Most packeted 'instant foods' (soups, cake and pudding mixes), most tinned and glacé cherries, tinned peas and strawberries, and margarines contain chemical colouring or flavouring or anti-oxidants – to name a few. Many savoury foods contain monosodium glutamate. Keep *Look Again at the Label* in your pocket for quick reference as you shop – for a few E numbers are actually good and desirable.

Home cooking, using fresh wholefoods, is the safe way to avoid unwanted ingredients.

Rebuild total health the foresight way

While allergic parents may readily produce children with even greater allergic tendencies, Foresight shows the way out of this downward spiral of diminishing health and vitality. You may be fortunate in having an enlightened doctor, Health Visitor or midwife who understands the wholistic nutritional approach of this book, and who will help you. Otherwise Foresight doctors, qualified nutritionists and naturopaths could help you achieve better health when you need professional guidance. As you see from this chapter, there are wholefood diets which can help rebuild health when we choose to implement them.

Start by assessing the situation. Examine your life-style and your eating and drinking habits. Look at your family tree and its history of inherited strengths and weaknesses, to see where preventive measures are appropriate. Track down and eliminate as many pollutant sources as you can. Re-examine your home and environment to see if improvements can be made (e.g. putting the gas boiler outside the house to avoid inhalation of gas fumes). Check the ingredients in the foods you buy. Search out sources of organic produce, free range eggs, unsprayed fresh garden produce. Read widely to increase your understanding of the problem and its solution (see Recommended Books, p. 190).

Ensure that your good wholefood diet includes all the vital trace minerals and vitamins you personally need; if necessary supplementing with a balanced programme e.g. Foresight Vitamins, Foresight Minerals and Foresight Iron Formula. These are made to Foresight's specifications to form a safe, comprehensive, balanced programme of interacting nutrients. Their formulation is regularly reviewed and updated when indicated by the latest proven research findings.

Produce vital, healthy meals and drinks. Cultivate a healthy life-style. In a word, choose to be responsible for your own and your family's good health. It is a way of living which can eventually bring greater harmony and wholeness to every aspect of our lives and our relationships. May God bless us in our journey to better health, greater understanding and deeper happiness.

Recommended Books

The wholistic approach to health: 1) physical, 2) mental, 3) spiritual and 4) emotional:

Nature's Plan for your Health by Thomas Bartram (Blandford Press)

Spiritual, Physical Survival thru' Living Foods by Ann Wigmore, D.D. N.D. (Hippocrates Press, U.S.A.)

Here's Health magazines

1 *Natural Remedies for Common Ailments* by Constance Mellor (Granada)

Health Secrets from Europe by Paavo O. Airola (Arco, U.S.A.)

My Healing Secrets by Boris R. Chaitov (Health Science Press)

Everybody's Guide to Nature Cure by Harry Benjamin, N.D. (Thorsons)

The Grape Cure by Basil Shackleton (Thorsons)

2 *Getting Well Again* by O. Carl Simonton, Stephanie Matthews-Simonton and James L. Creighton (Bantam Books, U.S.A.)

A Guide to Confident Living by Norman Vincent Peale (Cedar Books)

Psycho-dietetics by Dr. E. Cheraskin and Dr. W. M. Ringsdorf (Bantam Books)

3 *Your Healing Is Within You* by Canon Jim Glennon (Hodder and Stoughton)

The Prayer that Heals by Francis MacNutt (Hodder and Stoughton)

Anything You Ask by Colin Urquhart (Hodder Christian Paperbacks)

Inspiring Messages for Daily Living by Norman Vincent Peale (Cedar Books)

Receive Your Healing by Colin Urquhart (Hodder Christian Paperbacks)

4 *Handbook of the Bach Flower Remedies* by Philip M. Chancellor (Daniel)

Stay Alive All Your Life by Norman Vincent Peale (Cedar Books)

Love is Letting Go of Fear by Gerald G. Jampolsky, M.D. (Celestial Arts, U.S.A.)

Diet and Special Recipes:

Cook Yourself a Favour by Sheila Gibson, Louise Templeton and Robin Gibson (Johnston Green)

The Right Food for your Kids by Louise Templeton (Century Publishing)

Food Combining for Health by Doris Grant and Jean Joyce (Thorsons)

Rita Greer's Extraordinary Kitchen Notebook (Rita Greer)

Good Food, Grain-Free, Milk-Free by Hilda Cherry Hills (Roberts Publications)

Nutrition and Health:

Raw Energy by Leslie and Susannah Kenton (Guild Publishing)

Nutrition and Health by Sir Robert McCarrison (McCarrison Society Publication, London)

The Saccharine Disease by T. L. Cleave (John Wright and Sons, Bristol)

Nutrition and Physical Degeneration by Weston Price, M.D. (Price-Pottinger, U.S.A.)

Nutrition Against Disease by Dr. Roger J. Williams (Bantam Books, U.S.A.)

Mental and Elemental Nutrients by Carl C. Pfeiffer, Ph.D, M.D. (Keats Publishing Inc., U.S.A.)

Nutrition Almanac Nutrition Search Inc. (McGraw Hill Book Co., U.S.A.)

The Trace Elements and Man by Henry A. Schroeder, M.D. (Devin-Adair)

Ortho-Molecular Nutrition by Abram Hoffer, Ph.D., M.D. and Morton Walker (Keats Publishing Inc., U.S.A.)

Super Nutrition for Healthy Hearts by Richard Passwater, Ph.D. (Jove Publications, U.S.A.)

Body, Mind and Sugar by E. M. Abrahamson, M.D. and A. W. Pezet (Pyramid Books, U.S.A.)

Hypoglycaemia: A Better Approach by Dr. Paavo O. Airola (Health Plus, U.S.A.)

Hyperactivity:

The Hyperactive Child by Belinda Barnes and Irene Colquhoun (Thorsons)

Can Your Child Read? Is He Hyperactive? by William G. Crook, M.D. (Pedicenter Press, U.S.A.)

Allergies:

Allergies and Your Family by Doris J. Rapp, M.D. (Sterling Publishing, U.S.A.)

The Food Allergy Plan by Keith Mumby, M.B., Ch.B. (Unwin)

Allergies Your Hidden Enemy by Theron G. Randolph M.D. and Ralph Moss Ph.D. (Thorsons)

The Bitter Pill by Dr. Ellen Grant (Elm Tree Books)

Tracking Down Hidden Food Allergy by William G. Crook, M.D. (Professional Books, U.S.A.)

Chemical Victims by Dr. Richard Mackarness (Pan)

Food Allergy by Rita Greer and Robert Woodward, B. Pharm., Ph.D. (Roberts Publications)

Babies:

Having a Baby Easily by Margaret Braby, M. Sc. (Thorsons)

Breast is Best by A. and P. Stanway (Pan)

Let's Have Healthy Children by Adele Davis (Unwin)

Pre-Conceptual Care:

Guidelines for Future Parents (Foresight Publication★)

Environmental Factors and Foetal Health by Prof. J. Dickerson (Foresight Publication★)

The Next Generation – avoiding damage before birth in the 1980's (Foresight Publication★)

Running a Foresight Clinic (Foresight Publications★ available from Foresight, The Old Vicarage, Witley, Godalming, Surrey, GU8 5PN.)

International Journal of Environmental Studies, Vol. 17 No. 1 the Foresight Symposium of March, 1980 (Gordon and Breach, London and U.S.A.)

Food:

The Organic Food Guide (Henry Doubleday Research Assn.)

E for Additives by Maurice Hanssen (Thorsons)

Look Again at the Label (Soil Assn.)

Your Daily Food (A Recipe for Survival) by Doris Grant (Faber)

Gardening:

Organic Gardening by Lawrence D. Hills (Henry Doubleday Research Assn.)

Fertility without Fertilizers by Lawrence D. Hills (Henry Doubleday Research Assn.)

The Bug Book (Harmless insect controls) by H. & J. Philbrick (Garden Way Publishing, U.S.A.)

Useful Addresses

Action Against Allergy, Mrs Amelia Nathan Hill, 43 The Downs, Wimbledon, London, SW20

Association for Breastfeeding Mothers, Peggy Thomas, 131 Mayow Road, London, SE26 4HZ (01–778 4769). (For help with breastfeeding.)

Association for Children with Learning Difficulties, Quirral House, Pitch Place, Thursley, Godalming, Surrey

British Association of Holistic Health, 179 Gloucester Place, London, NW1 6DX (01–262 5299)

British Holistic Medical Association, 179 Gloucester Place, London, NW1 6DX (01–262 5299)

British Organic Farmers Assn., Leggatts Park, Potters Bar, Herts. EN6 1NZ

British Society for Clinical Ecology, Mrs Ina Mansell, Acorns, Romsey Road, Cadnum, Southampton, SO4 2NN (0703 812124)

British Society for Nutritional Medicine, Information Officer, 5 Somerhill Road, Hove, East Sussex, BN3 1RP

Cantassium Co. (makers of special products for gluten-free and grain-free diets, and Foresight Vitamins and Minerals), 225 Putney Bridge Road, London SW15 2PY

The Dyslexia Institute, 133 Gresham Road, Staines, Middx., TW18 2AJ (01–815 9498)

Foresight Assn. for the Promotion of Pre-Conceptual Care, The Old Vicarage, Witley, Godalming, Surrey, GU8 5PN

Guild of Health (The Church's Ministry of Healing), 26 Queen Anne Street, London W1M 9LB

Henry Doubleday Research Assn., Ryton on Dunsmore, Coventry, CV8 3LG

Hyperactive Children's Support Group, 59 Meadowside, Angmering, Sussex

La Leche League, Mr Spencer Lester, 30 Whimbrel Way, Banbury, Oxfordshire, OX16 9YN – for help with breastfeeding.

London Food Commission PO Box 291, London, N5 1DU (01–633 5782). (Voluntary body to inform and teach about food, and investigate agricultural, manufacturing, retailing and catering methods.)

McCarrison Society, Secretary, 36 Bowness Avenue, Headingly, Oxford, OX3 0AL

Natural Family Planning, NFP Centre, Birmingham Maternity Hospital, Queen Elizabeth Medical Centre, Birmingham, B15 2TG (021 472 1377 ex 102)

New Approaches to Cancer, Addington Park, Maidstone, Kent, ME19 5BL

The Nutrition Assn., 36 Wycombe Road, Marlow-on-Thames, Bucks, SL7 3HX

The Organic Food Service, Ashe, Churston Ferrers, Brixham, Devon. (Will provide addresses of places selling organic food.)

Pre-conceptual Care Inc., c/o Dr E. Lodge Rees, 21 Binnock Hill, Oakland, California 94618, USA. (The USA Foresight counterpart.)

Sanity, Marjorie Hall, 77 Moss Lane, Pinner, Middx, HA5 3AG

The Schizophrenia Assn. of Great Britain, Mrs G. Hennings, Llanfair Hall, Caernarvon, Gwynned, Wales.

The Soil Association, 86 Colston Street, Bristol, BS1 5BB (0272 290661).

Wholefoods, 24 & 31 Paddington Street, London, W1M 4DR (01–935 3924) (Suppliers of certified organic produce, health food ingredients and books relating to nutrition and health.)

Acknowledgement

The author gratefully acknowledges the influence, teaching and help of many –
my parents (the founders) colleagues and patients at Enton Hall Health Hydro,
my health-seeking family and friends, fellow nutritionists, Foresight, the McCarrison Society, New Approaches to Cancer, the Nutrition Association, and Guild
of Health lecturers and friends.

Fortunately I started life with wise parents devoted to attaining optimum
health of body, mind and spirit through natural methods. These included
wholefoods, a disciplined healthy life-style, and the peace of mind which comes
from honouring God, neighbour, oneself and the soil. Following these principles
in our lives and work, our children's health was similarly our concern before their
conception – and now we have four beautiful Foresight grandchildren!

To my darling husband and co-author, my most grateful thanks for contributing recipes intended for his long-planned Enton Hall recipe book. Particular
thanks to my dear friend, Nim Barnes, indefatigable founder and chairman of
Foresight, who inspired me to write this book, and kindly contributed the section
on infant feeding.

To Louise Templeton, SRD, I owe a tremendous debt of gratitude for her
painstaking assistance and constructive criticism throughout. Especial thanks
also to our daughter, Juliana Burden, and to Helen Thaxter for careful typing,
and to Professor John Dickerson for vetting my nutritional chapters to earn his
approval as Nutrition Adviser to Foresight.

I am most grateful to Aurum Press for producing this new edition and for the
opportunity to revise and improve this nutritional cookbook.

INDEX

195